The
Dow Jones-Irwin
Guide to
Real Estate Investing

The Dow Jones-Irwin Guide to Real Estate Investing

CHRIS MADER
The Wharton School
University of Pennsylvania

Dow Jones-Irwin
Homewood, Illinois 60430

First Printing, April 1975

Second Printing, December 1975

Third Printing, April 1976

Fourth Printing, September 1976

Fifth Printing, December 1976

Sixth Printing, June 1977

ISBN 0-87094-095-3
Library of Congress Catalog Card No. 74–25812

Printed in the United States of America

To Susan Johnson Mader

Preface

Real estate investing is both a common and a sophisticated practice. Almost two-thirds of all householders own their homes and are, therefore, real estate investors. Yet most find it too expensive, risky, or complicated to also own investment property. They cite problems of selection, financing, management, taxation, and so on—and are frightened away. Others may fear that real estate is not sufficiently profitable or too hard to sell if necessary. We confront these issues, showing who can benefit from real estate investing, how, and how much.

Experienced real estate investors and professionals will also find this book unique and useful. They know about the rewards and risks of *leverage* and *tax shelter*. But what about *inflation?* What does it mean for brokers, builders, bankers, and buyers? Shown here for the first time is a way to answer these questions. We discuss all types of real estate—home ownership, apartments, office buildings, shopping centers, land, and so on.

Over the last five years, many associates have contributed to refining the analysis published here. Also I appreciate the specific comments of:

Bukk Carleton, President, Landtect Corporation.

Dave Dunn, Founder, Synerex Partners.

Rod Hardy, President, Landplan, Inc.

Jim Lenz, President, Creative Home and Land, Inc.

Elizabeth and Stanley Mader, Retired Parents.

Don Rappaport, Partner, Price Waterhouse & Company.

Russ Redenbaugh, Investment Counsellor, Cooke & Bieler.

Erich Weissenberger, Account Executive, Smith, Barney & Company, Inc.

Bill Zucker, Administrative Director, Wharton Entrepreneurial Center.

Your comments and questions are also welcomed. Making correct decisions in real estate investing requires the best in all of us.

March 1975   CHRIS MADER

Contents

Part I

Analyzing Real Estate

1. **Real Estate and Inflation**
   Added profits from leverage and tax shelter are the often-cited special benefits of real estate investing. But inflation is now the most important factor of all, *if* you believe it will continue. Do you?

2. **Real Estate versus Other Investments**
   Investors' resources and objectives affect the suitability of various investment opportunities. Does real estate belong in your portfolio?

3. **The Real Estate Market**
   The participants, structure, and opportunities in the real estate market are reviewed, including how they can help you.

4. **Analyzing Real Estate Investments**
   Knowledge, experience, and judgment are needed to evaluate real estate. They still are. But the full effects of inflation, tax laws, financing alternatives, and holding periods can now be assessed.

5. **A Case Example — the Devine Property**
   The analysis approach is applied in a straight-forward, easily understood example — buying a residential property for investment and rental income.

1

6. *Risk Analysis*

Our case example is extended to an analysis of risk and the relative importance of 13 key factors in real estate investing.

1

Real Estate and Inflation

Leverage and tax shelter. These are the often-cited special benefits of real estate investing. But is there another good reason to consider real estate — profit and protection from inflation. *Inflation can actually boost your after-tax rate of return from real estate investing to 15% or even 25% compounded annually.*

This book helps you evaluate real estate opportunities. It includes the profit impact of owning real estate during inflation. In addition, we will analyze such factors as initial costs, mortgage terms, rental income, operating expenses, depreciation, and taxes for their effect on profits and risk. To do so, Part I explains how to analyze real estate using the latest and most complete techniques. Part II then looks at the various types of real estate investments, including homes, condominiums, apartments, office buildings, shopping centers, and land held for speculation or development. Part III is a unique set of reference tables enabling you to make quick, accurate estimates of the profitability and risk of any real estate opportunity.

ROLE OF LEVERAGE, TAX SHELTER, AND INFLATION

Why do real estate investors so often grow wealthy?
Leverage.

Why do the wealthy so often invest in real estate?
Tax shelter.

What is the unanalyzed factor behind these profits?
Inflation.

Leverage means borrowing money to multiply the impact of your own capital. A $100,000 investment can sometimes control a million-dollar property. Even with more modest means, you can buy and mortgage real estate worth four or five times your own investment. Few opportunities have such leverage potential. This is not an unbridled benefit, of course, as the multimillion dollar bankruptcies of William Zeckendorf and, more recently, Martin Decker and Walter Kassuba can attest. But legendary fortunes have also been made *and kept* in real estate — ask Trammell Crow, Harry Helmsley, Bob Hope, or Laurence Rockefeller.

Tax shelter means the legitimate shielding of income from the government's grasp. Various tax laws are designed to encourage investing. Real property, both for housing and commercial purposes, has been deemed a national need and worth stimulating. Federal income taxes (and most state statutes) offer shelter to the real estate investor. It's one way the wealthy stay that way.

Inflation is the third, and often the strongest, reason for the success of real estate investors. Inflation-swollen rents and selling prices have propelled the profitability of most properties. But sometimes inflation in operating expenses or interest rates can curtail these gains and even produce losses. The examples and analytical evidence of this book can be your guide to profiting from real estate investing by understanding the proper role of leverage, tax shelter, and inflation.

INFLATION—THE UNANALYZED FACTOR

Inflation's strong impact is often overlooked. Even some real estate professionals simplify their investment analysis by omitting its complicating effect. But this is no longer necessary—and the results are usually too good to ignore. Whether you are a professional or part-time investor, we hope to change your mind about the need to analyze real estate and inflation. We then provide you with a straightforward tool to do so.

You need only a quick look at the average selling price of new single family homes, shown in Figure 1.1, to be convinced of rising prices. While some quality improvements may be reflected in these figures, the cost of new construction has been inflating strongly for years. During 1974, increases in such items as land, lumber, metals, mortgage interest, and skilled labor boosted the price of new housing by about 15 percent. These increased costs depressed the supply of new housing. In turn, this tended to raise the market value of the existing, lower-priced, used homes.

Those who have owned homes over the last decade can now, in most cases, take comfort from their inflation-swollen value. It has become standard practice, in fact, to roll the sales gain on one home into the down payment on a more desirable one. Outsiders watching this escalating merry-go-round now fear they will be priced out of suitable housing altogether. The

FIGURE 1.1
Trend of U.S. Housing Prices

Average Sale Price (thousands of dollars)

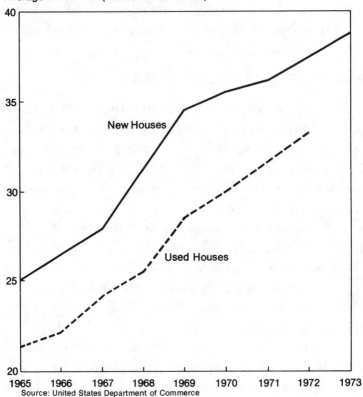

Source: United States Department of Commerce

cost of their dream house has risen faster than the savings they can accumulate to buy it.

This familiar scenario is recounted to "prove," at a personal and intuitive level, the theme that inflation usually helps real estate investors, while others miss out. In the chapters ahead we will take a more rigorous look at this and other factors affecting the various types of real estate. But the most important factor—*and the most overlooked*—is usually inflation.

FIGURE 1.2
Inflation as Measured by the Consumer Price Index

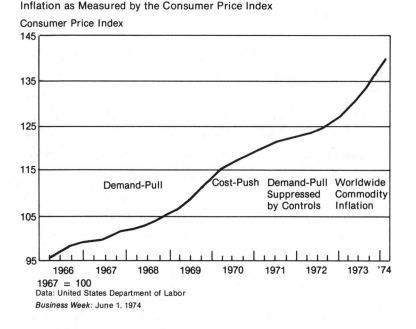

Consumer Price Index

Demand-Pull

Cost-Push

Demand-Pull Suppressed by Controls

Worldwide Commodity Inflation

1966 1967 1968 1969 1970 1971 1972 1973 '74

1967 = 100
Data: United States Department of Labor
Business Week: June 1, 1974

WHY INFLATION HELPS REAL ESTATE INVESTORS

Inflation (and real growth) has become the nation's major economic/political problem. President Gerald Ford once listed inflation as "public enemy number one." The *Wall Street Journal* said of inflation, "On no subject around is there more talk and less understanding."[1] And the *New York Times* editorialized that "of all the torrent of statistics pouring out of Washington, none exceeds in importance the monthly Consumer Price Index."[2] The CPI measures the ever-higher sum needed for the consumer's market basket of goods, as charted in Figure 1.2. It often seems that the flow

---

[1] *Wall Street Journal,* "The Outlook," September 23, 1974, p. 1.

[2] *New York Times,* "Inflation Gauge," June 22, 1974, p. 28.

of inflation statistics has itself become inflated. We might wryly wonder if inflation now troubles us only because we now measure it so much.

For those on fixed incomes, eroding purchasing power is no statistical artifact. The value of a constant dollar income, such as from an insurance annuity or debt security, has shrunk dramatically. The seemingly responsible 30 year old who purchased a whole life insurance policy in 1940, is now age 65 and each redeemable dollar has dropped 70 percent in purchasing power. Similarly, the dollars you choose to invest now face an uncertain future, if unguarded against inflation.

Making certain that incomes rise to meet inflation has become a prevalent concern today. Over 50 million citizens (those on Social Security, on certain government and private pension plans, or under cost of living labor contracts) now have the right to a larger paycheck from time to time just because of inflation. Similarly, many homeowner's insurance policies now escalate the coverage (and premiums) automatically to keep them current with inflating real estate values. Yet how can the investor seek protection — and profit — from inflation? How can he assure that his purchasing power will not be eroded and will, instead, actually expand?

Real estate, like most other forms of tangible ownership, has historically insulated investors' assets from erosion by inflation. Adequate, attractive, comfortable shelter — be it for residential or commercial purposes — is such a fundamental need that its price has risen about as rapidly as the average price level. Additionally, construction costs, including land, labor, materials, and financing, have zoomed in the last decade, propelling prices to higher and higher levels. The increasing number of households, higher incomes, and the fixed supply of land all act to nudge most real estate prices steadily upward.

Appreciation in real estate, both in its rental income and in its market value if sold, can result from factors other than mere price inflation. Tasteful design, regional development, shifting population, good maintenance, selective renovation, or just smart marketing can improve the economic value of a property beyond mere increases in the general Consumer Price Index. Whatever the cause—mere inflation or true appreciation—the profit impact of rising rents and selling prices is substantial.

ANALYZING REAL ESTATE INVESTMENTS

A typical case can show the favorable effects of *leverage, tax shelter,* and, most important, *inflation.*[3] Suppose that in 1967 you bought a six-office suburban medical building. It's price then was $100,000. By putting up $25,000 in equity and arranging a $75,000 mortgage, you could achieve good leverage on your own capital. A reasonable $250 per month for each suite ($3,000 per year) brings in gross income of $18,000 per year. Allowing $1,000 for possible vacancies results in $17,000 of effective gross income. Against this, you would probably experience about $7,000 of operating expenses annually, including maintenance, property taxes, utilities, supplies, insurance, and administration. This leaves $10,000 as the net operating income—a

---

[3] This case is analyzed more precisely in Chapter 4.

10% return on the $100,000 total invested, before considering leverage, tax shelter, and inflation. Table 1–1 shows the arithmetic for this example.

By using leverage, you incur the obligation of interest expense and debt repayment. But you tie up little of your own money compared to the total invested. All

TABLE 1–1
Sample Real Estate Investment During Inflation
Suburban Medical Office Building

Purchase:	Equity	$ 25,000	
	Mortgage...............................	75,000	
	Total Invested	$100,000	
I. *Holding Results:*	Gross Income	$ 18,000	
(Before Leverage,	Less: Vacancy......................	1,000	
Tax Shelter, and	Effective Gross........................	$ 17,000	
Inflation)	Less: Operating Expense	7,000	
	Net Operating Income............	$ 10,000	
Rate of return of:	$\dfrac{\text{Net Operating Income}}{\text{Total Invested}}$ is	$\dfrac{\$10,000}{\$100,000} = 10\%$	
II. *Holding Results:*	Net Operating Income...............	$ 10,000	
(After Leverage)	Less: Mortgage Interest	6,000	
	Amortization.................	1,000	
	Cash Flow	$ 3,000 (before tax)	
Rate of return of:	$\dfrac{\text{Before-Tax Cash Flow}}{\text{Equity}}$ is	$\dfrac{\$3,000}{\$25,000} = 12\%$	
III. *Holding Results:*	Actual Gross............................	$ 17,000	
(After Tax Shelter)	Less: Operating Expense	7,000	
	Mortgage Interest	6,000	
	Depreciation.................	4,000	
	Taxable Income.......................	$ 0	
	Cash Flow	$ 3,000 (after tax)	
Rate of return of:	$\dfrac{\text{After-Tax Cash Flow}}{\text{Equity}}$ is	$\dfrac{\$3,000}{\$25,000} = 12\%$	
IV. *Overall Results:*	Gross Sale Price	$150,000	
(After sale with	Less: Selling Costs...............	9,000	
8 years of	Debt Repayment...........	67,000 (after $8,000 of
about 5% annual	Capital Gain Tax...........	14,000 amortization)
inflation)	Cash Flow	$ 60,000 (after sale)	
Rate of return of:	$25,000 appreciating to $60,000 in 8 years is 11.6%		

appreciation in rents and resale value accrues to your account. In this case, annual mortgage payments during the first few years go, on average, for interest of $6,000 and loan amortization of $1,000. Of your $10,000 of net operating income, this leaves $3,000 as your in-pocket cash before taxes. This is called your "spendable" or before-tax "cash flow." This $3,000 amounts to a 12 percent rate of return on the $25,000 equity invested. Section II of Table 1–1 shows this computation.

Tax shelter is the next benefit. While your $17,000 of actual gross is taxable income, it is offset by the $7,000 of expenses and $6,000 of deductible interest payments. Tax laws also allow you to recoup your invested principal untaxed, via depreciation charges. About $4,000 per year, on average, could be deducted from taxable income in this case. Thus, for tax purposes, the deductible expenses fully offset your actual gross income. Your $3,000 of before-tax cash flow is completely sheltered and your after-tax rate of return is also 12 percent.

The real kicker is inflation. Assume that this property's market value has inflated (or appreciated) at about 5 percent per year, a likely occurrence. By 1975, its sale price would be nearly half again as great.[4] Selling costs for a property of this type and size are about 6 percent. (For smaller properties or land this percentage is usually higher, counting commissions, taxes, title, and closing costs; for larger properties it may be less.) After paying off the remaining mortgage balance and required capital gains tax, a bonanza still

---

[4] A 50 percent increase in sale price implies a 5.2 percent per year inflation rate compounded for the eight year holding period. Many, if not most, properties have experienced such appreciation during this period.

remains. Section IV of Table 1–1 shows this cash flow from sale to be $60,000.

Thus our investor not only had a 12 percent current income, but also more than doubled his initial $25,000 stake. And all of this was *after taxes*. The capital appreciation alone works out to 11.6 percent compounded annually over the eight year holding period. Thus the inflation-swollen sale price produced a rate of return nearly equalling the profits from holding. Combining these sources of profit—holding plus sale—produces an overall rate of return of over 20 percent compounded annually after taxes. Very impressive, but not at all unusual. In dollar terms, and even in purchasing power, our investor is well ahead of the inflation game.

WHEN INFLATION HURTS

During the last decade or two, inflation has significantly boosted the fortunes of most real estate owners, but not all. Rents and selling prices have increased, but so have financing costs and operating expenses such as property taxes, maintenance, fuel, utilities, and insurance. Unless paid by the tenant or unless lease terms and market and political conditions permit compensating rental increases, these rising costs can drive down net incomes and selling prices. Cities full of vandalized vacant buildings are mute testimony to this unfortunate effect.

On the leverage front, construction loans and permanent mortgages have become more costly. Lenders demand and borrowers tolerate high rates because of their growing fear of long-term inflation. To some extent, high mortgage rates reduce the property owner's leverage benefit, unless rents fully reflect such expenses. But precisely because these conflicting factors are so difficult to judge, this book provides a way to analyze them easily and accurately. After explaining and applying this analysis in the chapters ahead, the reference tables of Part III cover various mortgage terms and rent levels. In addition, they reflect the tax shelter from depreciation allowed on the different types of improved property and the likely impact of inflation.

Another inflation-related risk can also influence real estate investing. Properties are frequently valued at some particular multiple (called a capitalization factor, or "cap rate") of their annual net income. This concept is analogous to a price-earnings (P/E) ratio in common stock evaluation. For example, our medical office building was priced at $100,000, or ten times its net operating income. A bank, insurance company, or savings institution would almost certainly allow 75 percent of this valuation on a first mortgage. Thus this multiple provides a useful rule of thumb for translating from net income to an approximate selling price or to a collateral value.

What effect does inflation have on this valuation multiple? As interest rates rise to overcome increased inflation, investors may similarly demand higher current rates of return from real estate. In 1973–74, stocks and bonds fell in price so that their dividend yields and current returns increased along with interest rates. Just as P/E ratios may tend to decline in the face of competing high interest rates, real estate cap rates can come under similar pressure. Furthermore, a recession or oversupply can depress rental incomes, especially for commercial property. In London, for example, following a heady rise, and amid economic and energy crises, many real estate prices tumbled by 30 percent in 1974. However, long-term inflation and climbing construction costs both indicate rising, rather than falling, real estate prices in the years ahead.

WHAT HAS THE INFLATION RATE BEEN?

The many statistics leave no uncertainty on this question. Figure 1.2 showed the recent upward thrust of the U.S. Consumer Price Index. Figure 1.3 provides a longer-term and international perspective on

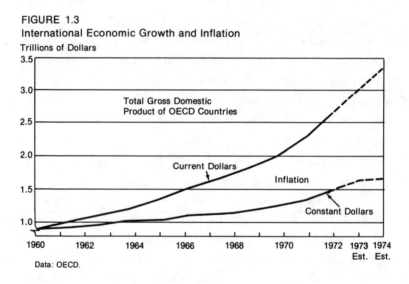

FIGURE 1.3
International Economic Growth and Inflation

the problem. It shows that most growth stems from inflation, which lately has gotten quite steep. And world-wide price levels have worked their way higher each of the last 15 years — rather a predictable trend.

WHAT WILL THE INFLATION RATE BE?

Trend projection from Figure 1.3 would suggest "double digit" inflation of 10 percent or more annually. However, slower inflation now seems likely. But "economists generally despair of seeing the rise in prices settle down to less than 5 percent a year."[5] Long-term interest rates of over 8 percent also imply expectations of at least a 5 percent long-term inflation rate. And in the twisted logic of an inflationary era, the old saying becomes "never a lender, but a borrower be."

The examples and tables in this book often assume a 5 percent annual inflation (appreciation) rate. What do *you* think the inflation rate will be? If your answer is *other than* 0%, then the discussion ahead may change your mind about real estate investing and change the way you analyze such opportunities.

---

[5] *U.S. News and World Report*, "New Era," March 3, 1975, p. 36.

2

Real Estate versus Other Investments

Real estate competes with other investments just as surely as one property competes with another. So if you invest, real estate belongs on your list of alternatives. But should it then leap from this list of maybe's and into your investment portfolio? To answer this issue, frank consideration must be given to:

1. Your investment objectives.
2. How the competing opportunities (such as real estate, stocks, bonds, and commodities) are likely to perform toward meeting those objectives.
3. Whether real estate should therefore be in *your* asset mix.

Our device for helping you decide is a discussion of investment objectives followed by a ranking of various investment opportunities according to these objectives. This Objectives-Opportunities Table is then personalized to your specific desires.

WHY INVEST?

Perhaps your most important personal resources are health, happiness, time, and money — but only money can be stored and, to a degree, exchanged for the others. Most of us feel we should invest to gain the satisfaction and security of knowing that this one resource will be available in times of want or need. Yet saving and investing continually compete with desires to spend now.

To attain the financial base that most people profess to want, our advice is *insure, invest, and spend the rest.*[1] This priority first assures income despite adversity and, second, income for the future before the daily thrust for consumption. How much you should set aside regularly depends on your current assets, your goals, the time remaining to reach them, and your comparative investment success. But you cannot profit at all from real estate, or any of the other competing opportunities, unless you first *decide to invest* some of your resources — time and usually money.

YOUR INVESTMENT OBJECTIVES

It might seem obvious that *profit*, usually measured as an investment rate of return, is your number one investment objective. You might also say it's the *only* objective (within legal and moral bounds) and, in retrospect, be correct. But investments are commitments to an uncertain future. Their after-the-fact profitability simply is not known at the time of investing. Therefore

---

[1] Robert Hagin and Chris Mader, *The New Science of Investing* (Homewood, Ill.: Dow Jones-Irwin, 1973), discusses personal investment objectives and the amount of ongoing investment needed to reach a particular financial goal.

investors claim to have the following more complete list of objectives when relying on foresight, rather than hindsight:

1. Investment Rate of Return

This first objective is the primary focus of this book — enabling you to forecast real estate rates of return. We will develop an evaluation procedure that translates your judgments of property costs, rents, mortgage terms, inflation rates, taxes, and other factors into a quantitative, consistent, and comparable measure of profitability. This analysis method is applicable to any property you might consider.

Investment rate of return is the *total return* from owning an investment. It includes both income and capital gains (or losses). The profitability of a savings account, for example, is easy to compute. The only cash inflows are the fixed, periodic interest payments with no change in the principal (unless interest income is reinvested). For assets with fluctuating prices, like real estate or common stocks, the total return concept includes both the current income from holding *and* any capital gains (or losses) upon sale.

This principle is well accepted by stock market investors, who look at more than just the current dividend yield. The effects of sale — such as a changed market value, selling expenses, and taxes due — are also relevant in real estate analysis, although often overlooked or oversimplified. The evaluation approach used here computes not only the current return from holding, both before and after taxes, but also the overall, total return including the effects of sale.

2. Low Risk

The evaluation method can also be used to assess risk, defined as adverse results from events other than those forecast. Investors' willingness and ability to accept risk varies with such factors as age, net worth, salary, and psychological temperament. For some, safety of capital rivals rate of return in importance. Others are more willing to gamble, hoping that good fluctuations will overcome the bad and produce total returns higher than from more conservative investments.

Empirical evidence only partially supports this widely held belief that high return accompanies high risk. Comprehensive stock market research, for example, has shown that medium risk investments offer somewhat more total return than low risk investments.[2] However, this same research shows that still higher risks actually provide *lower* overall returns. This paradoxical result extends also to the bond markets where medium grade bonds pay significantly more interest than the highest quality bonds — more so than is warranted by their only slightly higher default probability. But extremely speculative bonds have not done so well. Horse race fans also overbet both the favorites and the long shots, decreasing their relative returns.

There are two explanations for this seemingly irrational risk-taking behavior. First, investors, relying on foresight, tend to underestimate risk. They may, for example, have incomplete or unequal information about a potential investment. This imperfect forecasting

---

[2] Pratt, Shannon P., "Relationship Between Risk and Rate of Return for Common Stocks," D.B.A. Dissertation, Indiana University, 1966.

may then be magnified by economy-wide fluctuations and the mass psychology that usually exaggerates them.[3]

The second explanation for lower returns, on average, from both safe *and* speculative investments, is that people like to both insure *and* gamble. These activities yield an expected loss (the insurer's or casino's expenses plus profit). Yet individuals consistently choose the small, but certain, cost of insurance premiums rather than face large, but unlikely, losses. By contrast, state lotteries allow a cheap shot at a big payoff, although the odds are slim. The apparent demand for catastrophe-avoidance on the one hand and workless-wealth on the other, allows insurance and gambling to flourish, although neither offers positive expected returns.

Applying these phenomena to investing means that the very safe and very risky investments get overvalued by the "insure" and "gamble" instincts in each of us. But no two real estate properties are exactly alike. Furthermore, recent comparable transactions may not exist and prices usually are not widely disclosed. Smaller properties in particular tend to draw only local buyers because of the need for appraisal and supervision. Therefore, we may hope and expect to find some real estate opportunities offering exceptional return compared to their risk. Simultaneously, however, we cannot passively rely on the efficient mar-

---

[3] A market is called "efficient" if it has the ability to adjust prices quickly so that returns are comparable for comparable risks. The New York Stock Exchange, with its many participants and well-publicized prices, is considered an efficient market, although no one accuses it of *operating* or *paperwork* efficiency, but that is another story.

ket principle that high-risk (or at least medium-risk) in itself tends to result in a high return.

3. Leverage

This investment objective has a direct and dramatic influence on investment rate of return and risk. By borrowing, as in mortgaging a property, the capital of others magnifies the results achieved on your own money. For example, a project which returns 12 percent annually on the total invested can be levered favorably by borrowing at 8 percent or 10 percent. This magnifies the owner's return on equity (total invested less debt), because the borrowed capital is earning more than it costs. Naturally, a fall off in earnings can reverse the direction of this leverage, magnifying losses. Proper leverage, which is easily arranged and often used in real estate, serves to increase the investor's rate of return but also the risk.

4. Liquidity

Investors also strive for the availability, or liquidity, of their principal along with high return, low risk, and sometimes leverage. To a degree, these objectives are again in conflict. For example, readily available savings deposits may pay about 5 percent annual interest while four year certificates of deposit (CDs) may pay nearly 8 percent. Thus liquidity can be sacrificed to bolster return, but penalties are imposed for premature withdrawal.

The liquidity of real estate is also limited, unlike an ordinary savings account or publicly traded security. To sell, one must find a qualified and willing buyer and then induce him to act. This often takes time, effort, and expense. Liquidity can be hastened through a distress sale or auction, but the selling price (and thus the capital gain and total return) usually suffers.

5. Low Expenses

Investors typically are concerned with their *net* income from investing after deducting such expenses as *transaction costs, holding costs,* and *management fees.* The levels of these expenses vary from one type of investment to another. In real estate they are rather high. Transaction costs for executing a buy and a sell can easily include a broker's fee of 6 percent, financing commitment fees of perhaps 1 percent, legal, title insurance, and closing costs of another 1 percent or 2 percent and possibly transfer taxes. Total in and out costs, especially for smaller properties, may be eight to ten percent of the total invested. This impact of transaction costs can be softened by holding the investment at least a few years, further sacrificing liquidity.

Holding costs include deductions from income for operating expenses (e.g., property taxes, maintenance, utilities, insurance, and the like) and for interest on capital borrowed for leverage. Depreciation expenses (the accounting deductions allowed as a wearing out of the property over some allowable time period) are not a cash cost. However, they are deductible as an expense for tax purposes, thus sheltering available net income (or other income) from taxation.

Management fees, for hiring a professional property manager, may run 5 to 7 percent of gross income plus a surcharge for finding tenants. By comparison, the expenses for transactions, holding, and management of a securities portfolio tend to be less than in real estate (with such notable exceptions as mutual fund sales loads, over-the-counter stocks with wide dealer spreads, round-trip commissions on small investments, high portfolio turnover, or excessive counselling or custodial fees).

6. Tax Shelter

Investors seek *after-tax* returns and usually invest accordingly. As shown in Table 2–1, Your Objectives-Opportunities Table, various investments have different tax shelter characteristics. Tax exempt bonds and specialized oil/leasing/farming tax shelters are rated highest, along with various types of real estate.

As mentioned above, depreciation "expenses" shelter much or all of a property's net income, especially in a new project's early years. Interest costs for leverage and other holding costs or management fees are also deductible from ordinary income. Any profits from sale (after transaction costs) are typically taxed at long-term capital gains rates. For homeowners, while depreciation is not allowed, any gains on sale go untaxed if reinvested in another residence (of equal or greater cost) within one year (or within 18 months, if building a new home). Furthermore, such postponed capital gains are partially untaxed if the home seller is age 65 or over and go completely untaxed when entering his or her estate.

Refinancing (analyzed in detail in Chapter 11) provides another way to shelter real estate returns from

TABLE 2–1
Your Objectives-Opportunities Table

Investment Objectives	Real Estate			Savings			Bonds			Stocks			Tangibles		
	Home Ownership	Income Property	Development Property	Cash or Checking	Savings Account	Certificates of Deposit	Straight Bonds	Tax-exempt Bonds	Convertible Bonds	Option Writing Hedges	Common Stock	Option Buying	Commodities	Oil, Leasing, Farming Shelters	Art, Antiques, Gems, Stamps, Coins
1. Rate of return	+	+	+	–	–	+	+			+				+	
2. Low risk	+		–	+	+	+					–	–	–	–	–
3. Leverage	+	+	+									+	+	–	–
4. Liquidity	–	–	–	+	+	–	+	+	+		+		+	–	–
5. Low expense	–	–	–	+	+	+	+	+	+						
6. Tax shelter	+	+	+	–	–	–	–	+							
7. Inflation protection	+	+	+	–	–	–	–	–			+			+	+
8. Personal satisfaction	+	+	+	+											+

taxation. In this case the property is not sold, but rather re-mortgaged based on the collateral value of several years of amortization and/or property appreciation. The additional debt proceeds are nontaxable, being a loan to the owner rather than income. However, interest must be paid on the higher outstanding debt balance resulting from such a refinancing. Property trading (also discussed in Chapter 11) can similarly defer the taxable realization of capital gains.

7. Inflation Protection

Recent rampant inflation has raised investors' consciousness concerning this objective. History has shown, and this book seeks to prove, that real estate investing offers one of the best ways to protect your assets from erosion in purchasing power. Gains in real estate, particularly with proper leverage, often outrun increases in the cost of living. Thus you can achieve not only protection, but also *profit*, from inflation.

By contrast, a savings account involves a fixed, guaranteed rate of return. But, being denominated in dollars, it can lose purchasing power due to inflation. For example, $1,000 invested at 5 percent becomes $1,050 at year end (or $1,051.30 with daily compounding). If inflation during the year increases prices by 6 per cent, on average, then our saver is behind in terms of real goods his money can buy. Furthermore, interest income is taxable at ordinary income rates. On an after-tax basis, he or she might need 8 percent or 10 percent interest income just to break even with 6 percent inflation.

8. Personal Satisfaction

Since money is only one of your resources, it should not be the sole objective of investing. True, it can be used to buy time for leisure or retirement (health and longevity permitting), but if you don't enjoy investing, why bother? An investment in a personal home (or vacation property) is perhaps most satisfying. Next come such appreciating — and appreciable — assets as art, antiques, gems, stamps, and coins. Among the least satisfying, especially during recent recurrent bear markets, has been ownership of intangible securities. Real estate, in general, provides the attractive security and enjoyment of tangibility, creative development, or even personal use. But in this, as with each objective, you should decide what is important to *you*.

COMPARING OPPORTUNITIES

After assessing your personal objectives, you can judge the suitability of various opportunities and then decide which specific ones to pursue. The major categories include such real estate investments as your own home, income property, and development property — otherwise you and I wouldn't have bothered with this book. But in addition to real estate (the largest of all investment markets), there are common stocks (having better liquidity but higher risk), bonds (featuring low risk but sacrificing inflation protection), commodities (great leverage potential), and so forth. Each opportunity tends to have different characteristics with regard to the various objectives.

Real estate, for example, traditionally offers a comparatively high rate of return at moderate risk. Its leverage potential is large, but liquidity is restricted. Unfortunately, expenses—for transactions, operations, and supervision—are high compared to other investments. On the plus side again, real estate's tax shelter and inflation protection are almost unmatched and good personal satisfaction is often achieved.

By comparison, art/antiques/gems/stamps/coins tend to provide a moderate rate of return, again with modest risk, but allow little leverage, are terribly illiquid and expensive to buy, hold, and sell. They typically provide great personal satisfaction and excellent inflation protection based on tangibility and rarity—they simply aren't making any more (genuine) sets of circa 1740 Queen Anne walnut side chairs.

YOUR OBJECTIVES–OPPORTUNITIES TABLE

Table 2–1 rates these different investment opportunities for performance toward each of our eight objectives. This table is dubbed "Your Objectives-Opportunities Table" or, for short, the O–O Table. The plus signs indicate a high expected ability to fulfill that objective. The minus signs signal weakness along that performance dimension. A blank represents a medium, or neutral, expectation. The O–O Table can help you judge which types of investments best suit *your* needs.

In reading the O–O Table, the first horizontal line shows that the *Real Estate* category and "Option Writing Hedges" and "Oil, Leasing, Farming Shelters" score well on rate of return. The latter are both sophisticated money management vehicles. However, each has serious drawbacks when viewed by other investment objectives. Option writing hedges typically offer little tax shelter or inflation protection. The oil, leasing, farming deals are often very risky and usually illiquid.

The low risk objective is rated in row two of the O–O Table. The plus rating goes to the "Savings" category. The most risky opportunities are "Development Property," "Common Stock," "Option Buying," "Commodities," and "Oil, Leasing, Farming Shelters." Thus when read row by row, the O–O Table shows which investment opportunities most or least fulfill a particular objective.

By looking down a column, a particular type of investment can be judged. For example, "Income Property" rates a plus on rate of return, leverage, tax shelter, and inflation protection. It rates average (blank) on risk and personal satisfaction. It ranks poor (minus) in liquidity (often taking months to sell) and expenses (rather high for transactions, holding, and management).

These ratings, it should be noted, are *not* subjective. Rather, they reflect investment characteristics that are inherent in these different types of opportunities. Naturally, not all income property will provide a high rate of return despite its rating—such opportunities do entail some risk. Similarly not all common stocks will provide inflation protection—some go down in price, not up. But an objective consensus of experience and opinion indicates that the ratings assigned are those that all investors can typically expect from each type of opportunity.

DOES REAL ESTATE BELONG IN YOUR PORTFOLIO?

Many experts feel that decisions regarding the *types* of assets and their relative *proportions* in your portfolio are even more important than decisions on individual investments. For example: How much should you invest? At what overall risk level (or what portions at different risk levels)? How diversified should you be? How leveraged? How liquid? What is your present and projected tax bracket? Are you on a fixed income or will your salary probably rise with inflation? Does your personal satisfaction come from blowing money or building financial security?

In short, you should invest in light of your own objectives. The O–O Table allows you to decide in a consistent, unemotional way what types of opportunities suit you. Table 2–2 has the rating entries omitted and has an extra first column for you to rate your own objectives. Fill out the first column by assigning your most important objectives with a + rating. The least important ones earn a —. The moderately important ones stay as blanks. This completed first column describes an *objectives profile* that is uniquely yours.

For example, the stereotyped "wealthy young bachelor" might score rate of return and leverage as a plus while low risk and liquidity rate a minus for their unimportance to him. Expenses, tax shelter, inflation protection, and personal satisfaction might all rate a neutral blank. A far different set of objectives would be expected for an elderly retiree dependent on investment income or for a growing family of limited means and a need for liquidity.

Next, you can rate the various opportunities for suitability. You do this by comparing your objectives profile to each opportunity rating in Table 2–1. If your objective or the opportunity rates minus, score "zero." If not, one + scores "1"; two +'s score "2." Record the results in that row and column of Table 2–2. Then sum each column.

TABLE 2-2
Your Objectives-Opportunities Table

Investment Objectives / Your Objectives Profile	Real Estate			Savings			Bonds			Stocks			Tangibles		
	Home Owner-ship	Income Property	Develop-ment Property	Cash or Checking	Savings Account	Certifi-cates of Deposit	Straight Bonds	Tax-exempt Bonds	Convert-ible Bonds	Option Writing Hedges	Common Stock	Option Buying	Commod-ities	Oil, Leasing, Farming Shelters	Art, Antiques, Gems, Stamps, Coins
1. Rate of return															
2. Low risk															
3. Lever-age															
4. Liquidity															
5. Low ex-pense															
6. Tax shelter															
7. Inflation pro-tection															
8. Personal satis-faction															
Column totals															

Cash (or a checking account) is an easy opportunity to begin with. It is listed in the category "Savings." However, cash (or checking) provides no rate of return, tax shelter, or inflation protection and rates a minus for these objectives. So no matter what your objectives profile is, cash provides no benefits along these dimensions and scores "zero." Cash scores points if you favor such objectives as low risk, liquidity, low expenses and personal satisfaction, where it rates + because most people still like to have cash around, despite its deficiencies! After scoring cash along each of *your* objectives, total its scores and write this sum at the bottom of that column.

If your objectives lean toward high rate of return, leverage, tax shelter, and inflation protection and you can tolerate some risk and illiquidity, you will find from Table 2–2 that real estate is a high scoring investment opportunity. It need not be this way. For example, those foregoing rate of return, leverage, tax shelter, and inflation protection in favor of low risk and liquidity would find that a savings account and straight bonds score high. The question is, which opportunities are best for you?

Depending on the amount of your investable funds, it is wise to diversify into a few different investment opportunities. We have already spoken of an insurance need (before investing). Minimal needs for some low risk, liquid assets probably also dictate a role for some form of savings. Personal satisfaction (not to mention the favorable rate of return shown in Chapter 7) may also justify home ownership. What should you invest in next? For many — and maybe you — the answer is real estate.

3

The Real Estate Market

Real estate is the largest investment market, exceeding the value of stocks, bonds, commodities, or savings. Yet each property is unique and comparable data on profitability and risk are sparse. Investors have had to rely heavily on experience, judgment, and intuition. They still do. But increasingly, professionals and part-timers are seeking a better approach to investment analysis. The successes of the past did not have to contend with the problems of today: 10 percent mortgage rates, 15 percent construction loan interest, inflation, shortages, environmental impact studies, changing population and transportation patterns.

Ironically, real estate investing has been the subject of surprisingly little research and analysis. Stock market investing, by contrast, has been statistically analyzed for decades. And since 1960, when the first large-scale, computer-readable, stock price files were compiled, thousands of comprehensive studies have enumerated its rate of return, risk, liquidity, diversification, and so on. For reference, some historical results of securities investing are summarized in Table 3–1.

TABLE 3–1
Annual Total Rates of Return and Inflation (*total return* includes both income and capital gain or loss)

	Savings	Long-Term Bonds	S&P Stocks	Inflation
1926–29.............	4.0%	4.4%	19.2%	−0.6%
1930–39.............	0.8	6.9	−0.1	−2.1
1940–49.............	0.5	3.0	9.0	5.5
1950–59.............	1.9	0.9	19.2	2.0
1960–69.............	3.8	1.3	7.8	2.3
1970–73.............	5.2	9.3	4.6	5.4

Source: Roger G. Ibbotson and Rex A. Sinquefield, "Stocks, Bonds, Bills, and Inflation: The Past and the Future," Center for Research on Securities Prices, Chicago, Illinois, May, 1974.

In contrast with real estate, the market for stocks is centralized, publicized, and standardized. Three million investors own shares of A.T.&T. that are exactly identical. Their price and trading volume can be checked daily in the local newspaper. And financial disclosure of operating results, as mandated by law for any publicly-owned company, is prompt and detailed.

Instead, real estate investors have enjoyed decades of unscrutinized, but profitable, anonymity—bringing to mind the story about the unspectacular student who returned to his class reunion as a very successful restaurateur. When asked how he had made out so well, he replied, "I buy steaks for $1 each and sell them for $3, so I make 2 percent on every one." Something had made his investment profitable, but it certainly wasn't his analysis. Real estate investors have often enjoyed a similar kind of success. Overall, their record can be described by the kid writing home from camp, who said, "We are all having fun here, but we don't know how much."

Are today's real estate opportunities also worth pursuing? Is it still possible to someday tell others "How I turned $1,000 into a million in real estate—in my spare time," as William Nickerson did in his excellent book of that title, first published in 1959. It should be. But now is a time calling for different strategies and for analysis that, at the least, figures the percent return correctly. Good investment evaluation can help separate out the likely losers. It can also convince you and others about the profits realizable from the likely winners. And it can point to the risk factors that bear watching.

Real estate's institutions and techniques often seem foreboding and bewildering to the uninitiated. So to select, design, and implement profitable projects an overview of the real estate market is helpful. This chapter discusses the key *participants* in this market— brokers, builders, bankers, and buyers—and then the key *vehicles* for investing—direct ownership, partnerships, limited partnerships, real estate corporations, and REITs. The remainder of Part I then develops and illustrates our investment analysis procedure and Part II applies it to the different types of real estate, enabling you to judge the strategy that is right for you.

BROKERS

The most frequently encountered participant in the real estate market, and the most numerous, is a broker or a real estate salesperson. The latter must pass a state qualifying exam and usually works for a broker. Brokers have additional qualifications and experience. Firms belonging to a regional board affiliated with the National Association of Real Estate Boards (NAREB) may use the title Realtor. These professionals act to bring buyer and seller together. Their compensation is typically on commission, paid by the seller, for transactions arranged.

By dealing with a broker you get exposure to a broader list of properties and help with the screening and selection process. Usually a broker will also assist in transaction negotiation and financing. When you are ready to sell or trade, a broker's existing contacts and marketing capability can again be helpful, but now its your turn to pay the commission for these services.

Other specialized activities may be part of a real estate office's capabilities. Similarly, there are professional groups representing these additional functions. Examples include the Society of Industrial Realtors, the American Institute of Real Estate Appraisers, the Institute of Real Estate Management, and the American Society of Real Estate Counselors.

BUILDERS

Builders and developers create the supply of new housing. They create their own trade organizations as well, including the National Association of Home Builders and the Prefabricated Home Manufacturers Institute. The volume of their activity is highly cyclical. It responds mainly to interest rates, which affect both construction loan costs and the mortgage bite sustained by the buyer. Figure 3.1 shows this counter-cyclical relationship between new housing starts and mortgage

FIGURE 3.1

New Housing Starts and Mortgage Rates

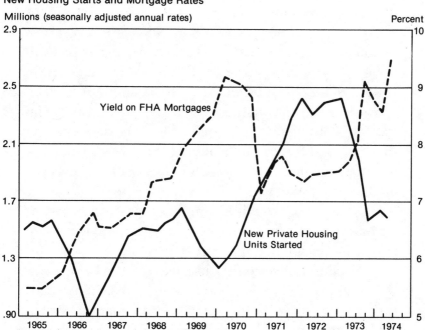

Millions (seasonally adjusted annual rates)

Yield on FHA Mortgages

New Private Housing Units Started

Data: Commerce Dept., Federal Housing Administration

rates. Additionally, the cost of building materials, population and demographic shifts, federal programs, zoning controls, rent regulations, fuel costs and so on can all influence the volume and location of residential construction.

Industrial and commercial construction follow the somewhat different pattern of the business cycle. Much of this building is specialized in nature and owned by the company that will operate the facility. Nonetheless, the commercial property market is a large one. These opportunities for investors are discussed in Chapter 9.

BANKERS

Strictly speaking, "banker" is too narrow a term for those providing financing in the real estate market. In addition to commercial banks, a sampling of institutions includes the Mortgage Bankers Association, the United States Savings and Loan League, the American Savings and Loan Institute, and the National Association of Mutual Savings Banks. Their members act as the main source of conventional mortgage loans. For example, savings institutions provide about 60 percent of all residential loans. Insurance companies supply money for larger deals or for packages composed of several individual mortgages. Foreign capital is becoming an increasingly important source.

The federal government has taken an active role in this field, especially in guaranteeing, subsidizing or arranging for resale of mortgages. The Federal Housing Administration (FHA) was created in 1934 to bring rationality to a depressed—and often foreclosed—real estate market. It does not lend money. Rather, it insures loans made by approved and supervised lending sources. FHA insured mortgages offer the advantage of lower interest rates based on the government's credit rating (provided for a charge of $\frac{1}{2}$ percent added on to the mortgage rate). They also feature high loan-to-value ratios, long loan life, monthly self-amortizing payments, and minimum specifications for building standards. By contrast, the Veterans Administration (VA) usually guarantees mortgages. But it also insures them and sometimes makes loans directly. This agency was created in the 1944 GI Bill, but Korean and Vietnam veterans now qualify too.

Three other agencies established by the government

are important in real estate finance—Fannie Mae, Freddie Mac, and Ginnie Mae. These offspring of Uncle Sam have recently been given enlarged roles. Fannie Mae, a now-public company traded on the New York Stock Exchange, buys mortgages. It conducts biweekly auctions (often by telephone, earning it the additional nickname of "call girl") in which qualified mortgage sellers competitively offer bundles of mortgages priced to provide a stated interest yield. By the end of the auction day, Fannie's management decides which offers to accept. In turn, Fannie buys these mortgages with funds raised in the conventional money markets, relying on its government credit rating to keep interest costs down. This process adds to the currently $30 billion in assets owned by the FNMA (for Federal National Mortgage Association, Fannie's full name).

Freddie Mac (really the Federal Home Loan Mortgage Corporation) was formed in 1970 to buy mortgage loans from federally chartered savings and loan associations. Ginnie Mae (the Government National Mortgage Association) was formed in 1968. It focuses on FHA–VA government-supported loans. Its creation of a "pass-through" security lets investors buy shares in a pool of mortgages, without the bother of collecting and administering them individually. In total, this powerful trio now provides about $15 billion annually, financing about 500,000 housing units a year.

BUYERS

The real estate buyer presumably is you (or your client). Your objectives in buying real estate—or not buying—were discussed in Chapter 2. Most people do purchase, since census data reveal that about 63 percent of households own where they live. (The economics of this important situation are analyzed in Chapter 7.) But far fewer also own *investment* real estate, of course. We discuss below the many vehicles and instruments for doing so.

DIRECT OWNERSHIP

This form of legal ownership (including joint ownership) is most frequent. It allows income and expenses to be taken directly into one's personal financial statements. Thus losses, as from depreciation, can shelter other income from ordinary taxation. The disadvantage is that the owner is liable to the full extent of his or her (or their) personal worth. Insurance, hopefully, protects against this risk. Also, a lending institution often requires the personal signature of a direct owner as backup mortgage collateral in addition to the property itself.

PARTNERSHIPS

Partnerships (as distinguished from limited partnerships, discussed below) have identical tax and liability features as direct ownership. That is, the partnership organization itself is untaxed. Rather it flows income and expense through to the partners, according to their interests. It is merely a legal, contractual binding of interests of the subscribers to the partnership agreement. Its advantage lies in the pooling of talents and capital combined with the efficiency of specializing responsibilities among the partners.

LIMITED PARTNERSHIPS

The limited partnership is the most frequently used legal entity for group investing in real estate. Often adopted by syndicates, this form of ownership features a general partner who has managerial authority over the property and full financial liability. The *limited* partners, in contrast, are actually restricted from being active in the management of their investment. Otherwise they risk loss of their limited partner status, which limits loss to "only" their investment. Thus limited partners abdicate management authority for relief from financial liability.

A limited partnership may have any number of limited partners. By contrast, a partnership gets unwieldy if sizable because one death, for instance, dissolves the partnership. Limited partnership interests are considered to be securities and, as such, come under state and federal regulation. However, most states and the federal Securities and Exchange Commission (SEC) exempt *small* groups of coinvestors from registration. By contrast, interests sold to the general public must meet stringent disclosure requirements. Risks and financial history must be spelled out, for example.

Limited partners (like direct owners or general partners) are allowed to deduct their allocated share of expenses from their current income. In a development situation, this benefit shelters other ordinary income with the deductible expenses of construction, particularly loan interest. When income is finally produced by the property, this in turn can often be fully sheltered by depreciation deductions. This means that total tax deductions (especially when including mortgage interest) may far exceed one's equity investment.

These tax advantages contribute to overall returns, as we will see. Such opportunities are often restricted because it is desirable that investors have high income needing shelter, and because the limited partner is comparatively illiquid and lacks control. For example, a prospective investor might have to invest at least $5,000 and certify to having some minimum income and net worth. These provisions tend to indicate that the investment is suitable for that investor.

REAL ESTATE CORPORATIONS

The advantages of this legal form are those of any corporation, namely:

1. Stockholder liability is limited to the invested amount.
2. Capital raising and liquidity are facilitated by the ability to sell and transfer shares.
3. Indefinite life of the entity itself.

The principal disadvantage is double taxation, first at the corporate level on earnings and then on dividends when distributed to shareholders. In real estate, it is also significant that losses of the corporation cannot be passed through for shareholders to deduct against their other current income. An attorney, tax advisor, or accountant should be consulted for particular rulings on the intricacies of these organizational, tax, and financial issues.

The shares of larger, publicly-held real estate corporations are listed on national stock exchanges. They may participate in one or several functions within the real estate market, such as homebuilding, development, land sales, or brokerage. Other companies have substantial real estate assets in order to carry out their businesses, such as lumber, mining, or farming operations. (Remember, however, that property ownership was supposed to be a strength of the now-bankrupt Penn Central Railroad!)

REITs

The number and size of REITs (Real Estate Investment Trusts) have mushroomed since their authorization in 1960. Most of this expansion has occurred in the last half dozen years as shown in Figure 3.2. Consequently, investors may be unfamiliar with this vehicle. REITs, in short, are pooled funds investing in real estate. That is, they sell shares of stock, and often con-

FIGURE 3.2
Number and Total Assets of REITs

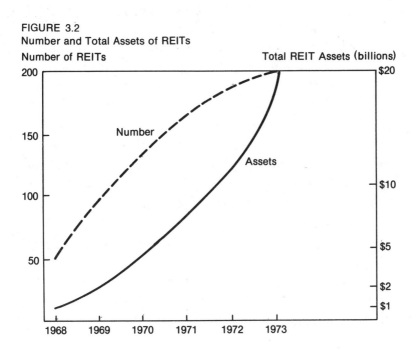

vertible bonds and other debt securities, and then invest the proceeds in the real estate market. The trust itself does not build or manage property. Rather, by pooling the capital of many, it provides the expertise, diversification, and administration that only size can buy.

REITs receive special tax treatment. Specifically, if they pay out 90 percent or more of their annual income to shareholders, then they themselves are exempt from income taxes. These dividends are then taxed at the recipient's personal rate, much like the functioning of a limited partnership. Here, however, a majority vote of shareholders can influence — or remove — the trust's management. But many REITs are named for, affiliated with, and managed by some respected financial institution, such as a bank or insurance company. So as a practical matter, terminating the trust's management contract just isn't done.

REITs are classified as *mortgage* or *equity* trusts, depending on whether they lend on or own property. A mortgage trust arranges either *short-term* (construction) loans or *long-term* (permanent) ones. Some trusts mix these types of assets for diversification beyond that afforded just by participation in many deals. Additionally, the REITs employ leverage to a significant degree, which is not allowed for any but the most specialized mutual funds. Therefore, REITs earn and pay income at rates highly dependent on interest levels and the yield curve (i.e., interest rates for various maturity dates). Accordingly, their overall investment performance has been very volatile, although current dividend yield is usually high. Many REITs are listed on the New York or American Stock Exchanges.

SUMMARY

Among the many institutions in real estate, the prime functions accomplished are those of the broker, builder, and banker. As the buyer in this market, your vehicles include direct ownership, general or limited partnerships, and real estate corporations or investment trusts.

4

Analyzing Real Estate Investments

Most books on real estate discuss operating problems, such as how to design, construct, sell, finance, or manage properties. They may also include a chapter on appraisal. This book is more specialized. We focus on what is perhaps the most important real estate decision: whether or not to *invest* in a property. The operating problems are important, but they begin — or don't begin — because of an investment commitment. The ensuing operations are then all in an effort to achieve the kinds of investment objectives we have already discussed.

This book's contention is that real estate investments should not — and need not — be based on oversimplified analysis. Our upcoming examples and the reference tables of Part III illustrate a comprehensive evaluation method that is easy to understand and apply. After screening many investment opportunities, then negotiating terms, and making judgmental estimates, why skimp on the analysis? You deserve, at that point, an accurate, timely method for assessing investment merit, including rate of return, risk, leverage, liquidity,

47

expenses, tax shelter, and inflation protection. The remaining goal, personal satisfaction, is subjective, but a good analysis ought to contribute even to that.

TRADITIONAL ANALYSIS

Real estate evaluation has been based on a series of methods that approximately compute a property's value. This task requires experience and judgment since each property is unique. For example, professional appraisers are encouraged to use each of three methods to determine a real estate parcel's value:

1. The current cost of reproducing a property less depreciation from deterioration and functional and economic obsolescence.
2. The value indicated by recent sales of comparable properties in the market.
3. The value which the property's net earning power will support, based upon a capitalization of net income.[1]

These are known as the *cost, market,* and *income* approaches.

A similar point of view is taken here. The value received from a property is compared to the resources invested. If the property is being developed, the amount invested is its *cost.* If it already exists and is being purchased, the amount invested is its *market* price (including transaction costs). In either case, the investor must determine—in advance—whether the property

---

[1] From *The Appraisal of Real Estate,* 5th ed.; Chicago, Ill.: American Institute of Real Estate Appraisers, 1967, p. 60.

will produce a sufficient *income* to justify investing this cost or market price.

Too often, property analysis for investment purposes has been inconsistent or incomparable. One method might deal with before-tax "cash flow" while another presents after-tax results. Sometimes a vacancy contingency is omitted. At other times transaction costs are overlooked. To avoid comparing apples and oranges indiscriminately, we will develop a standardized and comprehensive picture of the property's investment merit. We will look at results both in dollars and as percentage rates of return. Four important measures of profitability will be presented:

1. Net income to total invested (before leverage, tax shelter, and sale).
2. Cash flow to equity (after leverage).
3. Cash flow to equity (after tax shelter).
4. Overall cash flow to equity (after sale).

1. Net Income to Total Invested

This most elemental computation estimates the property's current rate of return, before leverage, tax shelter, and resale during inflation. As such it is akin to computing a common stock's dividend yield, which also omits the effects of borrowing (called "margin" for stocks), taxation, and stock price appreciation or decline. A property's net income is found by taking its historical or estimated rent roll and adjusting this for expected vacancy. This result is called "effective gross" or just gross income. From this, operating expenses must be subtracted. Table 4–1 shows the net

TABLE 4–1
Net Income of Medical Building

Rent Roll:	Suite #1 at monthly rental of..................	$	250
	#2		250
	#3		250
	#4		250
	#5		250
	#6		250
	Monthly rent roll	$	1,500
			×12
	Annual rent roll.......................		$18,000
	Less: Vacancy*		1,000
	Gross Income		$17,000
Operating Expenses:	Maintenance............................	$2,550	
	Taxes.....................................	1,950	
	Utilities	1,100	
	Supplies.................................	700	
	Insurance	300	
	Administration	400	
	Total......................................	$7,000	7,000
Net Operating Income:	(Gross Income less Operating Expenses)......................		$10,000

Rate of return of: $\dfrac{\text{Net Operating Income}}{\text{Total Invested}}$ is $\dfrac{\$10,000}{\$100,000} = 10\%$

* It should be noted that Vacancy can be shown as a deduction before Gross Income, as above, or as an item of Operating Expense. In either case the accounting and tax treatment produce an identical result.

income for our suburban medical office building cited in Chapter 1. The *minimum* data requirements for this computation are:

1. Total invested.
2. Gross income.
3. Operating expense.

2. Cash Flow to Equity (after leverage)

Since most properties are purchased subject to a mortgage, and we endorse doing so, the effect of leverage is analyzed next. After the 1930s Great Depression, one fundamental financial reform was a restructuring of standard mortgage contracts. Rather than calling for the loan principal to be due in full after only several years, mortgages now are self-amortizing and of longer life. That is, their monthly payments include both interest on the outstanding debt balance and partial repayment of the loan. The required monthly payment which exactly amortizes the mortgage when due can be computed from the:

1. Mortgage amount.
2. Mortgage interest rate.
3. Mortgage life.

Table 4–2 shows a schedule of annual mortgage payments. For general reference, a **$1,000** mortgage amount is assumed. Notice that each year's total pay-

TABLE 4–2
Mortgage Schedule per $1,000 of Mortgage Amount at 8 Percent Interest for 25 Years (monthly mortgage payment $7.72; yearly mortgage constant $93)

Year	Total Payment	Interest	Amortization	Loan Balance
1	$ 93	$ 80	$ 13	$987
2	93	79	14	973
3	93	77	16	957
4	93	76	17	940
5	93	75	18	922
10	93	66	27	808
15	93	53	40	636
20	93	33	60	381
25	93	4	89	0
Totals	$2,325	$1,325	$1,000	—

The yearly mortgage payments for a $75,000 loan are 75 times $93 or $6,975. This figure allows us to compute cash flow as follows:

Cash Flow = Gross Income − Operating Expense − Mortgage Payment
$3,025 = $17,000 − $7,000 − $6,975

$$\text{Rate of return of: } \frac{\text{Before-Tax Cash Flow}}{\text{Equity}} = \frac{\$3,025}{\$25,000} = 12.1\%$$

ment remains *constant*. However, the amount required for interest decreases, and the amortization portion increases, as the loan balance is paid off. To get dollar amounts applicable to our $75,000 mortgage, multiply these figures by 75. Then we can compute the owner's *cash flow*, or residual income after operating expenses and mortgage payments.

The mortgage has improved the owner's rate of return. That is, the effect of leverage here is positive. Furthermore, it is important to note that amortization provides a build-up of equity in the property. Although this benefit is not yet liberated as cash flowing to the owner, the amortization amount is sometimes added to the actual cash flow and the total called "economic income."

3. Cash Flow to Equity (after tax shelter)

Since income taxes take a significant bite from almost everyone's income, they must be included as relevant to investment analysis. Real estate's vaunted tax shelter stems from three tax law provisions:

1. Expenses incurred for investment purposes are deductible.
2. Depreciation is allowed, providing a tax-free recovery of capital.
3. Long-term capital gains are not recognized until sale and are then taxed at a lower rate.

In the early years of an income property, the owner can usually report expenses, including depreciation, that exceed the property's gross income. This loss for tax purposes shelters not only the cash flow but other

TABLE 4-3
Depreciation Schedules per $1,000 of Depreciation Amount with 25 Year Life

Year	Straight Line (100%)	125%	150%	200%
1......................	$ 40	$ 50	$ 60	$ 80
2......................	40	48	56	74
3......................	40	45	53	68
4......................	40	43	50	62
5......................	40	41	47	57
10......................	40	39	36	38
15......................	40	39	36	28
20......................	40	39	36	28
25......................	40	39	36	28
Totals	$1,000	$1,000	$1,000	$1,000

income as well. Over time, however, depreciation and deductible interest expenses usually decline and net income may rise. Then taxes may be due on part or all of cash flow. Table 4–3 lists the depreciation amounts allowed (again per $1,000) using the four currently applicable depreciation methods. The year 1 after-tax results from our medical building are then shown in Table 4–4. Notice that the tax loss causes a tax rebate

TABLE 4-4
Cash Flow to Equity (after tax shelter)

Taxable Income =	Gross Income..	$17,000
	Less: Operating Expense........................	7,000
	Mortgage Interest..........................	6,000
	Depreciation	4,800
		$ − 800
Income Tax =	Taxable Income	$ − 800
	× Tax Rate...	× .40
		$ − 320
Cash Flow (after tax) =	Cash Flow (before tax)	$ 3,025
	Less: Income Tax.................................	+ 320
		$ 3,345

Rate of return of: $\dfrac{\text{After-Tax Cash Flow}}{\text{Equity}} = \dfrac{\$3,345}{\$25,000} = 13.4\%$

that actually increases our cash flow from its before-tax level.

"Accelerated" types of depreciation are denoted by the percentage of straight line depreciation allowed in the first year. The faster write-off methods improve the tax shelter in the early years at the expense of later years. After varying periods, straight line write-off of the remaining value becomes best for each method and is adopted, as Table 4–3 shows. Accelerated depreciation is still desirable, of course, so Congress has declared a maximum depreciation rate for each class of real estate as follows:

200% for new residential property only.

150% for new commercial property.

125% for used residential having 20 years life or more.

100% for all other.

The factors required to compute this tax shelter effect, in addition to those already listed, are:

1. Depreciation amount.
2. Depreciation life.
3. Depreciation type.
4. Ordinary income tax rate.

4. Overall Cash Flow to Equity (after sale)

Measurement of a property's investment merit is not complete until the effects of sale are considered. Even if a near-term sale is not contemplated, amortization continually builds up equity while depreciation deductions tend to create a future tax liability. These countervailing forces, plus the important impact of inflation and transaction costs, make it necessary to compute (rather than guess or ignore) the after-liquidity results of our investment.

Let us at first assume, as is frequently done, that the property's sale price doesn't change and that selling costs can be overlooked. Then Table 4–5 computes this approximate sale cash flow.

TABLE 4–5
Cash Flow from Sale After Year 1

Sale Price.....................................	$100,000
Less: Debt Repayment...................	74,025 (after $975 amortization)
Taxes Due...........................	960 (20% of $4,800 depreciated)
Sale Cash Flow.........................	$ 25,015

Table 4–5 shows that the owner's capital after sale has nudged upward from the original $25,000 equity to $25,015. But it is wholly inadequate to ignore both inflation and transaction costs in this analysis. Also, a further tax liability stems from a provision called "recapture of excess depreciation." So we must add three final factors that are necessary to compute an overall rate of return:

1. Net sale price.
2. % Annual inflation.
3. Capital gains tax rate.

The first item reflects the transaction costs of selling, namely commissions and closing costs. Suppose these equal 6% of the total invested. Then immediate liquidation of our medical building would produce a net sale price of only $94,000, not the $100,000 assumed in Table 4–5. With inflation, however, we get a counterbalancing benefit. That is, we would expect the net sale price to rise over time. At 5% annual inflation, in one year the price gain would nearly cover the 6% transaction costs. After five or ten years, a worthwhile and tempting gain is available. But sale triggers a tax liability due on any gains beyond the property's book value, possibly including some taxation at ordinary income rates. By now the analysis is getting too tedious for hand calculation, so we will bring in bigger guns.

THE ROLE OF COMPUTERIZED ANALYSIS

Computers are really phenomenal tools. They can perform a CPA-day's worth of arithmetic — perfectly correct and researched to include the latest depreciation and tax rules — in only a few seconds. In fact, using computers for accounting has been likened to squirrel hunting with a cannon. If so, then relying only on a pencil to aid important real estate decisions is like elephant hunting with a peashooter.

Many larger firms routinely use computers for real estate analysis. An increasing number of professional articles have described various approaches and computer programs. But this technique has not been made widely available before. Now individual investors and professionals alike can judge for themselves the startling profit impact of inflation.

THE REAL ANALYSIS

Table 4–6 is the first of many similar tables in this book that result from using a computer program called

TABLE 4-6
Suburban Medical Office Building—Base Case

KEY FACTORS ARE ---

TOTAL INVESTED	MORTGAGE TERMS			OPERATING & INFLATION ASSUMPTIONS				DEPRECIATION			TAX RATES	
	AMOUNT	% INTR	LIFE	NET SALE PRICE	GROSS INCOME	OPERATING EXPENSE	% ANNUAL INFLATION	AMOUNT	LIFE	TYPE	INCOME	CAP GAIN
100000	75000	8.00	25	94000	17000	7000	0.0	80000	25	150%	40%	20%

COMPUTED SUMMARY ---

EQUITY AMOUNT	MORTGAGE TERMS			% INCOME TO TOTAL	% EXPENSE TO INCOME	% NET TO TOTAL	NET SALE PRICE	% NET SALE TO TOTAL	% DEPREC TO TOTAL
	% DEBT	MONTHLY	YEARLY						
25000	75.0	578.84	6946	17.0	41.2	10.0	94000	94.0	80.0

COMPUTED RESULTS ---

YR	HOLDING RESULTS BEFORE INCOME TAXES						HOLDING RESULTS AFTER TAXES					OVERALL RESULTS WITH SALE AT YEAR END					
	GROSS INCOME	OPERATE EXPENSE	MORTGAGE-- INTR	AMORT	CASH FLOW	% RE TURN	DEPREC IATION	TAXABLE INCOME	TAXES DUE	CASH FLOW	% RE TURN	SALE PRICE	DEBT REPAY	TAXES DUE	CASH FLOW	TOTAL PROFIT	% RE TURN
1	17000	7000	5965	982	3054	12.2	4800	-765	-306	3360	13.4	94000	74018	-240	20222	-1418	-5.7
2	17000	7000	5883	1063	3054	12.2	4512	-395	-158	3212	12.8	94000	72955	1245	19801	1372	2.9
3	17000	7000	5795	1151	3054	12.2	4241	-36	-14	3068	12.3	94000	71803	2301	19896	4536	6.5
4	17000	7000	5699	1247	3054	12.2	3987	314	126	2928	11.7	94000	70556	3256	20188	7756	8.4
5	17000	7000	5596	1350	3054	12.2	3748	657	263	2791	11.2	94000	69205	4115	20680	11039	9.5
6	17000	7000	5484	1463	3054	12.2	3523	994	397	2656	10.6	94000	67742	4884	21374	14390	10.3
7	17000	7000	5362	1584	3054	12.2	3311	1327	531	2523	10.1	94000	66158	5569	22273	17813	10.8
8	17000	7000	5231	1715	3054	12.2	3113	1657	663	2391	9.6	94000	64442	6174	23384	21314	11.2
9	17000	7000	5088	1858	3054	12.2	2926	1986	794	2260	9.0	94000	62585	6704	24711	24901	11.5
10	17000	7000	4934	2012	3054	12.2	2865	2201	880	2174	8.7	94000	60573	7210	26217	28581	11.7

REAL.[2] The name REAL could stand for Real Estate Analysis Liberation—a concise and fashionable description, but contrived. Alternately, the name could have been REAP, presumably suggesting Real Estate Analysis Profits. But let's stick with REAL, which simply stands for "real"—as in the real, accurate truth about analyzing real estate—really.

The title line of Table 4–6 shows that the analysis represents our suburban medical office building. The first report section is called "Key Factors Are—." This lists the values of the items already noted as necessary for an investment analysis. They are grouped in the report as:

1. Total invested.
2. Mortgage terms.
3. Operating and inflation assumptions.
4. Depreciation.
5. Tax rates.

The next report section lists a "Computed Summary," facts that are easily derived from the key factor values. For example, since the total invested is $100,000 and $75,000 is mortgaged, the equity amount is $25,000. Further to the right, the "% Net to Total" is shown. This is the first measure of rate of return that we discussed above. However, it omits leverage, tax shelter, and inflation.

The next report section entitled "Computed Results" takes these vital issues into account. It shows a year-by-year investment analysis of the property *before-tax, after-tax,* and *after-sale.* Thus this report

---

[2] The REAL program, written and kept updated by the author, has been used for five years in consulting to real estate professionals and investors.

format parallels the analysis we performed manually for year 1 of our medical building. The columns on the far left show the property's $17,000 annual gross income, its $7,000 annual operating expense, and then an accurate calculation of mortgage interest and amortization. This income, less expense and mortgage payments, produces a before-tax cash flow of $3,054.[3] As shown, this represents a 12.2% return on our $25,000 equity.

The after-tax results of holding the investment are presented in the middle third of the report. Allowable depreciation is $4,800 in year 1, but then drops as time marches on. Taxable income, which is gross income less operating expense, interest, and depreciation, is computed to be $—765. Thus we have sheltered cash flow completely and some other income as well. At a 40 percent ordinary income tax rate, this results in "taxes due" of $—306, really a refund of this amount. This boosts year 1's after-tax cash flow to $3,360, a 13.4 percent return on our equity.

The third of the analysis on the far right shows the effects of selling the property after holding it for any number of years. In Table 4–6 the sale price, which is net of 6 percent for transaction costs, is $94,000. The "Debt Repay" column shows the mortgage balance due at any year end. Taxes due, based on the latest

---

[3] Computers, like accountants, round off results for reporting purposes. Annual reports no longer carry figures out to pennies and large companies sometimes round off to the nearest thousand dollars. Unlike accountants, however, computers don't have the common sense to always arrange the rounding properly. Because each number is correctly, but *separately*, reported to the nearest dollar, an occasional sum might seem to be $1 off. This is no cause for concern, especially when you recall that the purpose of the analysis is to estimate the future and not to account for the past. Besides, each individual number *is* represented as accurately as possible.

federal legislation, also get deducted from the net sale price in arriving at the "Sale Cash Flow" figure: $20,222 in year 1.

What is our *total return*, including both holding income and capital gain or loss? The right-most two columns list these overall results. "Total profit" is the after-tax cash flow from holding through that year and then selling at year end. With sale after year 1, a $1,418 loss results. Why? Because stiff transaction costs are not overcome by an inflating sale price in this example. To be profitable, the property must be held longer.

By contrast, the year 3 total profit is $4,536. It is the sum of the $3,360, $3,212 and $3,068 yearly holding cash flows plus the $19,896 sale cash flow, less recouping the original $25,000 equity. This sequence of after-tax cash flows, for sale at the end of year 3, is then "discounted" to produce the right-most column.[4] Here this overall rate of return is an unexciting 6.5 percent, but it improves for longer holding periods.

THE INFLATION FACTOR

Table 4–6 lists among its key factors an annual inflation assumption of 0.0 percent. Do you believe that? If not, we can change this factor's value, as shown

---

[4] This discounted rate of return, called an internal rate of return, is that interest rate which equalizes future cash flows to the initial cash outlay. For example, receiving $1.08 one year hence implies an 8% annual return if $1.00 must be invested today to get it. Both the timing and amount of future cash flows are taken into account by this internal rate of return computation. Also, for greatest simplicity and consistency, the cash inflows are assumed to occur at year end. To the extent net income is actually received during the year and can draw interest, extra profits and slightly higher rates of return can be achieved. Thus rates of return are conservatively stated.

TABLE 4–7

Key Factors in Real Estate Investment Analysis

Project Title — *SUBURBAN MEDICAL OFFICE BLDG. - WITH INFLATION*

	1)	Total Invested (equity plus debt including closing costs)	$ *100,000*	
Mortgage Terms	2)	Mortgage Amount (show either $ or %)	$ *75,000* or _____ %	of Total Invested
	3)	Interest Rate	*8* % Annually	
	4)	Mortgage Life	*25* Years	
Operating and Inflation Assumptions	5)	Net Sale Price (currently, before inflation, net of transaction costs)	$ *94,000* or _____ %	of Total Invested
	6)	Gross Income (annually, before inflation)	$ *17,000* or _____ %	of Total Invested
	7)	Operating Expense (annually, before inflation)	$ *7,000* or _____ %	of Gross Income
	8)	Annual Inflation (in sale price, gross income, and operating expense)	*5* %	
Depreciation	9)	Depreciation Amount	$ *80,000* or _____ %	of Total Invested
	10)	Depreciation Life	*25* Years	
	11)	Depreciation Type (percent of straight line)	*150* %	200% for New Residential 150% for New Commercial 125% for Used Residential with 20 Years Life or More 100% for All Other
Tax Rates	12)	Ordinary Income	*40* %	
	13)	Capital Gains	*20* %	

in Table 4–7, a form for specifying our 13 key factors. Here a 5 percent annual inflation rate is to be applied to the property's sale price, gross income, and operating expense. For a hand-calculated analysis this would be a loathesome task. But a brief burst of computer power produces the revised results shown in Table 4–8.

Your trained and curious glance should immediately drift to the right-most column of results. It shows the overall rate of return after considering leverage, tax shelter, and sale with inflation. It presents an accurate, REAListic picture of the property's investment merit. In all, this report quantifies seven of our eight investment objectives: rate of return, risk (by comparing tables with different key factor values), leverage, liquidity, expenses, tax shelter, and inflation protection. Personal satisfaction is still for you to judge.

The no-inflation analysis may be interesting, and it has held sway in real estate circles for decades, but the impact of rising rents and sale prices is absolutely dynamite. By present standards, our 5 percent inflation assumption seems reasonable and perhaps conservative. It is, at the least, likely to be closer to the truth than assuming *no*-inflation. Yet such *inflation boosts the overall rate of return to double the no-inflation levels.*

Figure 4.1 compares the right-most columns of Tables 4–6 and 4–8. The inflation-swollen rate of return is nothing less than excellent. After-tax returns of 20 percent or more annually are attainable when the property is held at least a few years, thereby overcoming the effects of high transaction costs. To provide comparable results, a bond, for example, would

TABLE 4-8
Suburban Medical Office Building—Inflation

KEY FACTORS ARE ---

TOTAL INVESTED	---MORTGAGE TERMS--- AMOUNT	% INTR	LIFE	---OPERATING & INFLATION ASSUMPTIONS--- NET SALE PRICE	GROSS INCOME	OPERATING EXPENSE	% ANNUAL INFLATION	---TAX RATES--- INCOME	CAP GAIN	---DEPRECIATION--- AMOUNT	LIFE	TYPE
100000	75000	8.00	25	94000	17000	7000	5.0	40%	20%	80000	25	150%

COMPUTED SUMMARY ---

EQUITY AMOUNT	---MORTGAGE TERMS--- % DEBT	MONTHLY	YEARLY	% NET SALE TO TOTAL	% INCOME TO TOTAL	% EXPENSE TO INCOME	% NET TO TOTAL	% DEPREC TO TOTAL
25000	75.0	578.84	6946	94.0	17.0	41.2	10.0	80.0

COMPUTED RESULTS ---

YR	GROSS INCOME	OPERATE EXPENSE	INTR	AMORT	CASH FLOW	% RETURN	DEPRECIATION	TAXABLE INCOME	TAXES DUE	CASH FLOW	% RETURN	SALE PRICE	DEBT REPAY	TAXES DUE	CASH FLOW	TOTAL PROFIT	% RETURN
1	17000	7000	5965	982	3054	12.2	4800	-765	-306	3360	13.4	98700	74018	1020	23662	2022	8.1
2	17850	7350	5883	1063	3554	14.2	4512	105	42	3512	14.0	103635	72955	3172	27508	9380	18.3
3	18742	7717	5795	1151	4079	16.3	4241	989	396	3683	14.7	108816	71803	5265	31749	17304	21.3
4	19680	8103	5699	1247	4630	18.5	3987	1890	756	3874	15.5	114257	70556	7307	36394	25823	22.5
5	20664	8509	5596	1350	5209	20.8	3748	2812	1125	4084	16.3	119970	69205	9309	41456	34969	22.9
6	21657	8934	5484	1463	5817	23.3	3523	3756	1503	4314	17.3	125968	67742	11278	46948	44776	23.0
7	22782	9381	5362	1584	6455	25.8	3311	4727	1891	4564	18.3	132267	66158	13222	52887	55278	22.9
8	23921	9850	5231	1715	7125	28.5	3113	5728	2291	4834	19.3	138880	64442	15150	59288	66513	22.8
9	25117	10342	5088	1858	7828	31.3	2926	6760	2704	5124	20.5	145824	62585	17069	66170	78520	22.6
10	26372	10659	4934	2012	8567	34.3	2865	7714	3086	5481	21.9	153115	60573	19033	73509	91340	22.4

Section headers: ---HOLDING RESULTS BEFORE INCOME TAXES--- (GROSS INCOME, OPERATE EXPENSE, MORTGAGE INTR/AMORT, CASH FLOW, % RETURN); ---HOLDING RESULTS AFTER TAXES--- (DEPRECIATION, TAXABLE INCOME, TAXES DUE, CASH FLOW, % RETURN); ---OVERALL RESULTS WITH SALE AT YEAR END--- (SALE PRICE, DEBT REPAY, TAXES DUE, CASH FLOW, TOTAL PROFIT, % RETURN)

FIGURE 4.1
Comparison of 0 Percent Inflation and 5 Percent Inflation

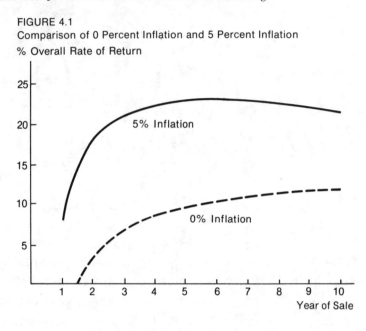

have to pay a 30 percent or higher interest rate, because its income is fully taxable. Clearly, real estate can be the key to profiting from inflation.

SUMMARY

An analysis method has been developed that includes only the minimum number of key factors — 13 in all — needed for real estate investment evaluation. You can use it to compute accurate, consistent rates of return that include the effects of leverage, tax shelter, and inflation. The results of our medical building analysis indicate that *inflation can double the overall rate of return from real estate*. However, such investments are illiquid and, if sold prematurely, can produce a loss.

5

A Case Example—
the Devine Property

This chapter illustrates an actual case example of using the REAL analysis developed in Chapter 4. We also discuss getting started in investment real estate and the steps toward successful buying, operating, and cashing in. In Chapter 6 we extend our case example, dissecting the individual benefits and risks of leverage, tax shelter, and inflation. Part II then analyzes the gamut of real estate opportunities, enabling you to conclude which types of properties seem right for you.

GETTING STARTED

The best initiation into real estate is home ownership. While noneconomic considerations usually take precedence in this decision, the investment aspects are also important. (The special features of this situation are analyzed in Chapter 7.) Furthermore, home ownership provides first-hand experience in selecting, financing, closing, and operating a property as well as insight into its tax and appreciation benefits. Presuming that you have already gone this route, or eschew this life style for personal reasons, we will now analyze a typical, "starter," real estate investment.

The first prerequisite is *attitude*. You must be ready to invest, willing to stay invested, and able to accept occasional operating responsibilities. Real estate does not have the safety and liquidity of savings, for example, or the liquidity and passive participation of mutual funds. The insecure should note that a property's price is not quoted daily in newspaper financial pages and that arranging rentals or sale may require some marketing savoir-faire. It also helps if you get personal satisfaction from the tangibility, uniqueness, and control of your property.

Next comes *knowledge*. Each real estate property is unique. The selling price is a negotiated, private, mutual decision, not a finely-adjusted balance of many publicized transactions as on national stock exchanges. Differential knowledge — such as understanding zoning possibilities or analyzing new highway plans — can lead to revised values that both parties may not be equally aware of. Even with the same knowledge of the property and of its "highest and best use," investors vary in their objectives and their analysis ability. As this book should demonstrate, the exact effect of leverage, tax shelter, inflation, and other factors is not intuitively obvious. Analyzing these factors rapidly and accurately provides an advantage, even with comparable information.

Third, you need *capital*, usually including some of your own. How much depends on the types of properties and degree of diversification you seek. But, at the minimum, you should plan on having equity of

20 to 25 percent of the total invested. For a building lot or a few acres of undeveloped country land, equity of a few thousand dollars might do. Somewhat grander designs — such as a duplex, a several-unit apartment, or diversification into two or three small properties — typically require a minimum of around $10,000 of investable funds. To assure that your personal insurance, liquidity and housing needs are met first, you probably should have a net worth of $25,000 or more before considering investment real estate. Furthermore, if your annual family income is about $20,000 or more, real estate's tax shelter will provide additional benefits relative to most other investment opportunities.

Fourth, you must *invest.* Not a nickel is earned on investment until you buy something. Your attitude, knowledge, and capital must be galvanized into action. And your commitment cannot be easily undone, given the time spent investigating, negotiating and financing, coupled with the high transaction costs and resale illiquidity of most properties. Getting started is a gutsy decision.

CHOOSING YOUR FIRST INVESTMENT PROPERTY

Exuberant speakers and journalists often extoll the virtues of:

> Country land.
> Waterfront property.
> Expanding suburbs.
> New highway intersections.
> Resort second homes.
> The growing South.

The growing West.
The growing Southwest.
And so on.

While legend has it that *location* is the first, second, and third most important factor, it should be obvious that no investing formula suits everyone. For your first property, choose something within your means, in a familiar location, and within your ability to oversee. Buying an existing income-producing property is less risky than development property or holding raw land while waiting for its ultimate user to enter the picture. Check the seller's credentials and verify the property's purported financial statements. Retain experts, but plan to study their methods and documents — your goal is an independent ability to evaluate property and negotiate terms.

Seek and shop for maximum *leverage*. Limit your capital investment by including necessary appliances, repairs, fixtures, and closing costs in the purchase price, when possible, because it is the main basis for setting the mortgage amount. With proven income property in a stable or upgrading location, your risk of not having rents meet the mortgage is slight. Naturally, smaller units or a single-family house suffer proportionately more if a vacancy persists.

Assume an existing, below-the-market mortgage, if available. A *non-recourse* loan limits your risk to the equity amount invested. Avoid prepayment penalty clauses. Remember, you will probably sell or refinance after several years. Make sure the seller is willing to pay any mortgage points demanded by the lender. ("Points" amount to prepaid, extra interest; each point is 1 percent of the loan amount.) See if a second mortgage can be arranged with the seller, although this may stiffen his negotiable selling price.

Above all, choose a property for its *appreciation* potential. View income as a means of paying the mortgage while providing an acceptable return on your down payment. The upside play is a capital gain from resale or a tax-free refinancing or trade. This gain on your first property can then become the cornerstone for your real estate pyramid. Beware, however, the long easy slide down from a pyramid's precarious pinnacle. In short, get carried, not buried, by your first investment.

For subsequent investments, these guidelines change. You can then more knowledgeably diversify or venture into development situations or more remote locations — again selecting properties for their appreciation potential. Look for factors like expanding development, population growth or shift, new infrastructure (roads, utilities, schools and shopping), and increasing status attached to the area. Remember that inflation works on all property, so try to find the extra advantage that real appreciation provides. For example, selective repairs to older properties can lead to both increased income and capital gains. In general, however, quality in location and construction appreciates the most.

THE INVESTMENT ANALYSIS

Having selected opportunities according to the qualitative guidelines above, a REAL analysis can be extremely useful. Our examples and Part III's tables let you do this easily. With these quantitative results you can discover the investment characteristics of each property and compare them. Additionally, you can investigate various possible terms, such as a 10 percent mortgage interest rate for 80 percent of the purchase price versus a $9\frac{1}{2}$ percent rate for only 70 percent financing. This sharpens your ability to make money-making and money-saving decisions.

A thorough investment analysis begins with a *base case*. This is a set of "best guesstimate" values for our thirteen key factors. The REAL analysis is then your mechanism for translating these judgments into measures of investment performance. Next, as done in Chapter 6, you can selectively vary the values of key factors to determine their individual impact on overall results. This is called a *sensitivity analysis* and it provides a great insight into the sources and degree of risk. The ensuing example's base case and risk analysis will demonstrate the role of each key factor.

THE BASE CASE

This actual investment, made by the author, involves a middle class, desirable-suburb, residential property. This fits our guidelines for your initial real estate investments. Its traditional four-bedroom plus family room design makes this property easily marketable, as does its quiet street location bordering on a secluded town park. Its appeal to a young family is further enhanced by the local school district's fine reputation. This is especially important because the largest percentage growth in any age group during

1975–80 will be in the 30–35 year olds. This maturing post World War II baby boom group will then need such family-oriented, metropolitan housing.

The property neighbors on rather expensive homes, typically owner-occupied. Thus, the property tax burden is mainly absorbed by others and the whole area exudes status and stability. The brick and stone construction (20 years old) should keep maintenance costs down. Additionally, by being relatively near the city center and mass transit, this location should benefit from consumer concern over the changing economics of transportation. For these reasons — and because the prior owners were named Devine — we call it "the Devine property." Now let's see if it is.

Before negotiating purchase and a mortgage we performed several variations of the REAL analysis, based on comparable sales, rentals, expenses, and available mortgage terms. Many of the key factors can be determined accurately, such as the depreciation allowance and your tax rates. Other factor values, such as rental rates and mortgage terms, are under your control or subject to known market conditions. The total to be invested is the major issue for negotiation. This leaves the net sale price, operating expense, and % annual inflation as most in doubt — and hence worth analyzing for their impact on profit and risk. Table 5–1 shows the key factor values for the purchase price, mortgage terms, and so forth actually applicable to this property. Then Table 5–2 shows the REAL investment results.

Note that the first section of Table 5–2 repeats the 13 key factor values. The second section computes some easily derived amounts and percentages. The

TABLE 5–1

Key Factors in Real Estate Investment Analysis

Project Title __*THE DEVINE PROPERTY*__

	1) Total Invested (equity plus debt including closing costs)	$ _37,800_

Mortgage Terms

2)	Mortgage Amount (show either $ or %)	$ _28,800_ or _____ % of Total Invested
3)	Interest Rate	_7½_ % Annually
4)	Mortgage Life	_25_ Years

Operating and Inflation Assumptions

5)	Net Sale Price (currently, before inflation, net of transaction costs)	$ _37,800_ or _____ % of Total Invested
6)	Gross Income (annually, before inflation)	$ _4,080_ or _____ % of Total Invested
7)	Operating Expense (annually, before inflation)	$ _1,200_ or _____ % of Gross Income
8)	Annual Inflation (in sale price, gross income, and operating expense)	_5_ %

Depreciation

9)	Depreciation Amount	$ _32,000_ or _____ % of Total Invested
10)	Depreciation Life	_20_ Years
11)	Depreciation Type (percent of straight line)	_125_ % { 200% for New Residential 150% for New Commercial 125% for Used Residential with 20 Years Life or More 100% for All Other

Tax Rates

12)	Ordinary Income	_40_ %
13)	Capital Gains	_20_ %

TABLE 5-2
The Devine Property—Base Case

KEY FACTORS ARE ----

TOTAL INVESTED	----MORTGAGE TERMS----			----OPERATING & INFLATION ASSUMPTIONS----				----DEPRECIATION----			----TAX RATES----	
	AMOUNT	% INTR	LIFE	NET SALE PRICE	GROSS INCOME	OPERATING EXPENSE	% ANNUAL INFLATION	AMOUNT	LIFE	TYPE	INCOME	CAP GAIN
37800	28800	7.50	25	37800	4080	1200	5.0	32000	20	125%	40%	20%

COMPUTED SUMMARY ----

EQUITY AMOUNT	----MORTGAGE TERMS----			% NET SALE TO TOTAL	% INCOME TO TOTAL	% EXPENSE TO INCOME	% NET TO TOTAL
	% DEBT	MONTHLY	YEARLY				
9000	76.2	212.82	2554	100.0	10.8	29.4	7.6

% DEPREC TO TOTAL
84.7

COMPUTED RESULTS ----

YR	----HOLDING RESULTS BEFORE INCOME TAXES----						----HOLDING RESULTS AFTER TAXES----					----OVERALL RESULTS WITH SALE AT YEAR END----					
	GROSS INCOME	OPERATE EXPENSE	--MORTGAGE-- INTR	AMORT	CASH FLOW	% RE TURN	DEPREC IATION	TAXABLE INCOME	TAXES DUE	CASH FLOW	% RE TURN	SALE PRICE	DEBT REPAY	TAXES DUE	CASH FLOW	TOTAL PROFIT	% RE TURN
1	4080	1200	2146	408	326	3.6	2000	-1266	-506	833	9.3	39690	28392	858	10440	2272	25.2
2	4284	1260	2115	439	470	5.2	1875	-966	-386	856	9.5	41674	27953	1685	12037	4726	24.4
3	4498	1323	2080	473	621	6.9	1758	-663	-265	887	9.9	43758	27480	2485	13794	7369	23.6
4	4723	1389	2044	510	780	8.7	1648	-358	-143	923	10.3	45946	26969	3262	15715	10214	23.0
5	4959	1459	2004	550	947	10.5	1545	-48	-19	966	10.7	48243	26420	4019	17805	13270	22.3
6	5207	1532	1961	592	1122	12.5	1545	169	68	1054	11.7	50655	25827	4799	20029	16548	21.8
7	5468	1608	1915	638	1306	14.5	1545	399	160	1146	12.7	53188	25189	5604	22395	20061	21.3
8	5741	1689	1866	688	1499	16.7	1545	642	257	1242	13.8	55847	24501	6434	24913	23820	20.8
9	6028	1773	1812	741	1701	18.9	1545	898	359	1342	14.9	58640	23759	7280	27600	27849	20.4
10	6329	1862	1755	799	1914	21.3	1545	1168	467	1447	16.1	61572	22960	8153	30459	32155	20.0

third section is the year-by-year display of investment results derived from the key factor values. Using the latest accounting, depreciation, and tax rules, these profitability results are computed on a "before tax," "after tax," and "after sale" basis. As discussed, the most crucial answers are at the far right — the after-tax, after-sale overall rate of return for each year. This base case suggests that our property is indeed "divine." For example, the overall rate of return ranges from 25 percent to 20 percent compounded annually after-tax.[1]

The "Total Profit" column (next to last on the right) shows the cumulative dollar profit from holding the property and then selling it at the end of the indicated year. As of year five, these profits total to $13,270, in large measure due to inflation working for us. Furthermore, some of these dollars come in earlier years and can be invested elsewhere before year five.

How much do we profit in the period before sale? The left-of-center columns labeled "Cash Flow" and "% Return" reveal first the before-tax cash flow from holding and then this "spendable" return as a percentage of the original equity. In this example, the before income taxes results are not exactly spectacular: $326 in cash flow (gross income, less operating expense and mortgage payments). As a percent of the $9,000 equity, this provides only a 3.6% return. Clearly this is an incomplete view of the property's investment merit.

---

[1] As the next chapter's risk analysis will show, this high return is principally dependent on two assumptions: that the property was bought cheaply enabling it to be resold with no loss, despite transaction costs; and that inflation would boost income, expenses, and sale price at 5% per year. To date these assumptions have been borne out. Furthermore, the mortgage has proven to be attractive relative to more recent interest rates.

The center columns show "Cash Flow" and "%
Return" on an after-tax basis. This is the full profit
from holding, counting tax shelter. It is $833 in the
first year (9.3% return on equity) and rises slightly
thereafter. But notice that the after-sale "% Return"
is much higher: 25.2% initially. Inflation has produced a
significant capital gain. In this case, the overall %
return then tapers off. This is because the leverage
and tax shelter benefits are eventually dissipated.

ARRANGING FINANCING

Having satisfied yourself that a particular opportunity meets your investment objectives, arranging to
buy it is the next step. We have suggested that maximum leverage be sought, especially for your earlier
projects when capital building (rather than safety or
liquidity) is probably the key goal. Telephone several
mortgage lenders and visit a few to ascertain the
availability and cost of a mortgage for the kind of
property you plan to finance. Inquire about "hidden"
costs such as points, prepayment penalties, insurance
premiums, and application, appraisal, and attorney's
fees. Be prepared to disclose your personal financial
status—a statement of assets, liabilities, and net
worth is usually required.

Mortgage rates are largely dictated by national
money market conditions, although somewhat restrained by state usury laws and federal agency programs. Mortgage terms still vary from lender to lender
at any particular time, so it may pay to shop around.
However, on specialized deals or when enlisting a
professional mortgage broker to obtain financing,

"shopping a deal" may be a poor practice. After drumming up alternatives, your major decision is choosing between various interest rates and mortgage amounts.

For example, a loan for 70 percent of the purchase price may be obtainable at a $9\frac{1}{2}$ percent interest rate. Alternately, an 80 percent "loan to value ratio" may be available at 10 percent interest. Both have a 25-year life. Which should you choose? A REAL analysis of each situation allows a dollar-by-dollar comparison. Usually—if you can stand the added risk—the larger mortgage would boost the rate of return on the smaller equity required. Is the larger mortgage worth it, despite your intuition to rebel at such high rates? You have to decide, but at least you can use more than the seat of your pants as a "base" for decision-making.

NEGOTIATING PURCHASE TERMS

Armed with assurances that acceptable financing is likely, you (or an intermediary) must negotiate terms with the seller. In addition to the purchase price, consider what appurtenances are included, the closing date, the form and timing of payment, any conditions to the sale, and access to the property or financial records prior to closing. Each party to the negotiation seeks varying objectives, ultimately concluding in a voluntary deal that, by definition, is advantageous to both.

Recognizing your adversary's position and desires has been called the first step toward successful bargaining. Then have good reasons why you are a qualified, interested, and desirable buyer—but explain why you feel the asking price is too high. Be prepared to raise your own initial offer if you expect the seller to change his. You can yield most favorably on those factors having greater importance to the seller, while insisting on terms you deem necessary. By offering compromise and articulating reasons for your firmer positions, a note of fairness and a chord of acquiescence may be struck.

Such negotiation ends successfully with the signing of an *agreement of sale.* This legal binder states what is being sold and for what consideration, subject to stated conditions. Signing is usually accompanied by a deposit toward the purchase price. If the proposed buyer defaults on this agreement, then this deposit can often be retained by the seller as liquidated damages and/or the buyer can be sued for "specific performance" of the sale contract. Consequently, the agreement of sale should be made subject to suitable financing and to any other conditions that might cause noncompliance.

CLOSING THE DEAL

The deal is not done, as they say, until checks have been deposited *and have cleared.* Closing is the event which transfers ownership, where old and new mortgage and tax accounts are consummated, and where professionals such as brokers, attorneys, and title insurers get paid. (Of course, some expenses are incurred whether or not closing takes place.) The process involves meeting to execute and confirm the purchase arithmetic, sign appropriate documents, and deliver — usually certified — payment.

RENTING THE PROPERTY

Assuming you have purchased income-producing property (as opposed to land or development property, discussed in Chapter 10), securing tenants is the next step. Your investment analysis estimated rental income and operating expense presumably based on the property's history or a market analysis of comparable situations. Existing and/or likely tenant types and rents have therefore been identified. Securing any additional tenants requires advertising and showing the property or delegating these tasks to a rental agent.

Sunday newspapers and broker listings are the standard advertising media. Selection of prospects should be made only after reviewing the full response to your marketing effort. Payment dependability, probable care for the property, and lease starting date and duration are factors to judge. One guideline is that housing—including utilities—averages about one fourth of a renter's gross income. (For a large or low-income family, with greater housing needs and lesser taxes, the guideline is one third). You can use this rule to judge the income level required of prospective tenants. The first month's rent in advance is the typical consideration upon lease signing, plus a security deposit of the same amount.

OPERATING GUIDELINES

Either you or someone hired as your agent will have to act as the property manager. Professional property managers charge 5% to 10% of gross income for residential properties with the higher rates applying to smaller properties. Management of commercial facilities may be obtained for somewhat less. Among the manager's functions — whether done by you or another — are:[2]

1. Establish rental rates.
2. Market the available space.
3. Qualify and investigate tenants' credit.
4. Prepare and execute leases.
5. Collect rents.
6. Supervise maintenance and repairs.
7. Direct purchasing.
8. Audit and pay bills.
9. Pay insurance premiums and taxes.
10. Maintain proper records and report to the owner.

In addition to these mechanistic responsibilities of the property manager, creative policies can also help you toward your financial goals: increased rent, decreased operating expenses, and assured appreciation. For example, broad marketing can increase the flow and quality of tenant applicants. A target tenant profile can be sought by such tactics as property design (i.e., high security areas for upper income or retired prospects), decoration, appurtenances, athletic facilities, social activities, and the like. Regular and prompt maintenance tends to gain tenant respect and restrain repair costs. Periodic rental adjustments tracking inflation and market trends are vital. This can be accomplished by short term lease contracts (if vacancy is not a problem) or by rent escalator clauses.

---

[2] *Reference Book*, Department of Real Estate, State of California, 1970, p. 383.

CASHING IN

Beyond seeking a suitable holding profit, capital appreciation is the main motivation for investing in real estate during times of inflation. You have three ways to cash in on such inflation/appreciation — sell, refinance, or trade. Sale is most common, but has the least favorable tax consequences and transaction costs. By referring to Table 5–2, our base case example, we can study the financial results of selling at any year end. (Refinancing and trading properties are analyzed in Chapter 11.)

Sale at the end of year 1 shows a net sale price of $39,690. This is the initial net sale price ($37,800) adjusted for the year's inflation — 5 percent in our base case assumption. From this sale proceeds, the mortgage balance due is $28,392 (because $408 of the original $28,800 debt was amortized during year 1). Taxes due are calculated on the difference between the net sale price and book value (cost less cumulative depreciation — here $37,800 less $2,000 or $35,800). Including recapture, the tax due from sale is $858.[3]

When should you sell? Each year's sale cash flow figure shows the actual amount that could be extracted

---

[3] Recapture means that, under certain conditions, the taxes postponed by accelerated depreciation are "recaptured" by taxing some profits at the ordinary tax rate. Here, straight line depreciation of $32,000 for 20 years implies a $1,600 deduction per year. However, 125 percent of that amount ($2,000) was taken under the post-1969 tax rules. Thus, $400 of this $2,000 deduction is considered "excess depreciation" and is subject to full recapture if the property is held less than 100 months. After 200 months ($16\frac{2}{3}$ years) there is no recapture for residential property. From 100 to 200 months it is *pro rata*. Thus, a 40 percent ordinary tax rate is applied to $400 of the $3,890 taxable gain. This yields $160 in taxes due. The capital gain rate applies to the remaining $3,490 gain, here yielding a $698 tax liability at the 20 percent rate. In total, the taxes due are $858 as shown in Table 5–2.

from the property by the act of sale. This is also the amount that you choose to parlay when you do *not* sell in a particular year. After year 1, holding leaves $10,440 of otherwise liquid funds "on the line."

What do you gain by holding? Each year produces an after-tax cash flow from holding (the center "Cash Flow" column) and an increased sale cash flow. The "Total Profit" column combines these two sources of return. Thus, the gain from holding for one more year is the amount by which this total profit increases from the prior year. In this case, not selling provides the $856 after-tax cash flow of holding for year 2 plus the increase in sale cash flow from $10,440 in year 1 to $12,037, a difference of $1,597. This holding gain plus sale gain add up to $2,453, the extra profit for holding through year 2.

Should you hold another year? For any year the amount kept at risk in the project can be stacked up against the extra profit achievable. For year 2, the extractable funds kept committed are $10,440 and the incremental profit from such patience is $2,453. This is nearly a 24 percent after-tax marginal rate of return for the year. As Table 5–2 shows, this good result nearly maintains the high overall rate of return, which declines only slightly as the years pass.

SUMMARY

A base case analysis provides a quick, convenient, accurate view of a proposed opportunity's economic merits. It should be an early step in checking out any situation. The REAL analysis incorporates several under-analyzed but important variables, such as transaction costs, equity build-up through amortization, and tax liability upon sale. But perhaps most importantly, it underscores the dramatic *profit impact of inflation.*

6

Risk Analysis

After performing a base case REAL analysis, it is helpful to evaluate *risk* — the results of adverse changes from the base case. For example, what would be the effect on rate of return if the total invested increased by 2 percent, 5 percent, or 10 percent? What if the project could be swung for 5 percent less investment than assumed in the base case? What would an increase in leverage be worth? What is the risk from higher than anticipated mortgage rates? From high vacancy? And so on.

To answer such questions, a risk analysis was performed for each of the 13 key factors of the Devine property. This chapter's brief discussion of each factor summarizes its impact. Some of the most significant results are displayed graphically for quick comprehension. This analysis of variations from the base case leads to practical decision guidelines for investors. The chapter closes with a table comparing the relative effect of each key factor.

1. Total Invested

One of the most important factors is the price you pay for your property. Overpaying always hurts your rate of return. But while the risk from mistakenly overpaying is great, you can soften the impact by leveraging more or by holding longer. Suppose, for example, that the Devine property had to be purchased for a price higher than that assumed in our base case. Adding 10 percent would raise its price from $37,800 to $41,580. Is this a disasterous blunder?

How much an overpayment hurts the rate of return depends mainly on two issues: how you financed it and your holding duration. Figure 6.1 shows this situation's risk — that is, the adverse change in its overall rate of return. The graph illustrates various holding periods and two financing possibilities:

1.   The overpayment was financed by a proportionally larger mortgage (because the mortgage amount was fixed as a percentage of the total invested).
2.   The overpayment was financed by all equity (because the mortgage amount was fixed in dollars rather than as a percentage of the total invested).

Figure 6.1 reveals that holding this property 5 years or more reduces the adverse impact from overpaying initially. The holding income then outweighs the shrunken capital gain experienced at sale because of the too-high purchase price. How the overpayment was financed also makes a difference. If your mortgage was determined as a fixed percentage of the purchase price (say 75 percent) rather than fixed in dollars, then the lender pays for most of your mistake. Naturally

FIGURE 6.1
Risk from Overpayment Varies with Financing and Holding Period
% Overall Rate of Return

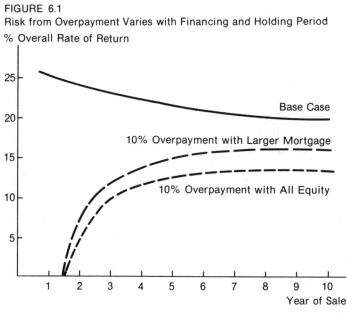

you pay more interest on the larger mortgage, but the project's returns are still favorable and your equity requirement is only slightly larger. With inflation, and if you hold on for several years, the overpayment risk is then moderated.

By contrast, with a short holding period (say one or two years) the results are disasterous. This is precisely how many developers go bankrupt, including some of the multimillion dollar ones mentioned in Chapter 1. For example, the John Hancock building in Chicago incurred a $5 million cost overrun because of originally faulty foundation work. Additional equity was needed to complete construction. This led to the eventual demise of one of the partners in the project, Jerry Wolman, whose highly-leveraged $80 million real estate empire tumbled from the lack of staying power to ride out this type of risk.

2. Mortgage Amount

This second key factor also influences the rate of return significantly. Usually, the more leverage the better, tempered by the increased risk from cost overruns, vacancy, low rents, rampant expenses or similar problems. Figure 6.2 shows that an increased mortgage on the Devine property would boost its rate of return on the lower equity required. For example, if

FIGURE 6.2
High Leverage Increases Rate of Return
% Overall Rate of Return

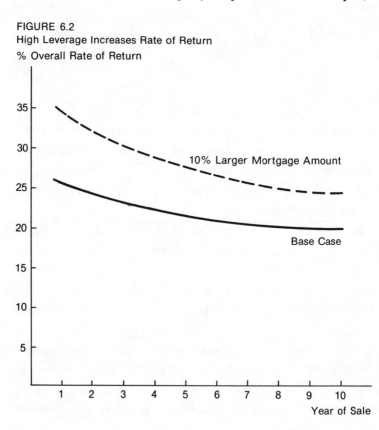

the mortgage amount is increased by 10 percent to $31,680 (83.8 percent of the total invested), then the year 5 rate of return jumps from 22.3 percent to 28.3 percent.

This extra leverage increases risk. The investment becomes very sensitive to a shortfall in income, as from low rents or vacancy. The relative levels of risk can be measured as a reduction in the rates of return. The 10 percent fall in gross income has a more adverse impact on rate of return when leverage is high. You must judge this trade off of return and risk for yourself. But a general rule is: If the project is worth doing, it is probably safe to borrow about 75 percent of the total invested.

3. Mortgage Interest Rate

This factor is perhaps the most discussed variable. Recent tight money has propelled residential mortgages to 10 percent or more while commercial properties face even higher rates. Should you invest with such mortgage terms? What would our base case results have been if a 10 percent interest rate had then prevailed? Our example property is again the context for this analysis, but the conclusions are broadly applicable.

Figure 6.3 shows the lower profit profile for the Devine property, if it had to be financed with a 10 percent mortgage (rather than at 7½ percent) *and all other factors remain unchanged.* Surprisingly, the REAL analysis suggests that mortgage interest rates are *not* as crucial as widely supposed. This large increase in the mortgage interest rate knocks down the overall

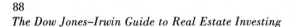

FIGURE 6.3
High Mortgage Rates Lower the Rate of Return

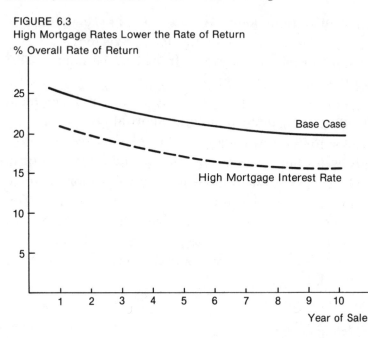

rate of return by a fairly modest amount. And since inflation has produced a very robust rate of return in the first place, the higher mortgage rate is hardly a death knell. Furthermore, should increased inflation accompany these higher interest rates, then rents and sale prices will probably go up more than the higher mortgage costs. Thus with higher inflation, despite the correspondingly higher interest rates, the real estate investor profits even more. The decision guideline is that you can afford to pay an inflated mortgage rate *if* you expect ongoing inflation.

4. Mortgage Life

This fourth factor proves to have little impact on your rate of return. (It is necessary for the correct mortgage computations, however). Longer mortgages stretch out amortization payments. This keeps up the owner's cash flow and leverage. For mortgages as long as 25 years, however, a 10 percent lengthening has little significance. For the Devine property, extending to a 27.5 year mortgage life (with other factors unchanged) boosts the rate of return by only 0.2 percent. It is usually more important to negotiate a favorable mortgage amount and interest rate than to be fussy about its duration.

5. Net Sale Price

This key factor shows the impact of selling costs on the real estate investor. The "total invested" factor includes your buying costs, but these are usually much less than selling costs because commissions are paid by the seller of the property. Thus when you want to liquidate your investment, sizable transaction costs should be anticipated. "Net Sale Price" is defined as the proceeds, after expenses, from immediately reselling your investment. If you expect to encounter 6 percent transaction costs, then the "% net sale to total" would be shown as 94.0 on the REAL report. Future sale prices, after inflation, would also encounter this same proportionate cost of liquidating.

Our base case assumed that the property was favorably bought so that it could be immediately resold, if need be, for the total invested. Suppose the more typical situation prevailed. By changing the net sale price to 94 percent of the total invested, we could guage the impact of selling costs. Figure 6.4 shows this factor's dramatic adverse impact on short holding periods. Over

FIGURE 6.4
Selling Costs Decrease the Rate of Return

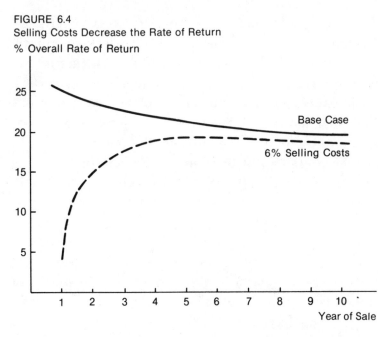

a decade, however, the selling commission has little effect on overall returns. The risk is in being forced to sell early, possibly because of too little income with too much leverage. Then transaction costs only add to your headaches.

6. Gross Income

Rental levels have an important influence on the rate of return throughout an investment. Usually, careful attention is paid to this factor because overestimating the market can lead to high vacancies. Yet too low a rent leaves "money on the table" that could have been earned. Our base case includes $4,080 annual gross income ($340 monthly with the renter paying for utilities). Rent is projected to increase, on average, at 5 percent per year. A 10 percent shortfall in gross income, of itself, only lowers the overall rate of return modestly.

However, two other risks stem from an income shortfall. The first is that the property may slip into a negative cash flow position. Any tax-rebate from depreciation tends to soften this blow, but the owner may still be forced to add to his commitment or to sell prematurely. If so, the second risk is that the net sale price is likely to reflect this lower than expected ability to generate income. And we have already seen that a lower net sale price substantially cuts the overall rate of return.

7. Operating Expense

Operating expenses, and possibly management fees, usually absorb a quarter to a half of gross rentals. Accordingly, elaborate expense projections typically precede the purchase of an income property. Certain expenses are sometimes made the tenant's responsibility to minimize this risk. Nonetheless, the real estate investor usually finds that operating cost control is his most visible and constant problem. Rental income is pretty much pegged for the short run, so any expense bulges are particularly distasteful.

What does the REAL analysis reveal? Again this highly visible variable has, like mortgage rates, received more fanfare than its due. We are not saying to ignore operating costs. But other factors — inflation for one — are dramatically under-analyzed by comparison. For our base case, a 10 percent increase above each year's budgeted operating costs lops less than 1 percent off the overall rate of return.

A much greater risk is stagnant rents (as from a long-term lease or rent controls) that cannot keep up with rising expenses.[1] With maintenance, taxes, fuel, security, and other costs escalating, a reduction—rather than an increase—in net operating income can result. For older properties held past the point of favorable leverage and tax shelter, the owner may have little incentive to hang on. But this trouble usually takes many years to develop. The conclusion? Be sure that rents can be raised at least enough, often enough, to cover inflating costs. And then beware of the political risk of doing so.

8. Percent Annual Inflation

As you have seen by now, inflation has a powerful profit impact. Study Figure 6.5 a moment as it is the major thrust behind this book. Just when inflation became a ubiquitous and growing problem, investors were thoroughly disappointed by stocks, bonds, and savings as a means of storing purchasing power. But what has happened in real estate? We have witnessed a reinvigorated appreciation in—and appreciation for—real estate values. The *after-tax* returns indicated above are

---

[1] A middle ground assumption is that rents will rise with inflation (say at 5% annually), while operating expenses rise somewhat faster (say at 7 percent annually). This would produce net income growth sufficient to support a rise in the sale price at 3 percent annually. Chapter 11 analyzes this perhaps more realistic, but probably conservative, pattern of rising rents, costs, and values. The resulting rates of return still confirm the highly profitable impact of inflation.

FIGURE 6.5
Inflation Boosts Real Estate's Overall Rate of Return
% Overall Rate of Return

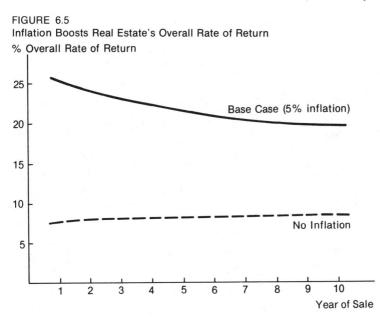

unparalleled by other investment opportunities. And real estate in this country is still undervalued relative to land and building prices in other developed countries. In urban Europe or Japan, for example, comparable housing might cost one and a half times what we would expect to pay.

The securities markets will bounce back and some real estate operators will choose unwisely or be unlucky. But as an investor, be your tendencies toward insurance or gambling, you should know the odds. If you believe the odds are that inflation will continue over the long run and have enough net worth to tolerate illiquidity and enough income to desire its shelter, then Figure 6.5 is a roadmap to real estate.

9. Depreciation Amount

Depreciation is the main source of real estate's tax shelter capability. Tax policy recognizes that a "wearing out" of a physical asset occurs across its economic lifetime. Thus a depreciation provision is allowed, providing an untaxed return of the capital invested. Highly codified standards have been stipulated for the amount, life, and type of such deductions. From the investor's viewpoint, depreciation represents a tax-deductible "expense" that is not a cash cost. Indeed, it often generates a rebate on income taxes otherwise due.

In our base case, the depreciation amount is $32,000 of the $37,800 total invested. The remainder is the implied value of the land, which is not depreciable because land never wears out. Suppose the building itself does not wear out as rapidly as it is depreciated. Suppose, in fact, that it actually appreciates/inflates in value as most properties do, at least until they become hopelessly outdated. Then, a taxable gain would be realized upon sale. So because the tax saving is partly paid back at sale, depreciation's effect is somewhat less dramatic than popularly supposed. For example, boosting the Devine property's depreciable amount by 10 percent (to $35,200) increases the overall rate of return by only 0.4 percent.

10. Depreciation Life

A shorter depreciation life, all other things being equal, fattens the overall return. This is because larger depreciation expenses are thereby allowed in the earlier years. This enhances the up-front tax shelter, while the counterbalancing tax recoupment upon sale is deferred and at preferential tax rates. However, the effect of shortening depreciation life — or the risk from its being longer than anticipated — is modest.

11. Depreciation Type

Various types of depreciation are now in use. The simplest, and least advantageous, is straight line. It deducts expenses for depreciation uniformly over the property's depreciation life. For our base case, with $32,000 depreciable over 20 years, this would result in a $1,600 annual deduction. Tax laws dictate which types of depreciation can be applied to various classes of investment real estate.

The examples of Part II and the reference tables of Part III illustrate four depreciation methods: straight line, 125 percent of straight line (as used in our base case), 150 percent, and 200 percent of straight line. The latter two methods now apply only to new commercial and new residential property, respectively. In each case, the REAL analysis switches to the straight line method when advantageous, as allowed. As will be seen, accelerated depreciation methods boost the overall return somewhat, but usually by only about 1 percent or 2 percent in overall rate of return. In summary, investors should take the largest, shortest, and most accelerated depreciation allowed, when income is available for shelter.

12. Ordinary Income Tax Rate and
13. Capital Gains Tax Rate

The legends about real estate's tax shelter potency are true. Regardless of the investor's tax bracket, his overall return from real estate remains practically constant. By contrast, interest from savings and most bonds is fully taxed. For example, the after-tax return is only half the before-tax interest rate for an investor in the 50 percent bracket. The decision guideline? The higher your ordinary income and capital gains tax rates, the greater the comparative attractiveness of investing in real estate.

COMPARING KEY FACTORS

This chapter has systematically analyzed each of our 13 key factors. It is useful now to compare each factor's impact on a consistent, standardized basis. Table 6–1 serves this purpose. It shows the *changes* in rate of return for selected holding periods caused by a *10 percent increase* in each key factor from its base case value. For example, the first column shows the impact of a 10 percent overpayment, while all other factors remain unchanged. As discussed, this drops the rate of return substantially, especially for short holding periods. This indicates substantial risk if this factor is mis-estimated, as in a development cost overrun.

In another example, the mortgage amount column reveals the impact of a ten percent increase in leverage. Since the base case investment has a favorable return, this incremental leverage boosts it even higher. For instance, the year 5 rate of return improves by 6.0 percent because of this change. Table 6–1, while developed for our base case, shows generally applicable results. You can use it to judge the relative strength of the 13 key factors and their effect on returns for various holding

TABLE 6–1
Risk Analysis for the Devine Property, Change in Overall Rate of Return Caused by a 10 Percent Increase in Key Factor Values (percent)

| Year | Total Invested | Mortgage Terms | | | Net Sale Price | Gross Income | Operating Expense | Annual Inflation | Depreciation | | | Tax Rates | |
		Amount	Interest	Life					Amount	Life	Type	Income	Cap. gain
2........	-17.8	8.5	-1.3	0.1	14.6	2.6	-0.8	1.5	0.4	-0.4	0.1	0.3	-0.7
5........	-8.5	6.0	-1.0	0.2	4.1	2.4	-0.7	1.2	0.4	-0.4	0.2	0.2	-0.4
10........	-5.1	4.1	-0.8	0.3	1.3	2.1	-0.6	0.9	0.4	-0.4	0.2	0.1	-0.2

periods. All investment analysis involves forecasting, but now you can gauge the risk from being wrong.

SUMMARY

Part I has been concerned with analyzing real estate. Since inflation has become a persistent problem, it is necessary to include its impact in your investment thinking. Indeed, real estate can offer a means for *profit*, as well as protection, from inflation. If your own objectives favor a high rate of return with leverage possibilities and tax shelter, and you can tolerate moderate risk and substantial illiquidity, then real estate probably belongs in your investment portfolio.

The real estate market is a large one. And while each property is unique, there are many professionals who can advise you. With the proper attitude and knowledge, anyone can profitably pyramid even a small capital base into substantial wealth. But each opportunity should be analyzed individually for its likely rate of return and sources of risk. Generally, we advise beginning with existing residential income properties. They typically yield good income, have the least risk, are least difficult to manage, and can offer protection plus profit from inflation.

Part II

Investing in Real Estate

12. Conclusions and Strategy

The real estate investor can get high returns at moderate risk, aided by leverage, tax shelter, and inflation. But it requires some management time and accepting illiquidity. The properties, terms, and tactics best suited to various objectives are summarized.

7

Home and Condominium Ownership

We have advocated home (or condominium) owner-ship as a logical and satisfying way to begin investing in real estate. Forty million households seem to agree, owning not only single-family homes, but also town-houses, condominium apartments, and mobile homes in increasing numbers. Admittedly, the economic aspects are only one of many motivations for home ownership. But for many families the steady increase in their home equity through appreciation and mortgage amortiza-tion has made it their best investment. The question remains, "Should *you* own your home?"

THE HOUSING MARKET

The housing market is changing. The traditional single-family detached house is being attacked from two sides. On one end of the scale, mobile homes now account for 97 percent of all homes priced under $15,-000. In 1973 over 560,000 were manufactured.

On another front, the rising cost of capital, land, materials, and labor has altered home design. Town-houses and condominiums allow a higher density of living units per acre. Their common walls also economize on materials and such operating costs as heating and cooling. Thus the condo concept combines the savings of apartment-style construction with the benefits of home ownership. As a result, the number of new condominiums built in 1974 increased 12 percent to nearly 250,000 units. By contrast, the number of new, single-family, "stick-built" homes (excluding mobile homes) declined by over 30 percent to less than 700,000. This represents under 50 percent of all new housing, down from their 75 percent share in the late 1950s. Figure 7.1 depicts these trends.

The location of new housing demand is in flux as well as the type of construction. For one thing, the popula-

FIGURE 7.1

Percent Share of Housing Starts

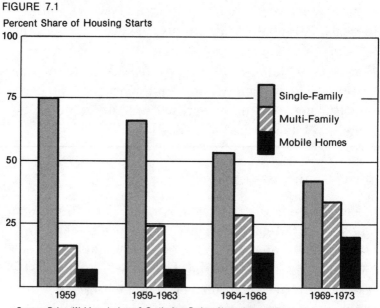

Source: Paine, Webber, Jackson & Curtis, Inc. *Forbes,* November 1, 1974.

tion explosion has become a "birth dearth." The number of children born per thousand women of childbearing age (15 to 44) dropped from 123 in 1957 to only 69 in 1973. This and higher-cost energy may thwart the long-standing trend toward suburban sprawl.

Also our citizenry is migrating toward the good weather (e.g., Arizona, California, and Florida), the good life (e.g., Oregon, Vermont, and selected resort areas), and the good cities (e.g., Atlanta, Denver, and San Francisco). This can have dramatic effects on real estate activity and values. For example, Fort Lauderdale alone added more new housing units in 1973–74 than all of New York City—turning a boom into a glut in the process.

Not all of this housing demand is absorbed by homeowners, but over six in ten households belong in this category. (The remaining renters form a market analyzed in the next chapter, Residential Income Property.) Homeowners face an entirely different set of depreciation and tax rules than do investors in real estate. Since most of this book focuses on investment property, we will deal in this chapter with the important issue of home ownership.

THE ECONOMICS OF HOME OWNERSHIP

First the rules. You can *not* depreciate your own home. This removes a usually significant tax shelter. On the other hand, capital gains taxation upon sale of your home is quite favorable. The rule: If you sell your house and buy a higher priced one within 12 months (or build and occupy within 18 months), you can defer paying any capital gains tax. At age 65 a further, one-time, tax break kicks in. Gains on a $20,000 house go untaxed, for instance. For a $70,000 house, two sevenths of any gain is tax free. The overall result is that home ownership can provide tax sheltered capital appreciation.

An additional feature is the tax deductibility of interest on mortgage money borrowed to finance a home purchase. (On all leveraged investments, except tax-free bonds, such interest expenses are deductible from income in figuring ordinary income tax.) Real estate taxes are similarly tax deductible. Thus the government pays part of the costs of home ownership. The surprise, however, results from correctly accounting for the *rent savings* afforded by ownership. We will use an example to prove this great economic benefit of home ownership.

HOME OWNERSHIP—AN EXAMPLE

A REAL analysis can shed light on the implied profitability of home ownership, as well as that of investment property. We use the term "implied" because homeowners don't actually pay rent to themselves, but rather *save* paying that amount. Suppose, for example, that a $40,000 home can be purchased using a $30,000 mortgage at $9\frac{1}{2}$ percent. Then the market value of comparable housing, if rented, would probably be about $375 per month, for a rent savings of $4,500 per year.

It is important to realize that rent must come from your *after-tax* or "take-home" pay. You have to earn an even greater sum in salary, which is taxable income.

Someone with a 25 percent tax rate would have to earn $6,000 annually just to net the $4,500 needed for rent. In the 50 percent bracket, after-tax consumable cash is only half of gross earnings. Because of income taxes, which Benjamin Franklin did not have to face, for this person "a penny saved is *two* pennies earned." And with inflation, those pennies had better be dollars by now!

The homeowner's rent savings must be adjusted downward for the maintenance, insurance, supplies, and other expenses that a renter would not have to pay. Also, these upkeep expenses are not tax deductible by the homeowner. Therefore, we must reduce the $375 rental savings by about $75 per month, the assumed outlay for these costs. (Condominium owners, where a paid maintenance staff is employed, might expect these costs to run about $100 per month for a property of this value.) This produces an "implied gross income" of ownership of $300 per month (or $275 for our condo). This equals $3,600 annually (or $3,300 for the condo) of after-tax savings. Now what are the offsetting costs?

One ownership expense is tax deductible—real estate taxes, assumed here at $750 per year. Expenses for utilities are often paid separately by both the renter and the owner, so can be excluded from this comparison. Mortgage payments include both interest and debt amortization. The interest portion, which is three quarters or more of each payment in the mortgage's early years, is also tax deductible.

Table 7–1 shows an investment analysis of home ownership, including the special no-depreciation and

TABLE 7-1
Home Ownership—Base Case—No Inflation

KEY FACTORS ARE ----

TOTAL INVESTED	----MORTGAGE TERMS----			----OPERATING & INFLATION ASSUMPTIONS----				----TAX RATES----		----DEPRECIATION----		
	AMOUNT	% INTR	LIFE	NET SALE PRICE	IMPLIED PROP. TAX GROSS INCOME	OPERATING EXPENSE	% ANNUAL INFLATION	INCOME	CAP GAIN	AMOUNT	LIFE	TYPE
40000	30000	9.50	25	37600	3600	750	0.0	30%	0%	0	0	0%

COMPUTED SUMMARY ----

EQUITY AMOUNT	----MORTGAGE TERMS----			% NET SALE TO TOTAL	% INCOME TO TOTAL	% EXPENSE TO INCOME	% NET TO TOTAL	% DEPREC TO TOTAL
	% DEBT	MONTHLY	YEARLY					
10000	75.0	262.11	3145	94.0	9.0	20.8	7.1	0.0

COMPUTED RESULTS ----

YR	----HOLDING RESULTS BEFORE INCOME TAXES----						----HOLDING RESULTS AFTER TAXES----					----OVERALL RESULTS WITH SALE AT YEAR END----					
	GROSS INCOME	OPERATE EXPENSE	--MORTGAGE-- INTR	AMORT	CASH FLOW	% RE TURN	DEPREC IATION	TAXABLE INCOME	TAXES DUE	CASH FLOW	% RE TURN	SALE PRICE	DEBT REPAY	TAXES DUE	CASH FLOW	TOTAL PROFIT	% RE TURN
1	3600	750	2837	308	-295	-3.0	0	-3587	-1076	781	7.8	37600	29692	0	7908	-1311	-13.1
2	3600	750	2806	339	-295	-3.0	0	-3556	-1067	772	7.7	37600	29352	0	8248	-200	-1.0
3	3600	750	2773	372	-295	-3.0	0	-3523	-1057	761	7.6	37600	28980	0	8620	934	3.3
4	3600	750	2736	410	-295	-3.0	0	-3486	-1046	750	7.5	37600	28570	0	9030	2094	5.4
5	3600	750	2695	450	-295	-3.0	0	-3445	-1033	738	7.4	37600	28119	0	9481	3283	6.7
6	3600	750	2650	455	-295	-3.0	0	-3400	-1020	725	7.2	37600	27624	0	9976	4503	7.5
7	3600	750	2601	544	-295	-3.0	0	-3351	-1005	710	7.1	37600	27080	0	10520	5757	8.1
8	3600	750	2547	558	-295	-3.0	0	-3297	-989	694	6.9	37600	26482	0	11118	7049	8.5
9	3600	750	2488	658	-295	-3.0	0	-3238	-971	676	6.8	37600	25824	0	11776	8383	8.8
10	3600	750	2422	723	-295	-3.0	0	-3172	-952	656	6.6	37600	25101	0	12499	9762	9.0

no-capital-gains tax rules.[1] For example, because depreciation is not allowed, that column of the analysis shows all zeros. But then so does the right-most "Taxes Due" column when the property is sold. Since this type of analysis applies to so many — all homeowners — and the overall results are so surprising, let us review the year 1 computation in detail.

The column labeled "Gross Income" represents our $3,600 annual rent savings after adjustment for upkeep expenses. This is after-tax money that would otherwise go to rent a home of equal quality. The "Operating Expense" column shows only the amount of property taxes, an expense item that homeowners are allowed to deduct (whereas all expenses are deductible for investment property). The next column lists "Mortgage Interest," the other tax deductible cost. The amortization column shows the annual amounts applied to mortgage repayment. "Cash Flow" is the net rent savings less outlays for property taxes and mortgage payments. Then the "% Return" column shows this cash flow as a percentage of the equity invested.

For tax purposes, a homeowner's property generates no income, but still provides deductible expenses even though depreciation is not allowed. Here the $750 of assumed property taxes plus year 1's mortgage interest provide a sizable tax deduction. This results in income taxes due of $—1076, really a rebate on taxes

---

[1] Note that we have assumed sale is followed by purchase of a more costly home, thereby deferring capital gains taxation. If a less expensive home is purchased (or none), taxes are due on the amount not reinvested in housing or on the full capital gain, whichever is less. This tax-free trading up can be parlayed for a lifetime. Your heirs then pay no capital gains taxes on any appreciation during your lifetime. Using this reasoning, we have used a capital gains tax rate of zero for this home ownership analysis.

otherwise due. The after-tax cash flow of ownership during this first year is shown as $781. This adjusts the before-tax cash flow figure for the tax rebate. In the next column, this figure is expressed as a 7.8 percent return on the original equity invested.

The right-most third of the report shows the effects of sale at the end of any particular year. The "Sale Price" is shown net of assumed selling costs. Here 94 percent of the total invested is recouped, after a 6 percent allowance for commissions. "Debt Repay" lists the mortgage balance due upon sale at that year end. "Taxes Due" are zero, as discussed, because of capital gains benefits accorded homeowners. "Cash Flow" is the net proceeds of sale after the mortgage repayment. The "Total Profit" is an implied one, including the effect of rent savings. It tallies the cumulative after-tax cash flows of holding the property through any year, plus the cash flow from sale at that year end. The right-most column shows this total profit as a compound annual rate of return.

INFLATION'S IMPACT

Few of us really expect an inflation rate of 0% annually. The analysis used here allows you to assume otherwise and to compute easily the investment impact of inflation. Suppose it is 5 percent annually. Table 7–2 shows our homeowner example revised for this effect. Now the story is dramatically different – and better.

The amount saved (rather than being true income) goes up over time as comparable properties command

TABLE 7-2
Home Ownership—Revised Case—5 Percent Inflation

KEY FACTORS ARE ---

----OPERATING & INFLATION ASSUMPTIONS----

NET SALE PRICE	IMPLIED PROP. TAX GROSS INCOME	OPERATING EXPENSE	% ANNUAL INFLATION
37600	3600	750	5.0

----DEPRECIATION----			----TAX RATES----	
AMOUNT	LIFE	TYPE	INCOME	CAP GAIN
0	0	0%	30%	0%

TOTAL INVESTED	----MORTGAGE TERMS----		
	AMOUNT	% INTR	LIFE
40000	30000	9.50	25

COMPUTED SUMMARY ---

EQUITY AMOUNT	----MORTGAGE TERMS----		
	% DEBT	MONTHLY	YEARLY
10000	75.0	262.11	3145

% NET SALE TO TOTAL	% INCOME TO TOTAL	% EXPENSE TO INCOME
94.0	9.0	20.8

% DEPREC TO TOTAL	% NET TO TOTAL
0.0	7.1

COMPUTED RESULTS ---

----HOLDING RESULTS BEFORE INCOME TAXES----

YR	GROSS INCOME	OPERATE EXPENSE	--MORTGAGE-- INTR	AMORT	CASH FLOW	% RETURN
1	3600	750	2837	308	-295	-3.0
2	3780	787	2806	339	-153	-1.5
3	3969	827	2773	373	-3	-0.0
4	4167	868	2736	410	154	1.5
5	4376	912	2695	450	319	3.2
6	4595	957	2650	495	492	4.9
7	4824	1005	2601	544	674	6.7
8	5066	1055	2547	598	865	8.6
9	5319	1108	2488	658	1065	10.7
10	5585	1163	2422	723	1276	12.8

----HOLDING RESULTS AFTER TAXES----

YR	DEPRECIATION	TAXABLE INCOME	TAXES DUE	CASH FLOW	% RETURN
1	0	-3587	-1076	781	7.8
2	0	-3594	-1078	925	9.3
3	0	-3599	-1080	1077	10.8
4	0	-3604	-1081	1235	12.4
5	0	-3606	-1082	1401	14.0
6	0	-3607	-1082	1574	15.7
7	0	-3606	-1082	1756	17.6
8	0	-3602	-1081	1946	19.5
9	0	-3596	-1079	2144	21.4
10	0	-3586	-1076	2352	23.5

----OVERALL RESULTS WITH SALE AT YEAR END----

YR	SALE PRICE	DEBT REPAY	TAXES DUE	CASH FLOW	TOTAL PROFIT	% RETURN
1	39480	29692	0	9788	569	5.7
2	41454	29352	0	12102	3808	18.1
3	43527	28980	0	14547	7330	21.4
4	45703	28570	0	17133	11151	22.5
5	47988	28119	0	19869	15287	22.8
6	50387	27624	0	22763	19756	22.7
7	52907	27080	0	25827	24576	22.6
8	55552	26482	0	29070	29765	22.3
9	58330	25824	0	32505	35344	22.0
10	61246	25101	0	36145	41335	21.8

more rent in the marketplace. Maintenance and taxes also rise, but the conventional mortgage payments stay fixed. The interest portion of these payments slowly decreases, however, reducing that tax deduction. Best of all the sale price balloons from inflation, even after considering transaction costs. This boosts the overall rate of return significantly, as shown.

This overall rate of return, when compared to renting, is very attractive. With personal satisfaction factored in, it is no wonder that most households choose ownership. But isn't it somewhat curious that so few then extend this successful pattern into also owning investment property?

Figure 7.2 compares the overall rates of return of our no-inflation and inflation examples. Each curve improves sharply in the early years as the adverse impact

FIGURE 7.2
Impact of Inflation on Homeowner Rate of Return

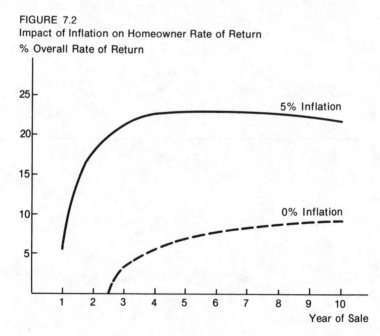

of transaction costs gets spread over a longer holding period. But the 5 percent annual inflation case literally rockets to an excellent level. Here the after-tax rate of return, based on rent saved, reaches over 20 percent compounded annually after taxes. With somewhat higher rates of inflation, it is possible that each year's accruing capital gain will equal or exceed your after-tax mortgage and expense outlays. Thus, in the overall sense, your housing would have been absolutely free!

SUMMARY

Buying your home is one of the best possible investments if you plan to stay in a particular location two years or longer. In inflationary times, its fast-rising equity is a source of satisfaction and emergency funds. Perhaps most important, the rent you save by ownership is *after-tax* money. By contrast, two major costs of ownership, mortgage interest and property taxes, are deductible and reduce income taxes otherwise due. And while you cannot take depreciation deductions, homeowners do benefit from favorable capital gains taxation upon sale.

Historically, waiting to purchase a home has been a poor policy. If ever there was cause to borrow, especially for younger families with a rising income, home ownership is it. The startling rate of return, especially when leveraged, ought to convince any prospective home or condominium buyer.

8

Residential Income Property

After home ownership, residential income property is perhaps your best, low risk, possibly small-scale, next step. We have already discussed the selection, financing, buying, renting, maintenance, appreciation, and selling aspects of such investing. And home ownership, presuming you have by now taken this step, has provided some firsthand experience with these issues. Therefore, we will continue to focus on the *investment merits* of real estate. In this chapter we analyze some typical residential income properties, followed by Chapter 9's look at Commercial Property and Chapter 10's Land Investing and Development.

ANALYSIS APPROACH

Our analysis approach here and for the next chapters' examples is to provide a base case to determine *expected profitability* and then to discuss *risk*. We will also illustrate the use of Part III's reference tables. This unique feature — literally a handbook — allows you to estimate, both quickly and accurately, the profitability and risk of any real estate opportunity.

113

As always, you must use skilled judgment, experience, and knowledge of local market data, current mortgage terms, taxation guidelines, and the like. This blend allows you to estimate the 13 key factors that determine a property's investment merit. Then a REAL analysis, or the tables of Part III, can be used to translate these assumptions into measures of investment performance. At that point, your judgment is again required to assess whether the results suit your investment objectives.

Stated simply, real estate investing becomes a four-step process:

1. Define your investment objectives.
2. Estimate the thirteen key factors for each opportunity.
3. Project the investment outcome of each property.
4. Choose by comparing outcomes to objectives.

The weak link—and unnecessarily so—has been the analytical third step of projecting investment outcomes. Historically these forecasts have been incomplete, no-inflation, first-year-only, before-sale, no-transaction-costs, seat-of-the-pants guesses. The results have often been inaccurate and misleading. Worse yet, this destroys the value of solid work on the other three investing steps and leads to misguided investment decisions. Isn't there a better way?

SAMPLE MULTI-UNIT APARTMENT BUILDING

This first example features the type of property you can reasonably aspire to own after experience with pyramiding smaller buildings and/or individual homes. Let's assume a 20-unit low-rise design commonly available in metropolitan areas. It need not be an elevator building, might feature a mix of studios, one and two bedrooms, and offer off-street parking. The property could be about 10 years old with a remaining life, for depreciation purposes, of 25 years.

Having defined your investment objectives (per Chapter 2), the second step is developing the 13 key factor values. This example's values are shown in Table 8–1. This form indicates that our 20-unit apartment building requires $250,000 of total investment, of which 75 percent can be financed by a 25-year mortgage bearing 10 percent annual interest. Such mortgage rates are high by historical terms but have become typical during recent periods of tight money. Should such rates scare us away from investing?

The next key factor in Table 8–1 assumes that the property could be readily liquidated to net $235,000, based on a 6 percent allowance for transaction costs. The next factor shows that gross income of $42,000 can be expected in the first year. This averages $2,100 per unit, or a typical rent of $175 per month. From this a vacancy allowance of 5 percent (or $2,100) is deducted. Then annual expenses are initially expected to be:

Vacancy allowance at 5 percent*	$ 2,100
Maintenance	5,500
Property taxes	5,000
Utilities	3,000
Supplies	1,100
Insurance	700
Administration	600
	$18,000

* A vacancy allowance of 5% implies, for example, a 19-month occupancy followed by a one-month vacancy, for a 1/20 or 5% vacancy average. This factor may be accounted for as a reduction to gross income or as an operating expense, either way the analysis results are the same. The maintenance cost might include a rent subsidy to a resident part-time supervisor. Utilities expenses are those paid by the owner and exclude services billable to individual tenants.

TABLE 8–1
Key Factors in Real Estate Investment Analysis

Project Title *MULTI-UNIT APARTMENT BUILDING*

	1) Total Invested (equity plus debt including closing costs) $ *250,000*
Mortgage Terms	2) Mortgage Amount (show either $ or %) $_____ or *75* % of Total Invested
	3) Interest Rate *10* % Annually
	4) Mortgage Life *25* Years
Operating and Inflation Assumptions	5) Net Sale Price (currently, before inflation, net of transaction costs) $_____ or *94* % of Total Invested
	6) Gross Income (annually, before inflation) $ *42,000* or _____ % of Total Invested
	7) Operating Expense (annually, before inflation) $ *18,000* or _____ % of Gross Income
	8) Annual Inflation (in sale price, gross income, and operating expense) *5* %
Depreciation	9) Depreciation Amount $ *200,000* or _____ % of Total Invested
	10) Depreciation Life *25* Years
	11) Depreciation Type (percent of straight line) *125* % { 200% for New Residential / 150% for New Commercial / 125% for Used Residential with 20 Years Life or More / 100% for All Other }
Tax Rates	12) Ordinary income *40* %
	13) Capital gains *20* %

The next factor is vital to a financial analysis, yet often overlooked. Average annual inflation assumed in this example is 5 percent. This rate of increase is automatically factored into the gross income, operating expense, and sale price projections. After all, we bought the property seeking capital gains in addition to income. We ought to include such hoped-for — and probable — inflation/appreciation in our analysis. If unhappy with the inflation rate assumed, use risk analysis to project the results of a lower rate or the benefit of a higher one. The case of expenses inflating *faster* than income and sale price can also be analyzed.

The depreciation factors can usually be determined precisely. Based on tax laws and IRS guidelines (125 percent of straight line depreciation is allowed if used residential property has a useful life of 20 years or more), this property is presumed to have:

Depreciation amount.................. $200,000 ($50,000 is land)
Depreciation life....................... 25 years*
Depreciation type .... 125% (of straight line)

* It is likely that at least two separate depreciation schedules would, in fact, be maintained — one for the building and one for shorter–lived replaceable items like appliances. For simplicity and clarity, the REAL analysis works with a single depreciation life and rate, which can represent the weighted average of a multiple schedule accounting system.

Finally, the investor's applicable tax rates are illustrated in this example as 40% on ordinary income and 20% on capital gains.

Table 8–2 presents the results of analyzing our sample multi-unit apartment building. Glancing swiftly to the right-most column (as the trained and curious may already have done), you can see that the overall, after-tax, rate of return is nearly 20 percent for holding periods beyond a few years. This favorable result is above

TABLE 8-2
Sample Multi-Unit Apartment Building — Base Case

KEY FACTORS ARE ---

TOTAL INVESTED	---MORTGAGE TERMS--- AMOUNT	% INTR	LIFE	NET SALE PRICE	---CPERATING & INFLATION ASSUMPTIONS--- GROSS INCOME	OPERATING EXPENSE	% ANNUAL INFLATION	---DEPRECIATION--- AMOUNT	LIFE	TYPE	---TAX RATES--- INCOME	CAP GAIN
250000	187500	10.00	25	235000	42000	18000	5.0	200000	25	125%	40%	20%

COMPUTED SUMMARY ---

EQUITY AMCUNT	---MORTGAGE TERMS--- % DEBT	MONTHLY	YEARLY	% NET SALE TO TCTAL	% INCME TO TOTAL	% EXPENSE TO INCCME	% DEPREC TO TOTAL	% NET TO TOTAL
62500	75.0	1703.80	20446	94.0	16.8	42.9	80.0	9.6

COMPUTED RESULTS ---

YR	---HOLDING RESULTS BEFORE INCCME TAXES--- GRCSS INCOME	OPERATE EXPENSE	---MORTGAGE--- INTR	AMCRT	CASH FLOW	% RE TURN	---HOLDING RESULTS AFTER TAXES--- DEPREC IATION	TAXABLE INCOME	TAXFS DUE	CASH FLOW	% RE TURN	---OVERALL RESULTS WITH SALE AT YEAR END--- SALE PRICE	DEBT REPAY	TAXES DUE	CASH FLOW	TOTAL PROFIT	% RE TURN
1	42000	18000	18670	1776	3554	5.7	10000	-4670	-1868	5422	8.7	246750	185724	1750	59276	2198	3.5
2	44100	18500	18484	1962	4754	7.6	9500	-2784	-1114	5868	9.4	259087	183762	6417	68907	17698	13.8
3	46305	19845	18279	2167	6014	9.6	9025	-844	-337	6352	10.2	272041	181595	11018	79428	34570	17.0
4	48620	20837	18052	2394	7337	11.7	8574	1158	463	6874	11.0	285643	179200	15568	90875	52891	18.3
5	51051	21879	17801	2645	8726	14.0	8145	3226	1290	7436	11.9	299925	176555	20082	103287	72739	18.9
6	53604	22973	17524	2922	10185	16.3	7738	5369	2148	8037	12.9	314921	173633	24577	116711	94200	19.2
7	56284	24122	17218	3228	11717	18.7	7738	7206	2883	8834	14.1	330667	170405	29221	131040	117364	19.2
8	59098	25328	16880	3566	13325	21.3	7738	9152	3661	9664	15.5	347200	166839	34023	146338	142325	19.2
9	62053	26594	16507	3939	15013	24.0	7738	11214	4486	10527	16.8	364560	162900	38923	162737	169251	19.2
10	65155	27924	16094	4352	16786	26.9	7738	13400	5360	11426	18.3	382787	158548	43973	180266	198206	19.1

that routinely achievable from *any other common form of investment,* despite our assumption of a mortgage bearing 10 percent interest.

Naturally, there are risks to this investment. What if vacancy averages 15 percent? What if an adverse or premature sale must be made? How about inflation of expenses, but not of rents? What if your tax brackets, or the tax laws, change? What happens if catastrophic maintenance or personal liability strikes? These dire cases can be probed by risk analysis.

RISK ANALYSIS

Table 8–3 shows the results of a pessimistic turn in particular key factors as compared with their base case values. For example, suppose our $250,000 total invested figure turns out to be understated by 10 percent, *and all else remains the same.* We would then need $275,000 for the investment and $87,500 in equity. Under such circumstances, the rate of return declines —especially for shorter holding periods — as shown in Table 8–3. This particular decline has two causes. First, profits are spread over a larger equity require-

TABLE 8–3
Risk Analysis for Sample Multi-Unit Apartment Building

Year	*Change in Overall Rate of Return Caused by a 10 Percent Adverse Change in Selected Key Factor Values*				
	Total Invested	*Mortgage Percent Interest*	*Net Sale Price*	*Gross Income*	*Operating Expense*
2	−15.2%	−1.8%	−14.2%	−4.0%	−1.7%
5	−7.9	−1.4	−4.1	−3.7	−1.6
10	−4.9	−1.1	−1.3	−3.3	−1.4

ment. Second, the profits are lowered because the initial overpayment lessens the ultimate capital gain, since the sale price is assumed to be unchanged. The larger equity requirement and lower profits are both factors that knock down the rate of return.

To answer our query about the risk from high vacancy, look at the column reflecting shrunken gross income. The base case includes a 5 percent vacancy allowance. If vacancy is at the feared 15 percent level, then another 10 percent or $4,200 gets lopped off our $42,000 gross income. Table 8–3 shows the decrease in rate of return due to this 10 percent gross income shortfall relative to the base case. For example, the year 5 rate of return in Table 8–2, the base case, is 18.9 percent. Table 8–3 shows that the higher than projected vacancy lowers this 3.7 percent (to 15.2), which might be judged a moderate risk and worth taking.

Other risks in this property can be similarly investigated. Premature sale is perhaps the biggest worry. As the base case (Table 8–2) shows, sale after year 1 results in a slightly positive rate of return. If sale must be rushed or the property unexpectedly drops in price, a loss might result. But, for perspective, look also at the loss possibilities in other types of investing. For instance, the Dow Jones Industrial Average first reached 800 in early 1964. Ten years later it had plummeted below 600 — 25 percent lower. Counting dividends, one would have been barely ahead for that "bearly" decade.

USING PART III's TABLES

A REAL analysis can be tailored to each opportunity you consider. But for a quick approximation of key results, you can use the reference tables of Part III. Each chapter's tables feature the applicable depreciation and tax rules for a different category of real estate. The tables in Chapters 13 and 14 cover new residential and new commercial property respectively. Those of Chapter 15 (Used Residential Property) apply to the sample multi-unit apartment building just studied. Chapter 16 features straight line depreciation, which is applicable to used commercial property and used residential having a remaining useful life less than 20 years. Chapter 17 covers Land Investing and Development and Chapter 18 reflects the special depreciation and tax treatment accorded to homeowners.

Part III's tables also show the REAL analysis on a *per $1,000 invested* basis. That is, the "total invested" factor is $1,000 in each case. This makes the tables easy to use, and since rates of return are percentages, these results apply to *any size investment.* Dollar values — such as total profit — can be easily scaled up to reflect the actual investment level. Within each chapter, the different tables reflect variations in:

1. The percent mortgaged.
2. The mortgage interest rate.
3. The percent net income to total invested.[1]

For instance, our example $250,000 apartment has a $187,500 (or 75 percent) mortgage at 10 percent interest. The net operating income is $42,000 gross, less $18,000 of expenses, or $24,000. This amount is 9.6

---

[1] The percent net to total invested is used because it combines two factors into one. It is the surplus of income over expense, taxable as ordinary income. Thus your proposed investment's gross income and operating expense figures need not match those in the reference table. It is enough that the percent net to total be close to that in the reference table.

percent of the $250,000 total invested (as Table 8–2 shows). These three values—the percent mortgaged, the mortgage interest rate, and the percent net to total invested—dictate which table to consult within the appropriate chapter. In this case, the nearest table is found on page 200. It displays a REAL analysis for a 75 percent mortgage at 10 percent interest and 10 percent net to total invested. (All tables in that chapter also use 125 percent of straight line depreciation, per IRS allowances for such property.) The remaining key factor values common to all reference tables are:

1. A 25 year mortgage.
2. Transaction costs of 6 percent upon sale.
3. Operating expenses approximating 42 percent of gross income.
4. 0 percent and 5 percent inflation (combined on the same page).
5. 80 percent of the total invested is the depreciation amount (hence 20 percent is land).
6. A depreciation life of 25 years (except 30 years for new residential property and 35 years for new commercial property).
7. Tax rate of 40 percent for ordinary income.
8. Tax rate of 20 percent for capital gains.

The chosen reference table closely approximates our sample multi-unit apartment building. In fact, it has identically proportioned data except that the actual 9.6 percent net to total is not quite the 10 percent portrayed in the reference table. The dollar figures in this table also reflect the $1,000 assumed investment, of course. But all percentage figures—including the rate of return results—*are closely applicable to our example.*

Rates of return are easily estimated by referring to one or more appropriate reference tables. The reference table shows a total invested of $1,000, whereas it is really 250 times that large, or $250,000. So to determine any dollar amount for our multi-unit apartment, simply multiply by the scale factor: 250 times in this case. For example, the year 5 sale price—shown as $1,200 in the table—multiplies into $300,000 for the actual property.

The reference table shows both the no-inflation and the 5 percent inflation results. However, we know that with only a 9.6 percent net to total (rather than the 10 percent assumed in the reference table), our investment is not quite as rosy. From a knowledge of risk analysis, we can adjust this reference table figure down about one percentage point to adjust for our slightly lower net income expectations.

IMPACT OF INFLATION

The sample 20-unit apartment seems a reasonably good investment, especially when sacrificing near-term liquidity by holding at least three to five years. The 10 percent mortgage rate, which appears prohibitive on an historical basis, proves not too burdensome. A 9 percent rate would be better, of course, boosting the year 5 overall return by 1.5 percent. *But neither of these mortgage rates would be acceptable if it were not for inflation.*

Our analysis assumed 5 percent annual inflation in gross income, operating expense, and sale price. What happens if there is no inflation? Today, that seems an unlikely prospect. Nonetheless, the traditional analysis of real estate does assume constant rents, expenses,

FIGURE 8.1
Impact of Inflation

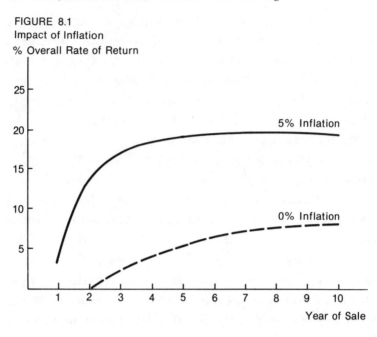

% Overall Rate of Return

Year of Sale

and selling prices — or, said another way, ignores inflation. Figure 8.1 graphs the results of the 5 percent inflation case (Table 8–2) compared to the results for 0 percent inflation. All other factors are unchanged including the 10 percent mortgage. A glance shows that our good investment sours in the absence of inflation. In fact, high mortgage rates *assume* inflation will continue and *require* that it does. A valid analysis certainly must include this profitability and risk from inflation.

NEW, LARGE APARTMENT COMPLEX

Next we will analyze a new, larger residential income property. Available for $6,400,000, it may be thought of as a 360 unit garden apartment complex (currently costing nearly $18,000 per unit for land and construction) or a 200 unit urban mid-rise (costing nearly double for each apartment). As new residential housing it is eligible for double declining balance depreciation—the most accelerated, beneficial category allowed.

Table 8–4 presents the REAL analysis of this example, shown in thousands of dollars. As the "Key Factors Are" section shows, a $4,800,000 mortgage at 10 percent is thought obtainable for 25 years. Anticipated transactions costs are 4 percent. (Multimillion dollar properties generally encounter lower brokerage commissions and other closing costs, when figured as a percentage of the total invested.) Annual gross income of $1,200,000 is expected. This corresponds to about $275 per month for the garden apartment units or to $500 per month for the urban mid-rise case. Annual expenses, including utilities, may be expected to approximate 45 percent of rents or $540,000. Inflation of 5 percent is projected. Double declining balance depreciation (200 percent of straight line) is applicable on $5,120,000 of the investment with a 30 year average depreciation life. (The mid-rise might incur a somewhat longer average depreciation life.) The investor's tax rates are shown as 50 percent for income and 25 percent for capital gains.

From the "Computed Summary" section of Table 8–4, we can see that $1,600,000 of equity is required, resulting in 75% leverage. Also, the percent net to total is 10.3 percent. This data, which is easily hand calculated, allows us to estimate overall rates of return for various holding periods by using the reference tables of Part III. Chapter 13, New Residential Prop-

TABLE 8-4
New, Large Residential Income Property—Base Case ($000 omitted)

KEY FACTORS ARE ----

TOTAL INVESTED	MORTGAGE TERMS			OPERATING & INFLATION ASSUMPTIONS				DEPRECIATION			TAX RATES	
	AMOUNT	% INTR	LIFE	NET SALE PRICE	GROSS INCOME	OPERATING EXPENSE	% ANNUAL INFLATION	AMOUNT	LIFE	TYPE	INCOME	CAP GAIN
6400	4800	10.00	25	6144	1200	540	5.0	5120	30	200%	50%	25%

COMPUTED SUMMARY ----

EQUITY AMOUNT	MORTGAGE TERMS			% NET SALE TO TOTAL	% INCOME TO TOTAL	% EXPENSE TO INCOME	% NET TO TOTAL	% DEPREC TO TOTAL
	% DEBT	MONTHLY	YEARLY					
1600	75.0	43.62	523	96.0	18.8	45.0	10.3	80.0

COMPUTED RESULTS ----

	HOLDING RESULTS BEFORE INCOME TAXES						HOLDING RESULTS AFTER TAXES					OVERALL RESULTS WITH SALE AT YEAR END					
YR	GROSS INCOME	OPERATE EXPENSE	MORTGAGE INTR	MORTGAGE AMORT	CASH FLOW	% RE TURN	DEPRECIATION	TAXABLE INCOME	TAXES DUE	CASH FLOW	% RE TURN	SALE PRICE	DEBT REPAY	TAXES DUE	CASH FLOW	TOTAL PROFIT	% RE TURN
1	1200	540	478	45	137	8.5	341	-159	-80	216	13.5	6451	4755	141	1556	172	10.8
2	1260	567	473	50	170	10.6	319	-99	-49	219	13.7	6774	4704	338	1731	567	17.4
3	1323	595	468	55	204	12.8	297	-38	-19	223	13.9	7112	4649	529	1935	993	19.5
4	1389	625	462	61	241	15.0	278	24	12	228	14.3	7468	4587	714	2167	1454	20.4
5	1459	656	456	68	279	17.4	259	88	44	235	14.7	7841	4520	894	2428	1950	20.8
6	1532	689	449	75	319	19.9	242	152	76	243	15.2	8233	4445	1070	2718	2483	20.9
7	1608	724	441	83	361	22.6	226	218	109	252	15.8	8645	4362	1243	3040	3056	20.9
8	1689	760	432	91	405	25.3	211	286	143	262	16.4	9077	4271	1414	3393	3672	20.9
9	1773	798	423	101	452	28.2	197	356	178	274	17.1	9531	4170	1566	3795	4348	20.8
10	1862	838	412	111	500	31.3	183	428	214	286	17.9	10008	4059	1709	4240	5079	20.7

erty, features the 200 percent depreciation tables applicable here. The table on page 180 is closest to our example. The only differences are its 10 percent net to total (versus our example's 10.3 percent), its 6 percent transaction costs (versus our 4 percent), and its tax rates of 40 percent and 20 percent (versus our 50 percent and 25 percent brackets). This reference table proves to be a good approximation of our specific situation, as seen by comparison with Table 8–4.

RISK ANALYSIS

Again it is appropriate to ask, "What can go wrong?" But even Solomon couldn't answer that. For example, a doubling of fuel costs (who foresaw that one?) adds mightily to operating expenses, especially when heat and hot water are furnished in the rent as just presumed. Rent controls or rent stabilization programs — a disconcerting surprise to some property owners — have been legislated. And inflation itself not only pro-propels profits but also penalizes their purchasing power. To be sure, it is better to receive an inflating number of dollars (unlike interest on a bond), but don't count on retiring comfortably on today's income levels.

To analyze risk, you can compute a revised rate of return based on a change in the key factor values. Table 8–5 lists the impact on rate of return from each 10 percent of adverse change in selected factors. Fear a fuel cost price rise? Suppose it would add 10 percent to operating expenses. Looking at the year 5 return as a benchmark, we see in Table 8–5 that each 10 percent rise in operating expense changes the overall return by −1.6 percent. Thus we would expect spiraling fuel

TABLE 8–5
Risk Analysis for New Large Residential Income Property

Year	Change in Overall Rate of Return Caused by a 10 Percent Adverse Change in Selected Key Factor Values				
	Total Invested	Mortgage Interest	Net Sale Price	Gross Income	Operating Expense
2	−15.4%	−1.4%	−13.5%	−3.8%	−1.7%
5	−8.4	−1.2	−4.0	−3.6	−1.6
10	−5.5	−0.9	−1.2	−3.3	−1.5

costs to diminish returns by this amount if rents and other factors remain unchanged. If this cost rise is passed through, the risk is lowered or eliminated.

SUMMARY

Should you invest in residential income property? It seems a reasonable place to begin, possibly on a small scale and after the experience of home ownership. Our examples show nice rates of return available from current market conditions, including the prospect of inflation. *New* residential property has the advantage of fast depreciation (at 200 percent of straight line), which is particularly helpful if you are in high tax brackets. On the other hand, *used* residential property has an already established market and financial history, lowering the risk of incorrect assumptions. Current high mortgage rates are acceptable only if overcome by rising rents and an inflation-swollen sale price. But doesn't this seem likely? Again, you must judge the returns and risks involved.

9

Commercial Property

The commercial property market is surprisingly large and robust. In 1974, business and industry spent $55 billion on new buildings — up from $48 billion in 1973. By contrast, the 1974 residential housing market slipped below $50 billion in new construction from $58 billion in 1973. But just as the majority of housing is owner-occupied, so, too, is a large portion of commercial property, especially manufacturing facilities. This still leaves many opportunities for investors, including the four examples discussed here: an office building, warehouse, shopping center, and indoor tennis courts.

OFFICE BUILDINGS

Urban and suburban office space has been in increasing demand for decades as the economy has shifted from a manufacturing to a service orientation and from blue-collar to white-collar jobs. Offices are also general purpose facilities readily usable by a large market of prospective tenants. And many corporations prefer to

129

rent rather than own space. This gives them location and expansion flexibility and keeps depreciation "expenses" from reducing the accounting profits they report to shareholders.

This large demand for office space has, naturally enough, stimulated a large supply. And periodic overbuilding plus occasional business recessions make office building ownership more risky than investing in residential income property. Rental rates and occupancy fluctuate more and are particularly affected by location, transportation, parking, architecture, floor size, lease length, and features such as an attractive lobby, adequate elevators, reliable heating and air conditioning, carpeting, cleaning services, and so forth. Happily these risks are balanced by potential gross rents of $10 or more per square foot annually for a downtown urban high-rise or up to $7 a square foot for suburban space.

Before our example, a final qualitative observation is in order. Location has been emphasized before, but for office space it is crucial. Think about it. Demand for offices is derived from business needs, including proximity to other offices, hotels, and restaurants and to multi-mode transportation hubs. Good locations tend to get even better. Manufacturing or warehousing facilities, by contrast, often need large land areas and can create jobs rather than relying on existing local demand. Also, a business spends a lower percentage of its revenues on rent than does a homeowner or apartment renter. It can afford to buy the best. You should be choosy, too. "Bargain" office space in a wrong or declining area may prove too troublesome to rent profitably.

EXAMPLE HIGH RISE OFFICE BUILDING

Today's office buildings are literally cities, occupied by day when demands for services and utilities are highest. New York's twin 110-story World Trade Center Towers can accommodate nearly 50,000 people, for example. Highly automated elevator and security systems can reduce operating personnel, but cleaning services remain excruciatingly labor intensive.

We have analyzed a typical 30-story office building in Table 9–1. Dollar figures are shown in thousands for this mammoth undertaking. One caution, however. Lease length is usually quite long, often no less than 5 years and frequently 20. This means rents do not escalate smoothly with inflation as they generally do with residential properties. Furthermore, the per square foot rentals can swing widely on renewed leases due to local capacity and economic factors, despite inflation. Wall Street structures commanding up to $12 per square foot in 1969 went for only $8.50 in 1974. Unless protected by an expense escalator clause, the rising costs of utilities and other services can further squeeze building owners.

The key factor values used in Table 9–1 reflect these special considerations of office buildings. The initial outlay for a high-rise is huge. Also, it may take two years or more from ground-breaking to rent-check-cashing. Here we have stipulated a $30,000,000 total invested. This averages one million dollars for the 20,000 square feet on each floor. Mortgages of fairly long duration can be arranged. But the lender, usually an insurance company, frequently holds back on financing until certain occupancy goals are met. This makes delay and vacancy an even greater risk.

TABLE 9-1
Sample High-Rise Office Building—Base Case ($000 omitted)

KEY FACTORS ARE ----

TOTAL INVESTED	----MORTGAGE TERMS----			----OPERATING & INFLATION ASSUMPTIONS----				----TAX RATES----		----DEPRECIATION----		
	AMOUNT	% INTR	LIFE	NET SALE PRICE	GROSS INCOME	OPERATING EXPENSE	% ANNUAL INFLATION	INCOME	CAP GAIN	AMOUNT	LIFE	TYPE
30000	22500	10.00	30	29100	5000	2400	5.0	50%	30%	24000	40	150%

COMPUTED SUMMARY ----

EQUITY AMOUNT	----MORTGAGE TERMS----			% NET SALE TO TOTAL	% INCOME TO TOTAL	% EXPENSE TO INCOME	% NET TO TOTAL	% DEPREC TO TOTAL
	% DEBT	MONTHLY	YEARLY					
7500	75.0	157.45	2369	97.0	16.7	48.0	8.7	80.0

COMPUTED RESULTS ----

	----HOLDING RESULTS BEFORE INCOME TAXES----						----HOLDING RESULTS AFTER TAXES----					----OVERALL RESULTS WITH SALE AT YEAR END----					
YR	GROSS INCOME	OPERATE EXPENSE	--MORTGAGE-- INTR	AMORT	CASH FLOW	% RE TURN	DEPREC IATION	TAXABLE INCOME	TAXES DUE	CASH FLOW	% RE TURN	SALE PRICE	DEBT REPAY	TAXES DUE	CASH FLOW	TOTAL PROFIT	% RE TURN
1	5000	2400	2244	125	231	3.1	900	-544	-272	503	6.7	30555	22375	496	7684	686	9.2
2	5250	2520	2231	138	361	4.8	866	-368	-184	544	7.3	32083	22237	1268	8578	2125	13.7
3	5512	2646	2217	153	497	6.6	834	-184	-92	589	7.9	33687	22084	2046	9557	3693	15.1
4	5788	2778	2201	169	640	8.5	802	6	3	637	8.5	35371	21916	2833	10623	5396	15.7
5	6078	2917	2183	186	791	10.5	772	205	102	689	9.2	37140	21729	3629	11781	7243	16.0
6	6381	3063	2164	206	949	12.7	743	411	206	743	9.9	38997	21524	4438	13035	9240	16.1
7	6700	3216	2142	227	1115	14.9	716	627	313	802	10.7	40946	21296	5261	14389	11396	16.2
8	7035	3377	2118	251	1289	17.2	689	851	426	863	11.5	42994	21045	6099	15849	13719	16.2
9	7387	3546	2092	277	1472	19.6	663	1086	543	929	12.4	45143	20768	6956	17420	16219	16.2
10	7757	3723	2063	306	1664	22.2	638	1332	666	998	13.3	47400	20461	7832	19107	18904	16.1

High gross rents meet commensurably high operating expenses, as shown. Both leasing agents and property managers are typically retained, for instance, and between-tenant remodeling costs are usually necessary. Average rents of $8.33 per square foot of gross space can be expected. But about 15 percent of the gross area goes for unrentable space like elevators, ventilating shafts, stairways, and restrooms. Net space rentals of about $10 per square foot would then produce a $5,000,000 initial rent roll, before vacancy.

Inflation of 5 percent per year is illustrated, although for the reasons cited above, there may be a lag in realizing such rent increases. (In Chapter 11, Advanced Analysis, we look at *different* inflation rates for the sale price, income, and expense factors as well as the effect of long-term leases.) A further risk is having to re-lease during a weak market period. Such a decline in income can dry up the owner's cash flow, especially if the available tax shelter cannot be applied to other income, as assumed by the REAL analysis.

In this example, depreciation is taken at 150 percent of straight line, the currently allowed rate for new commercial construction. The average depreciation life is 40 years, even considering the shorter life of some mechanical equipment and fixtures. A corporate ownership vehicle is assumed. Therefore the applicable tax rates are 50 percent on income (say 48 percent federal and 2 percent net state tax) and 30 percent on capital gains (the federal corporate rate).

How do you interpret this analysis? As always, its nice to have high income with low expenses, leverage, tax shelter, and appreciation. But commercial property has less tax shelter than residential. Only 150 percent declining balance depreciation is allowed on new commercial property (versus 200 percent for new residential) and only 100 percent of straight line with used commercial (versus 125 percent for used residential with a remaining life of 20 years or more). Also the *minimum* depreciation life allowed for some types of structures extends out to 50 years.

Total investment and expenses typically run higher per square foot of space than for a residential building, but so does the income. Unless marred by bad location or design, a weak local market, or persistent vacancies, an office building should return more than residential property. The risk is that lowered income might not cover mortgage payments and operating expenses. Also, changing demand for a location or the building's functional obsolescence can retard growth in its sale price. Without additional cash you may be forced to sell disadvantageously.

It takes big bucks and professional management in the office building game — something to try with your second million. And structures of the size illustrated above are the province of large corporations and major financial institutions. Only a very few individuals have the assets and expertise to consider high-rise office investments. However, syndication can bring these opportunities within the ownership scope of investors participating in a group.

DISTRIBUTION WAREHOUSE

Trammell Crow, the respected Dallas real estate entrepreneur, initially specialized in this type of facility. Located on cheap land, but in the path of growth, it is easily leasable and appreciates nicely. Because a warehouse facility is typically dedicated to one or a few tenants who can control its use, a "net" lease is often written so that the user pays the operating expenses. This keeps the owner's management time down as well as his operating risk. The goal is a stream of leveraged, tax sheltered, cash flow with inflation/appreciation in the property's collateral value and sale price.

The economics of a typical warehouse deal differ significantly from our high rise analysis. Warehouses are inexpensive and quickly built. With a quality long-term lease, mortgage credit is easily obtainable. The building yields a much lower gross income per square foot than the high rise, but also has lower operating expenses. In view of its low cost, this produces an acceptable "% net to total."

Tax shelter has improved. It is still restricted to 150 percent of straight line, but the allowable depreciation life is shorter than for the high-rise. Also, if cheap, outlying land is used, the depreciation amount can be 85 percent or more of the total invested. This positive effect is counterbalanced by the lesser leverage of a shorter mortgage. Thus a somewhat earlier sale or refinancing of the distribution warehouse may be in order.

SHOPPING CENTER

Stores and shopping centers, be they community "strip malls" or giant regional "enclosed malls," also attract sophisticated owners. The risks are high, unless dealing with triple-A credit rated tenants on long-term

TABLE 9-2
Shopping Center—Base Case (per $1,000 of Total Invested)

KEY FACTORS ARE ---

TOTAL INVESTED	---MORTGAGE TERMS---			---OPERATING & INFLATION ASSUMPTIONS---				---DEPRECIATION---			---TAX RATES---	
	AMOUNT	% INTR	LIFE	NET SALE PRICE	GROSS INCOME	OPERATING EXPENSE	% ANNUAL INFLATION	AMOUNT	LIFE	TYPE	INCOME	CAP GAIN
1000	750	10.00	25	960	130	30	5.0	700	30	150%	50%	30%

COMPUTED SUMMARY ---

EQUITY AMOUNT	---MORTGAGE TERMS---			% NET SALE TO TOTAL	% INCOME TO TOTAL	% EXPENSE TO INCOME	% NET TO TOTAL	% DEPREC TO TOTAL
	% DEBT	MONTHLY	YEARLY					
250	75.0	6.82	82	96.0	13.0	23.1	10.0	70.0

COMPUTED RESULTS ---

YR	---HOLDING RESULTS BEFORE INCOME TAXES---						---HOLDING RESULTS AFTER TAXES---					---OVERALL RESULTS WITH SALE AT YEAR END---					
	GROSS INCOME	OPERATE EXPENSE	---MORTGAGE--- INTR	AMORT	CASH FLOW	% RE TURN	DEPREC IATION	TAXABLE INCOME	TAXES DUE	CASH FLOW	% RE TURN	SALE PRICE	DEBT REPAY	TAXES DUE	CASH FLOW	TOTAL PROFIT	% RE TURN
1	130	30	75	7	18	7.3	35	-10	-5	23	9.2	1008	743	15	250	23	9.2
2	136	31	74	8	23	9.3	33	-2	-1	24	9.7	1058	735	42	281	78	15.2
3	143	33	73	9	28	11.4	32	6	3	26	10.3	1111	726	69	316	139	17.1
4	150	35	72	10	34	13.6	30	14	7	27	10.9	1167	717	96	354	204	17.9
5	158	36	71	11	40	15.9	29	22	11	29	11.5	1225	706	123	396	275	18.2
6	166	38	70	12	46	18.3	27	30	15	31	12.2	1286	695	151	441	351	18.4
7	174	40	69	13	52	20.9	26	39	20	33	13.0	1351	682	178	491	433	18.4
8	183	42	68	14	59	23.6	24	49	24	35	13.8	1418	667	206	545	522	18.4
9	192	44	66	16	66	26.4	23	58	29	37	14.7	1489	652	234	603	617	18.3
10	202	47	64	17	73	29.3	22	69	34	39	15.6	1564	634	263	667	719	18.2

leases. Financing is often relatively short and costly because of the specialized design and potential for new, near-by competition. Tax shelter is limited. Much of the investment is attributable to nondepreciable land. So why invest?

Store leases frequently charge a percentage of sales beyond their fixed minimum rent. So just pick the right location, get a good participation, and ride it with inflation. But to produce the steadily rising rents shown in Table 9–2 you will need "anchor" stores, such as a department store, giant discounter, or a food and drug store pair. They are important traffic builders and consequently can pay the lowest rents. Your profits stem from an override on growing sales and from the many smaller specialty shops.

Shopping center owners have done well in the last two decades. Such property is almost synonymous with shopping-by-auto and suburban sprawl. Rezoning and rising land values have contributed to their hefty gains. Inflation has driven up their rent receipts with pleasing regularity. But hindsight can be like looking in a mirror. It shows what is going on behind you as if it were in front, while obscuring what truly lies ahead. Will we see a shift to the cities, mass transit, and below-zero population growth? Place your bets.

INDOOR TENNIS COURTS

This final example of commercial property is representative of highly-specialized facilities. The risk and potential reward are highest here. Whether it be the tennis courts cited below or a motel, restaurant, bowling alley, or parking garage, you are marketing a *service*, not just a building. Success depends on business operations in addition to construction, financing, and property management expertise.

To spice up our illustration, an actual situation will be described including the limited partnership syndicate formed to do the deal. An innovative proposal was presented to the partners of a prestigious investment banking firm. A city-owned, unused, riverside pier structure would be leased and renovated for indoor tennis. Land so near the city center was prohibitive for this use, so why not locate over water? The proposal, complete with a REAL analysis, was accepted.

The development firm became the general partner and the investment bankers put up the major equity and became limited partners. Work was initiated on the eight-court facility, but ran nearly 7 percent over budget by completion. To their chagrin, a schedule slippage crimped three weeks from the first 30-week prime season and disgruntled the newly enrolled members. Worse still, the city slowed completion of the planned below-ground highway passing by the pier while designing out its two nearest exit ramps. Attempting to cross the existing highway was like rushing the net while facing a slam. And tennis-dressed women patrons were continually congratulated on their contours in constructionese, enough to ruffle any Ms.

The projections of profitability and risk had been based on 70 percent, 80 percent, and 90 percent occupancy assumptions. Other courts in the region, which were not then numerous or close by, were packed from 8 A.M. until midnight. Suffice it to say that for the first two years court utilization averaged only 50 percent. This was below break-even, after operating expenses and payments on the ten-year mortgage and pier lease. The third year was nicely profitable, however, due to revamped marketing and creation of a pier-front parking alcove.

What is the lesson? As verified in psychological research, people tend to underestimate risk. Optimism kept the organizers and investors from projecting the results of such low occupancy. Even so, 80 percent or 90 percent occupancy might have seemed more likely. But the somewhat uncontrollable business risks proved to outweigh the real estate risks, such as the construction cost and time overruns. With tennis booming nationwide, and indoor play gaining devotees during both winter and summer, it was difficult *not* to make a fortune on indoor courts. Instead, this case documents the *risk* of a specialized facility and underscores the need for a complete analysis.

SUMMARY

Commercial property generally offers higher returns and risks than residential income property. Its more specialized nature and typically larger scale make it the province of sophisticated, experienced investors. Financing is more difficult to obtain and may be subject to occupancy goals and minimum standards on lease quality. The construction cycle can be lengthy with interior finishing and renovation surprisingly costly. And single-purpose properties, like manufacturing facilities or resorts, are particularly illiquid.

An attractive, well-located structure that becomes available during good economic times can do very well. But overbuilding, especially in urban markets, can drop rental rates sharply or produce sustained high vacancies. Demand for commercial space simply is *not* as responsive to price cutting as is residential property. A business operation has too many other considerations that dominate minor changes in rental expenses.

If you can assure occupancy, as in a medical building owned by members of a group practice, then risk is lowered. Longer term leases and a longer holding period should be a part of your plan. If you want to operate a service, such as a motel, restaurant, or sports facility, then operating issues take precedence over the real estate aspects of your investment. The investor profiles best met by commercial property seem to be those of the wealthy or the occupant-owner.

10

Land Investing and Development

Will Rogers said, "Buy land. They aren't making any more of it." Not a particularly funny line for Will and not particularly true either. For example, *Forbes* magazine has noted that "at least 25 percent of Manhattan Island has been created by landfill"[1] — a "New Amsterdam" even the Dutch would be proud of. Malcolm Forbes, himself, has opened up his giant 250,000 acre Trinchera Ranch for homesteads and development. It is such new land *use* that creates investment values and this goes on all the time.

WHY OWN LAND?

To this point, we have focused on analyzing income property. Usually, rental income fully offsets both the leverage and operating expenses and provides a residual cash flow. Then depreciation acts to shield this return from taxation. True, some land also generates

---

[1] "Has the Land Boom Crested?" *Forbes* Magazine, June 15, 1974, p. 36.

income from crops, grazing, a driving range, sod farm, or whatever. But these are essentially specialized activities, like our indoor tennis courts. They require marketing of a product or service to get the income. The landowner may lease his acreage to remain a passive investor, but its rentable value then depends on its usefulness to others. So raw land derives income only from operations using it or none at all.

Land is really held for appreciation. Your yard or neighboring wooded lot also yields personal satisfaction perhaps, but we will focus on economic objectives. Upgrading the economic usefulness of land, plus inflation, is the source of capital gains. But in the absence of current income, this appreciation must provide a return not only on the initial outlay, but also on the carrying costs. When leveraging land with minimal equity, small changes in value or short delays in upgrading have a magnified impact on return. Leveraged land investment, analyzed in Table 10–1, is the most volatile way to invest in real estate.

"You can't go wrong in buying land." It's a common euphemism, but untrue. People *expect* land to rise in price and it almost always does. But with only modest appreciation (5 percent per year) or even with good growth (10 percent per year), the carrying costs can prove damaging. Add to this the typically higher transaction costs for sales commissions and the investment can prove mediocre unless held a long time. Figure 10.1 shows various rates of land appreciation. The overall rate of return is very sensitive to both the holding period and this appreciation factor.

Despite the success stories of some speculators, unless you are in the path of immediate development

TABLE 10-1
Land Held for Investment—10 Percent Inflation—75 Percent Mortgage

KEY FACTORS ARE ----

TOTAL INVESTED	----MORTGAGE TERMS----			----OPERATING & INFLATION ASSUMPTIONS----				----DEPRECIATION----			----TAX RATES----	
	AMOUNT	% INTR	LIFE	NET SALE PRICE	GROSS INCOME	OPERATING EXPENSE	% ANNUAL INFLATION	AMOUNT	LIFE	TYPE	INCOME	CAP GAIN
1000	750	8.00	20	900	0	20	10.0	0	0	0%	40%	20%

COMPUTED SUMMARY ----

EQUITY AMOUNT	----MORTGAGE TERMS----		% NET SALE TO TOTAL	% INCOME TO TOTAL	% EXPENSE TO INCOME	% NET TO TOTAL	% DEPREC TO TOTAL
	% DEBT	MONTHLY YEARLY					
250	75.0	6.27 75	50.0	0.0	0.0	-2.0	0.0

COMPUTED RESULTS ----

YR	----HOLDING RESULTS BEFORE INCOME TAXES----						----HOLDING RESULTS AFTER TAXES----					----OVERALL RESULTS WITH SALE AT YEAR END----					
	GROSS INCOME	OPERATE EXPENSE	MORTGAGE INTR	MORTGAGE AMORT	CASH FLOW	% RE TURN	DEPREC IATION	TAXABLE INCOME	TAXES DUE	CASH FLOW	% RE TURN	SALE PRICE	DEBT REPAY	TAXES DUE	CASH FLOW	TOTAL PROFIT	% RE TURN
1	0	20	59	16	-95	-38.1	0	-79	-32	-64	-25.4	990	734	-2	258	-56	-22.3
2	0	22	58	17	-97	-38.9	0	-80	-32	-65	-26.1	1089	717	18	354	-25	-4.4
3	0	24	57	19	-99	-39.8	0	-81	-32	-67	-26.8	1198	698	40	460	14	1.5
4	0	27	55	20	-102	-40.8	0	-82	-33	-69	-27.7	1318	678	64	576	61	4.2
5	0	29	53	22	-105	-41.8	0	-83	-33	-71	-28.6	1449	656	90	703	117	5.6
6	0	32	52	24	-107	-43.0	0	-84	-34	-74	-29.6	1594	633	119	843	182	6.4
7	0	35	50	26	-111	-44.3	0	-85	-34	-77	-30.7	1754	607	151	996	259	6.9
8	0	39	48	28	-114	-45.7	0	-87	-35	-80	-31.9	1929	580	186	1164	347	7.3
9	0	43	45	30	-118	-47.3	0	-88	-35	-83	-33.2	2122	550	224	1348	449	7.5
10	0	47	43	32	-122	-49.0	0	-90	-36	-86	-34.6	2334	517	267	1550	564	7.7

FIGURE 10.1
Land Profitability for Various Appreciation Rates

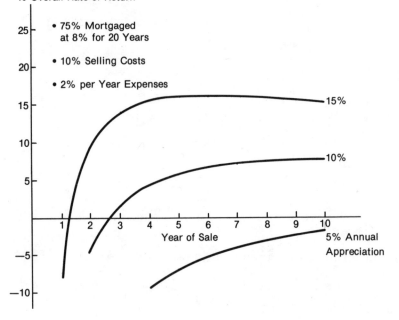

(perhaps undertaken by yourself), land values rise gradually. Land that moves only with inflation is not profitable when it must carry a mortgage. The 5 percent appreciation curve shows this. Real appreciation comes from economic upgrading of the land's actual or potential use. The 10 percent appreciation curve (say 5 percent real appreciation plus 5 percent inflation) produces modest profitability. But faster appreciation rates verify the speculators' war stories. When financed with high leverage, spurting land prices can indeed make millionaires of modest investors. This is the happy side of risk, also shown in Figure 10.1.

THREE FORTUNES MADE IN LAND

Three strategies for investing in land can be classified as:

1. Speculative purchase and quick resale.
2. Land packaging.
3. Long-term buy and hold.

Each strategy is illustrated below by citing an actual success story.

LAND SPECULATION

The *Wall Street Journal* has reported on lifestyles and how inflation affects incomes and purchasing patterns. One person cited was a Mr. Ingram, a self-made millionaire, who had parlayed several successful real estate deals into a comfortably lavish living for himself, Mrs. Ingram, and their young daughter. In one instance, our first land investment strategy was used.

As part of a syndicate, Ingram speculated in acreage in the path of eminent development. The parcel was bought and then sold within a year for nearly double the prices, leaving Ingram with a nice personal profit, even after overhead and taxes. Rapid development of the Dallas-Forth Worth Metroplex, centered around the new airport/industrial complex, had created this significant land speculation opportunity.[2]

The speculator pits his knowledge and judgment against that of the seller and other potential buyers in the marketplace. He hopes that risk-taking, differ-

---

[2] *Wall Street Journal*, June 12, 1974, p. 1.

ential knowledge, unpublicized negotiations, creative financing, or similar factors can produce an extraordinary rate of return. Naturally, timing is crucial. It is said that one definition of a long-term investor is a speculator who lost.

LAND PACKAGING

Land packaging is another route to riches, if it succeeds. This is the concept of buying at wholesale and selling at retail, usually to a new class of user. Land is purchased or optioned—possibly in secret and over a few years—until a suitable contiguous "package" is controlled. Then plans are announced for upgrading, redevelopment, or new construction. The pieces or the entire property are then resold at values reflecting the now-possible higher usefulness of the land. Alternately, as at Disney World in Florida, the land can be held for income from business operations rather than resold.

Zeckendorf is a name that sparks images of daring, creativity, and ultimately bankruptcy, among real estate afficianados. In perhaps his most famous deal, William Zeckendorf used land packaging as a vehicle for profit and publicity. He noticed that mid-town land on Manhattan's East River, while close to the city center, was a slaughterhouse district that lowered neighboring land values. But take away the smell and that area *and its neighborhood* would be suddenly more valuable.[3]

---

[3] A similar, more recent transaction was the March 11, 1975, agreement by Penn Central Transportation Co. to sell 144 acres of mid-Manhattan's West Side for about 1 million dollars per acre. Donald J. Trump, the purchaser, plans to upgrade these former freight yards into choice, water-front, residential and business locations.

Zeckendorf's plan was to upgrade this land by development consistent with a higher use. But control of the whole district was necessary and adjacent purchases were also desirable. Working covertly, he acquired properties at $17 per square foot and up. A few blocks west, Grand Central and Fifth Avenue locations then commanded up to $300 per square foot. The surprising dramatic conclusion was that the United Nations, which had just abandoned efforts to find a suitable urban site, was offered the package for a mere $2 million profit. The Rockefellers, donors of the land under the U.N., jumped at the chance and the resale was negotiated within a week.

LONG-TERM LAND INVESTMENT

This third strategy has the least risk but requires the most patience and staying power. A long-term land investor usually sustains a negative cash flow until the property is developed to generate income or is resold. Yet fabulous capital gains can be produced over decades of inflation/appreciation. And our tax structure encourages exactly this type of holding since expenses are immediately deductible against ordinary income while capital gains taxes are at lower rates and deferred until realized.

One extremely successful holding, producing a 200-fold capital gain, was made by Philadelphia's Seltzer family. In addition to their industrial land holdings in northern New Jersey's metropolitan suburbs, the Seltzers until recently owned some acreage adjacent to Philadelphia's city line. The parcel, situated between the city and its Main Line residential suburb, lay on a plateau overlooking the river — and the subsequently-developed expressway—as it flowed into town. Originally bought for $1,000 an acre in 1934, the last acre was sold in 1972 for $200,000.

The magnitude of a 200-fold multiple seems staggering until we compute the compound annual rate of return involved. The 38-year holding period is one that aggressive youths or habitual speculators will find hard to comprehend. It literally spans a working lifetime, say from age 24 to 62. Yet reduced to a compound annual rate of return, the result is 14.9 percent per year.[4] This is hardly staggering, although very good indeed. Furthermore, property taxes and other holding costs would lower this rate of return. On the other hand, leverage would improve the return on equity. And such long-term capital gains enjoy favored tax treatment.

We can put this example into further perspective by recalling that the long-term rate of return from the stock market has been under 10% compounded annually. By contrast, the best example of the long-term return customarily attainable from land is Manhattan Island itself. Purchased in 1624 for $24, it has appreciated at only 6 percent compounded annually during the intervening 351 years. But this produces a land value of $20 billion today! (If the Indians had

---

[4] A convenient way to estimate compound annual rates of return relies on the "rule of 72." Based on logarithms, this rule says that a doubling is achieved by any combination of years and rates multiplying to 72. For example, 7.2 years of 10 percent compound annual growth doubles your money (before tax considerations). Also 10 years at 7.2 percent growth provides a double. So does 5 years at 14.4 percent, or 72 years at 1 percent (a terrible thought). Our 200-fold gain represents nearly eight consecutive doubles. This is about one doubling every 5 years during the 38-year holding period. Applying the rule of 72, a double in 5 years indicates a 14.4 percent compound annual rate of return, close to the actual 14.9 percent figure.

bought $24 in certificates of deposit at 8 percent, they would now be way ahead, before taxes, expropriation, and assorted other mistreatment.)

The conclusion? Land almost certainly appreciates over time. Whether bought for short-term speculative gain, repackaged for a higher economic use, or held for the long pull, profit opportunities exist. But the question is: Will the land appreciate *fast enough* to produce worthwhile profits? And staying power is required to pay ongoing taxes and expenses.

Most of all, patience provides impressive rewards. Ask the thankful third-generation descendants of property-owning Californians, or second-generation Floridians, or first-generation Hawaiians about the wealth produced by land and time. While the rates of appreciation may vary, and some speculators will get higher, quicker returns, the gains from long-term investing are usually satisfying (and taxed at capital gains rates). Even a fourth- or fifth-generation Bostonian can be grateful for his property-holding ancestors' wisdom in not selling before he inherited the land. Buildings usually appreciate with inflation for a few decades, but eventually come to naught. Land endures.

LAND DEVELOPMENT

Land speculation, packaging, and long-term investment each seek appreciation based on the land's improved income-producing *potential*. This can stem from mere inflation — the same potential use, for which more dollars must be paid. Or it can result from true appreciation, such as from population growth exceeding new land availability or from greater per capita expenditures directed towards land. Closing this gap between the land's potential and its developed usage decreases a major risk — much like the leap from theory to practice. To the land developer, therefore, the marketplace accords the highest level of returns and risk.

Development, from the investor's perspective, pits construction cost against market value. Sometimes years pass before an income stream is produced. Some costs during the development phase are tax deductible as incurred (mainly construction mortgage interest), assuming that the owner has otherwise taxable income to offset them with. Most development costs — including the building, but also property closing costs, architect's fees, landscaping, and the like — must be capitalized. These costs can then be deducted only through depreciation charges over the improvement's useful life.

The magnitude of the income stream and of the partially offsetting operating expenses depend on the type of development undertaken. As we have seen, a net lease on industrial property has a low rent/low expense pattern. A motel/restaurant, by contrast, would generate high income (with acceptable occupancy) but half or more might go for operating expenses.

The leverage employed is also a key determinant of the rate of return. Here the developer has a major advantage. He might buy raw land at its existing price, then package it, get it rezoned, arrange "in the ground" improvements like roads, utilities, sewers and water, and upgrade its use through further development. By keeping his land profits and builder's profits invested, it may be possible to borrow the full amount of his out-of-pocket development costs. This happy situation is called "mortgaging out." That is, the loan amount equals total costs so the developer recoups his working capital untaxed. He then has a "free" equity ride on the finished project. The computed rate of return can be infinite as there is then no out-of-pocket equity.

Many developers have bootstrapped themselves in exactly this way. But during tight money, with inflation escalating materials and labor costs, and with shortages causing construction delays, the developer may be called on for additional capital beyond that allowed on a mortgage. This whipsaw effect can easily wipe out his working capital. The stalled project then defaults on mortgage interest. As it deteriorates in value, even the loan principal is threatened. Foreclosed and sold at auction, the property may be a bargain for another developer but represents the end of the first one. In 1974, for example, some REITs had as many as half their construction loans in such troubled abeyance. The risk is again commensurate with the potential for return.

NEW RULES FOR DEVELOPERS

Along with other businesses, developers must increasingly deal with consumer concern, government regulation, and an evolving philosophy of corporate social responsibility. Environmental impact statements, no-growth referendums, securities regulations, recalcitrant zoning boards, rent controls, and warranties to housing consumers are now part of the milieu. These make the developer's job more complex, and thus construction more costly, partly offsetting the social benefits.

Government programs aiding and prodding development also exist. Urban homestake programs offer much hope for generating homeowner equity from abandoned buildings. Section 235's rapid depreciation allowance (straight line over only five years) has spurred renovation of substandard housing. HUD's program for funding new towns tried to meet needs for urban diffusion based on sensible land use planning. Mortgage insurance and subsidy programs dampen the competition between housing and business needs for loan capital.

Finally there is a trend toward consolidation in what has always been a fragmented industry. The hundred largest homebuilders, for example, have improved their market share in the last decade, partly by acquisition. Counterbalancing this trend, many large corporations who ventured into development, such as Boise Cascade, Chrysler, ITT, and Westinghouse, have since regrouped. It seems that entrepreneurial skill and risk-taking are still vital elements of the business.

SUMMARY

Land can be held with a view toward short-term resale, upgrading in usage, or for long-term investment. Unless farmed or operated in some enterprise, land produces negligible income. Yet ongoing tax, insurance, and upkeep costs must be met. Leveraged holdings also face the drain of interest payments. All this means that land must appreciate heartily to provide suitable returns. Yet holders receive some tax benefits since actual costs are deductible and sale profits (after transaction costs) are capital gains. Combined with long holding periods, this can build up impressive multiples of capital.

Development requires management skill and experience beyond that of mere ownership. But in this labor-intensive, highly-leveraged, delays-are-costly environment, the potential rewards and risks are highest. Successful developers can sometimes "come out" on a project with no residual investment on their part. The returns are then incalculable — even for a computer!

11

Advanced Analysis

In addition to probing the investment merits of the different types of real estate—homes, apartments, commercial property, and land—we can use the REAL analysis to determine operating policies. That is: What leverage level is best? How long should leases be? How vital is it to control operating costs? Should you sell, trade, or refinance your property? When? Can a particular investment be syndicated on favorable terms? And so on. These crucial policy issues are explored in this chapter.

LEVERAGE ALTERNATIVES

The method by which you finance your investment has a major impact on profitability and risk. It dictates the degree of your leverage and also influences your other investing objectives: liquidity, expenses, tax shelter, and inflation protection. We have focused on "conventional" mortgages, self-amortizing loans of fairly long duration. But a multitude of financing alternatives can be created.

155

A *purchase money mortgage,* where the seller extends credit to the buyer, is not unusual, especially for land sales. The technique can also have tax benefits for the seller. He can report his capital gains over a stretched out period of years (thereby lowering his effective tax rate) by accepting less than 30 percent of the price in the first year. Thus terms of "29 percent down" plus the balance over five to ten years, with interest, are common.

A *second mortgage* might be used to obtain leverage beyond that granted by a probably conventional first mortgage. The second loan is subordinated in legal rights to the first. Many mortgages are "non-recourse" loans that look only to the property for security, as they are not guaranteed personally by the borrower. Thus the second mortgage holder takes a greater risk and usually receives a higher interest rate (unless, perhaps, the seller takes back the second mortgage to assure the sale, in which case a higher rate of interest may be less important).

Some mortgages, especially second or third ones, feature interest-only payments with a *balloon payment* of principal at the end. This improves the buyer's cash flow and maintains high leverage. Often the property is sold or refinanced prior to mortgage expiration so that the lump sum payment need not come from working capital, but rather from the resale or refinancing proceeds.

Another technique for achieving or restoring high leverage is called a *wrap around mortgage.* If a long-standing, low-interest mortgage exists, then because of amortization and/or appreciation, the property can usually sustain increased debt. A second mortgage, for the full leverage sought, can be arranged to "wrap around" this first mortgage. That is, the borrower makes payments only on the new loan, while the lender assumes responsibility for paying off the old one. The lender is happy to do this because he then benefits from the favorable terms of the old mortgage while receiving interest at the current, higher rate.

Another means of controlling property with little of your own cash involves *optioning.* A small, usually non-refundable amount may be sufficient to cause a willing seller to allow you the right or option to buy his property at a stated price during some defined length of time. Land packaging, requiring consummation of several transactions, often uses this technique. If the option period is fairly long, significant appreciation can occur, especially in conjunction with a higher use of the property. Financing can then be arranged reflecting this higher value, thus conserving the developer's own funds.

And what about *variable-interest-rate mortgages?* Will they be the wave of the future as lenders try to balance the returns and costs of money? Will the risks of fluctuating interest rates thereby be transferred to the consumer? Only time will tell. But for analysis purposes, perhaps the best estimate of average interest rates over the long term is the current long-term rate. In this case, our fixed-interest mortgage analysis applies as is. The only complication in evaluating such financing is that it introduces another significant factor for risk analysis. That is, if the average mortgage rate should prove to be higher or lower than your assumption, what would that do to the investment's rate of return?

LEVERAGE POLICY

A conventional mortgage on investment property might be limited to about 75 percent of value, but greater leverage is often achievable if it suits your objectives. The incremental loan funds may be costly, but a good project will nonetheless show a higher rate of return. In Figure 11.1, we have graphed the year 5 rate of return (a convenient, representative benchmark) for various leverage levels. The effects of 0 percent and 5 percent inflation are shown as an index of risk. This property, like those analyzed in Part III, shows typical investment characteristics so as to lend generality to our conclusions.

Figure 11.1 shows the main incentive for high leverage — the inflation/appreciation factor. Counting transaction costs and high mortgage rates but also a reasonably long holding period (five years), price in-

FIGURE 11.1
Year 5 Rate of Return for Various Leverage Levels

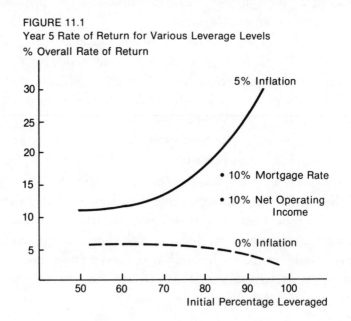

creases account for most of the profits. No inflation, no extraordinary gains. But with inflation, the greater leverage lets your money control proportionately more property so you benefit more from swollen prices.

The catch, of course, is risk. The highly leveraged policy is correct, despite high rates, with inflation and no operating problems. But it becomes a nightmare with high vacancy, deterioration, maintenance cost overruns, rent controls that tend to keep sale prices down as well as rents, a downgrading of the neighborhood, or *any other cause of constant or declining resale value.* Your experience, reserve capital, personal goals, and other factors should be considered in arriving at your own policy on leverage.

LEASE LENGTH

Many real estate investors try to contract for relatively long leases. And while businesses in particular seek such long-term locational and price stability, it may not be in the owner's best interests. For residential property, the usual remedy for lease-breaking by the renter is merely forfeiture of the security deposit. Thus the long lease binds the landlord as much as the tenant. During inflation, the inability to raise rents may mean a missed opportunity, or worse, a shrinking profit due to rising expenses.

On the other hand, tenant turnover is expensive and good renter relationships are valuable. Advertising, showing the space, agent commissions, renovation, and redecorating are all typical but expensive ingredients in re-marketing vacancies. What is a proper policy on lease length? And which cost increases can and should be passed on automatically by lease escalator clauses?

Dealing first with residential property, a one-to-three year initial lease, depending on tenant preferences and apartment marketing costs, plus optional one-year renewals, seems best. For shorter leases, an expense escalator clause might be included, but not used until renewal time. But for longer leases, with today's utility, fuel, supplies, labor, and tax cost increases, it is an increasingly desirable and acceptable practice to include a rent escalator clause.

With commercial property, lease length is typically five years at the minimum. Most leases then allow tenant renewal, perhaps with rental levels readjusted to the then-current market values based on appraisal. Since marketing commercial space can be costly, these longer leases are in the owner's best interests as well as the occupant's. But some form of rent escalation is necessary to bring about protection and profit from inflation.

With shopping centers, rent rates often include a percentage of sales (called "overage" because rents then increase proportionally with sales). By contrast, a net-net-net lease has the tenant pay all operating costs and hence all increases. But only at rental adjustment time (sometimes after 20 years) does the owner then increase his income due to inflation. The property's sale price would be expected to rise, however, but even this appreciation would be retarded by the long-term, fixed-income lease. The important factor is to catch up with inflation relatively often. Annually is great, and 5 years is acceptable, but 10 to 20 years of constant net rents restrains the owner's rate of return significantly, and perhaps unnecessarily.

ESCALATING EXPENSES

What if the market won't accept rental boosts as fast as expenses go up? After all, the building, whether new or used, gets older and out of style with the passage of time, despite good maintenance and administrative policies. The REAL analysis helps us to develop an understanding of this contingency also.

Suppose that instead of sale price, gross income, and operating expense all rising uniformly at 5 percent per year, we assume the following:

1. 3 percent inflation of the sale price, recognizing aging.
2. 5 percent increases, on average, in annual gross rents.
3. 7 percent jumps in annual operating expenses.

FIGURE 11.2
Effect of Escalating Expenses and Restrained Sale Prices
% Overall Rate of Return

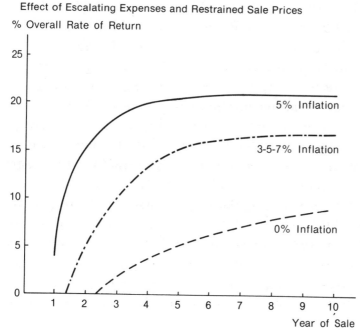

Many experts feel that this is a more accurate, and at least more conservative, estimate of inflation's impact on the investment merits of income property. What does this pattern of operating results do to the overall rate of return?

Figure 11.2 graphs the same typical property as Figure 11.1, but fixes the initial leverage level at 75 percent. This time we show the overall rate of return for various holding periods and the effect of 0 percent inflation, a uniform 5 percent annually, and our 3–5–7 percent inflation pattern defined above. As you can see, inflation still makes a big impact on rate of return — an impact too large and too attractive to ignore.

DECLINING PROPERTY VALUES

We have asserted that appreciation/inflation is the major driving force behind high real estate returns, even for income-producing property. But what if sale prices do not go up, or worse, what if they decline? The answer is: You are in trouble, more so than traditional analysis approaches might suggest if they ignore sale price and transaction costs effects.

Suppose our typical property has a net income before leverage that is 10 percent of the total invested. A price decline of 3 percent per year would cut the total return (income plus capital gains) to 7 percent annually, before considering leverage, taxes, and transaction costs. But with leverage, all of the sale price decline is attributable to the equity owner, just as the benefits of a price rise would be. With 75 percent leverage and 25 percent equity, the net income to equity might swell to 12 percent, as with our suburban medical office building. But now a 3 percent price drop, when taken as a percentage of the equity, gets magnified fourfold to 12 percent. This price drop completely negates the income from holding.

Suppose you choose to hold the property, so as not to realize this accumulating loss. Fine. But to exclude the effect of your accruing loss from your estimate of profits is to deceive yourself. The property still provides a cash flow from holding, of course. But it amounts to a return *of* investment, not a return *on* investment, because when you sell you will not get your full equity back. You have created an annuity which consumes principal to pay income. That may be fine for some investors, based on their objectives. But they should recognize the impact of what they have done. Appreciation, not milking declining properties, is the true provider of high returns.

REFINANCING

Refinancing, or periodically rejuvenating your leverage level, lets long-term investors achieve a major boost in their overall rate of return. Suppose you decide, as a matter of systematic policy, to increase your leverage back to the 75 percent level whenever it gets below 60 percent. This reduced leverage can result from property appreciation or mortgage amortization or, most likely, both.

For example, a $400,000 property with a $300,000 mortgage might appreciate/inflate in sale price at 5 percent per year. In five years we could expect a 25 percent higher market value, equalling $500,000 (or more counting compounded growth). Meanwhile, amortization of about $20,000 has been paid (assuming a 25 year mortgage at 9 percent). The $280,000 of remaining debt is then only 56 percent of the current $500,000 value—time to refinance. Figure 11.3 illustrates this scenario. It shows the sale price, debt level, and cash inflow from holding with a policy of refinancing to 75 percent of market value every five years.

Figure 11.3 shows the cash inflow from holding, including those delicious lumps in years 5 and 10 due to refinancing. And this is *after-tax* cash because the net proceeds from the larger loans are not taxable since they are not income. Yet refinancing has brought liquidity to the owner, realizing his inflation gains, without the need for selling.

However, this is not the complete bonanza it seems.

FIGURE 11.3
Market Value, Debt Balance, and Cash Inflow of a Refinanced Property (in $1,000)

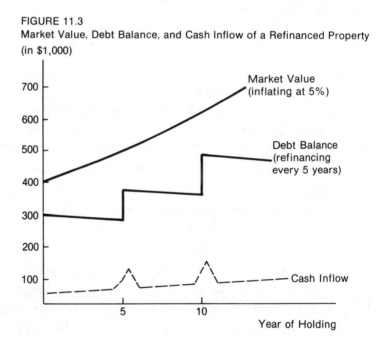

Because "profits" are taken out, the higher debt balance requires more of the net rental income to service it. Also, with the passage of time, depreciation (especially if accelerated) will have lost most of its zip. This lowers the property's tax shelter capability. And, most significant, an ever-larger tax liability and higher transaction costs are building up for when you *do* sell. Figure 11.4 shows the overall results for our year 5 refinancing example.

Since leverage boosts the overall returns of good projects, maintaining high leverage through refinancing helps even further. Figure 11.4 assumes that the refinancing carries the same mortgage terms as the original financing. Yet the profitability difference is

FIGURE 11.4
Overall Rates of Return With and Without Refinancing
% Overall Rate of Return

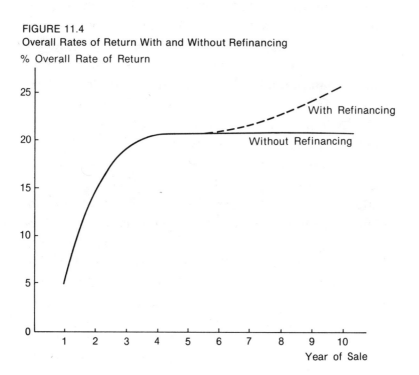

significant. Furthermore, a later refinancing jacks up the overall returns again. And liquidity is better due to the periodic inflow of the net loan proceeds. If you choose never to sell the property, the accruing capital gain tax liability is not your problem nor, under current law, is it your heirs' problem. Their tax basis is the property's market value upon their acquiring it as part of your estate. Thus refinancing is a sound policy for long-term investors desiring liquidity and capable of withstanding the heightened risk.

PROPERTY TRADING

Property trading is another useful, and somewhat sophisticated, technique for maintaining leverage and parlaying principal untaxed. A "tax-free exchange of assets of like kind," as allowed by the tax code, means that one real estate property can be swapped for another without either side being required to "recognize" gains as from a sale. As a practical matter, the properties will not have identical market values or equal equity portions. And one party may really want liquidity rather than another property. So trades must be engineered to meet these various needs.

Many advertised properties note that the owner is willing to trade. In many other instances, the would-be seller may also be persuaded to trade instead. Or a third party can be found to immediately buy from the reluctant trader, giving him (taxable) liquidity. Being interested in capital growth, you will probably want a larger property in swap for your existing equity. The trade terms may include assuming or obtaining a first mortgage on the property being acquired, plus a second mortgage note taken back by the former owner who is "trading down," plus perhaps some additional cash, called "boot."

Both refinancing and trading let you paying postpone your accruing capital gain tax liability. More importantly, you can own a larger property on which inflation can boost his profits. But arranging the trade generally costs more in broker commissions, any transfer taxes, title, appraisal and closing costs than would a refinancing. The main consideration, therefore, is your operating forecast for your present property. If it no longer suits your appreciation, tax shelter, or other goals, trade it or, failing that, sell it. Otherwise, refinancing and holding can be the easiest as well as most profitable policy.

PARTNERSHIP SYNDICATES

When a property is too large for one owner, or when a group wishes to participate in rather than manage an investment, a syndicate is often formed. In its simplest form it may be two partners sharing responsibility and liability. It may be a joint venture of two operating entities and organized as a corporation. Most likely, however, is the limited partnership. Usually organized by a developer or professional syndicator acting as general partner, it offers qualified investors a passive, limited-liability entree to real estate deals.

How should you analyze a piece of such a syndicate if offered to you? The most knowledgeable source is the general partner. But unfortunately, except for a commissioned salesman, he may be the least objective. The SEC requires that, in public offerings, all material data and risks be disclosed in a prospectus. A private offering memorandum should be equally comprehensive and forthright. The general partner's obligations and compensation must be spelled out. The limited partner's expectations should be presented. And the integrity and track record of the developer/manager is crucial. Finally, you must judge whether the degree of risk, liquidity, tax shelter, and so forth suits your needs. But if you are willing to be an active investor, you can avoid the overhead of syndicates.

12

Conclusions and Strategy

Many books discuss real estate. And many provide insight and distilled experience on how to select, develop, appraise, finance, improve, operate, and sell real property. But few adequately determine its investment merits and none other quantifies inflation's impact. We have addressed this gap because the answers are too important and too attractive to oversimplify. Both fact and theory verify that, with inflation, investors can reasonably hope to achieve *after tax rates of return of 15 percent to 25 percent compounded annually.*

Favorable results have been achieved by most, but not all, real estate investors. Just take homeowner's for example. One friend, a stockbroker, made more money on the sale of his house than he had in several years from his stock market trading. Perhaps an acquaintance of yours could tell the same story. And in every town large enough to spread a rumor, certain somebodies are always "making a fortune in real estate."

While such intuitive and unsubstantiated evidence

abounds, we have sought more comprehensive, consistent, and accurate measures of real estate investment performance. The respectable literature is sparse. But what does exist, coupled with both professional and firsthand experience, leads us to conclude that real estate suits the objectives of many investors. Its rate of return, highly tax sheltered, is unsurpassed by savings, bonds, stocks, or tangibles as investment alternatives. But the kicker is inflation. Rising rents and sale prices, coupled with leverage even at high mortgage rates, provide not only inflation protection but also inflated profits.

We developed and applied the REAL analysis to deal with these issues. It has served three broad purposes:

1. To illuminate the general characteristics of real estate investing.
2. To discover the specific merits of particular opportunities.
3. To analyze operating policies.

Part I discussed investing during inflation and offered a guide for determining your own objectives. We described the real estate market and presented two example investments plus a risk analysis. Part II reviewed various types of properties and operating policies. You are invited to use the reference tables of Part III for more exact application of the REAL analysis to your specific opportunities.

LEVERAGE, TAX SHELTER, AND INFLATION

We have seen that real estate's traditional advantages are a good rate of return, augmented by *leverage* and *tax shelter*. But *inflation*, which generally causes rising net incomes and sale prices, can double the investor's overall rate of return. Other key factors also influence returns and risks. The major ones are the total invested relative to immediate liquidation value, the percentage leveraged, and net operating income. Of important but lesser influence is the mortgage interest rate. Perhaps surprisingly, changes in the mortgage life, in the amount, life, and type of depreciation, and in the investor's tax rates cause only minor changes in overall rates of return. Figure 12.1 summarizes the before-tax, after-tax, and after-sale rates of return provided by a typical, leveraged, income property.

Clearly it is not sufficient to compute just the year 1

FIGURE 12.1
Before-Tax, after-Tax, and after-Sale Rates of Return

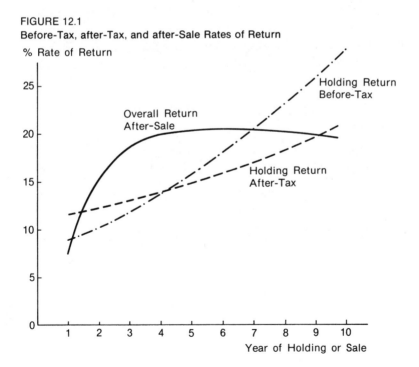

results when making such an investment analysis. Nor can transaction costs be ignored because they provide a strong incentive for holding a few years (or until about 25 percent appreciation). Tax shelter has a perverse effect — at first increasing the holding returns (after tax) before succumbing partially to the tax collector's grasp. Least of all can one afford to ignore inflation — or the risk of decline — in the property's sale price.

If you decide to invest in real estate, following home ownership, we suggest existing residential income property as the best beginning point. High leverage — around 75 percent or somewhat more — is a must. Appreciation, which enhances mere inflation, is the most important selection criterion. Then rental and operating policies should try to provide maximum and growing net income. Sale, or possibly refinancing or trading, should be used to pyramid to larger, similar properties and to multiple properties. Invest for yourself, guided by the counsel of professionals. Then hire someone to run the place so as to preserve your time for investing and supervision — and before you know it, leisure.

Part III

Real Estate Investment Analysis Tables

13. *New Residential Property*

Eight reference tables are presented using 200% of straight line depreciation, the most favorable tax treatment allowed for this class of real estate. The separate cases span different mortgage rates (8% annual interest and 10%), mortgage amounts (from 60% financed to 90%), and various income-after-expense levels (from 8% annually on the total invested to 12%). Profitability results are computed assuming both 0% and 5% inflation. Each table is computed per $1,000 of the total invested. The rates of return, being percentages, apply to any invested amount. The actual dollar figures are easily scaled to correspond to any size project.

14. *New Commercial Property*

Eight more tables span this class of real estate, which qualifies for 150% of straight line depreciation. The same mortgage, net income, and inflation values are used as in the prior chapter, but with this depreciation method and the typically longer depreciation life.

15. *Used Residential Property*

A third set of eight reference tables spans this class of real estate, which qualifies for 125% of straight line depreciation if the property's useful life is 20 years or more.

173

The same mortgage, net income, and inflation values are used as before but with this depreciation method and the typically shorter depreciation life.

16. *Used Commercial Property*

This fourth set of eight tables employs straight line depreciation, applicable to all used commercial property and to used residential property having a remaining useful life less than 20 years.

17. *Land Investing and Development Property*

Holding raw land, which is not depreciable, is illustrated in four tables. Various mortgage and inflation rates are used.

18. *Home or Condominium Property*

This final set of eight tables employs the special no-depreciation and tax rules applicable to owner-occupied residences. Various mortgage, inflation, and "implied" income (rent savings) levels are illustrated.

13

New Residential Property

This chapter presents eight reference tables detailing the profitability of *new residential property*, which qualifies for *200 percent of straight line depreciation*. Below is an index to this chapter's specific tables, showing their key factor values and summarized results.

Percent Mortgaged	Percent Mortgage Interest Rate	Percent Net Income to Total Invested	Percent Year 5 Rates of Return			Page Number of Table
			0% Inflation	3–5–7% Inflation	5% Inflation	
60	8	8	4.3	10.3	13.9	176
60	8	10	7.5	13.4	16.8	177
75	8	8	4.0	13.4	18.4	178
75	8	10	9.3	18.1	22.9	179
75	10	10	5.4	15.0	20.1	180
75	10	12	10.8	19.9	24.6	181
90	10	10	4.3	26.6	35.5	182
90	10	12	19.8	37.8	45.6	183

TABLE 13-1
New Residential—200 Percent of Straight Line Depreciation (per $1,000)

KEY FACTORS ARE ----

TOTAL INVESTED	----MORTGAGE TERMS----			----OPERATING & INFLATION ASSUMPTIONS----				----DEPRECIATION----			----TAX RATES----	
	AMOUNT	% INTR	LIFE	NET SALE PRICE	GROSS INCOME	OPERATING EXPENSE	% ANNUAL INFLATION	AMOUNT	LIFE	TYPE	INCOME	CAP GAIN
1000	600	8.00	25	940	140	60	0.0	800	30	200%	40%	20%

COMPUTED SUMMARY ----

EQUITY AMOUNT	----MORTGAGE TERMS----			% NET SALE TO TOTAL	% INCOME TO TOTAL	% EXPENSE TO INCOME	% NET TO TOTAL	% DEPREC TO TOTAL
	% DEBT	MONTHLY	YEARLY					
400	60.0	4.63	56	94.0	14.0	42.9	8.0	80.0

COMPUTED RESULTS ----

YR	----HOLDING RESULTS BEFORE INCOME TAXES----						----HOLDING RESULTS AFTER TAXES----					----OVERALL RESULTS WITH SALE AT YEAR END----					
	GROSS INCOME	OPERATE EXPENSE	----MORTGAGE---- INTR	AMORT	CASH FLOW	% RETURN	DEPRECIATION	TAXABLE INCOME	TAXES DUE	CASH FLOW	% RETURN	SALE PRICE	DEBT REPAY	TAXES DUE	TOTAL PROFIT	CASH FLOW	% RETURN
1	140	60	48	8	24	6.1	53	-21	-8	33	8.2	940	592	-1	-18	349	-4.5
2	140	60	47	9	24	6.1	50	-17	-7	31	7.8	940	584	17	3	339	0.4
3	140	60	46	9	24	6.1	46	-13	-5	30	7.4	940	574	32	27	334	2.4
5	140	60	45	11	24	6.1	40	-5	-2	27	6.6	940	554	55	80	332	4.3
7	140	60	43	13	24	6.1	35	2	1	24	5.9	940	529	73	134	337	5.2
10	140	60	39	16	24	6.1	29	12	5	20	4.9	940	485	89	226	367	6.0

---- INFLATION OF SALE PRICE, INCOME, AND EXPENSE AT 5% ANNUALLY ----

YR	GROSS INCOME	OPERATE EXPENSE	----MORTGAGE---- INTR	AMORT	CASH FLOW	% RETURN	DEPRECIATION	TAXABLE INCOME	TAXES DUE	CASH FLOW	% RETURN	SALE PRICE	DEBT REPAY	TAXES DUE	TOTAL PROFIT	CASH FLOW	% RETURN
1	140	60	48	8	24	6.1	53	-21	-8	33	8.2	987	592	13	14	381	3.6
2	147	63	47	9	28	7.1	50	-13	-5	34	8.4	1036	584	38	81	415	10.1
3	154	66	46	9	33	8.2	46	-5	-2	34	8.6	1088	574	61	153	452	12.3
5	170	73	45	11	42	10.4	40	12	5	37	9.2	1200	554	107	313	539	13.9
7	188	80	43	13	52	12.9	35	29	12	40	10.0	1323	529	150	495	644	14.4
10	217	93	39	16	69	17.1	29	56	22	46	11.5	1531	485	207	823	839	14.7

TABLE 13-2
New Residential—200 Percent of Straight Line Depreciation (per $1,000)

KEY FACTORS ARE ----

TOTAL INVESTED	MORTGAGE TERMS			OPERATING & INFLATION ASSUMPTIONS				DEPRECIATION			TAX RATES	
	AMOUNT	% INTR	LIFE	NET SALE PRICE	GROSS INCOME	OPERATING EXPENSE	% ANNUAL INFLATION	AMOUNT	LIFE	TYPE	INCOME	CAP GAIN
1000	600	8.00	25	940	170	70	0.0	800	30	200%	40%	20%

COMPUTED SUMMARY ----

EQUITY AMOUNT	MORTGAGE TERMS			NET SALE TO TOTAL	% INCOME TO TOTAL	% EXPENSE TO INCOME	% DEPREC TO TOTAL	% NET TO TOTAL
	% DEBT	MONTHLY	YEARLY					
400	60.0	4.63	56	94.0	17.0	41.2	80.0	10.0

COMPUTED RESULTS ----

YR	HOLDING RESULTS BEFORE INCOME TAXES						HOLDING RESULTS AFTER TAXES					OVERALL RESULTS WITH SALE AT YEAR END					
	GROSS INCOME	OPERATE EXPENSE	MORTGAGE INTR	MORTGAGE AMORT	CASH FLOW	%RE TURN	DEPREC IATION	TAXABLE INCOME	TAXES DUE	CASH FLOW	%RE TURN	SALE PRICE	DEBT REPAY	TAXES DUE	CASH FLOW	TOTAL PROFIT	%RE TURN
1	170	70	48	8	44	11.1	53	-1	0	45	11.2	940	592	-1	349	-6	-1.5
2	170	70	47	9	44	11.1	50	3	1	43	10.8	940	584	17	339	27	3.5
3	170	70	46	9	44	11.1	46	7	3	42	10.4	940	574	32	334	63	5.6
5	170	70	45	11	44	11.1	40	15	6	39	9.6	940	554	55	332	140	7.5
7	170	70	43	13	44	11.1	35	22	9	36	8.9	940	529	73	337	218	8.4
10	170	70	39	16	44	11.1	29	32	13	32	7.9	940	485	89	367	346	9.2

- - - - I N F L A T I O N   O F   SALE PRICE, INCOME, AND EXPENSE   A T   5%   A N N U A L L Y - - - - -

YR	GROSS INCOME	OPERATE EXPENSE	MORTGAGE INTR	MORTGAGE AMORT	CASH FLOW	%RE TURN	DEPREC IATION	TAXABLE INCOME	TAXES DUE	CASH FLOW	%RE TURN	SALE PRICE	DEBT REPAY	TAXES DUE	CASH FLOW	TOTAL PROFIT	%RE TURN
1	170	70	48	8	44	11.1	53	-1	0	45	11.2	987	592	13	381	26	6.6
2	178	73	47	9	49	12.4	50	8	3	46	11.5	1036	584	38	415	106	13.1
3	187	77	46	9	55	13.7	46	17	7	48	11.9	1088	574	61	452	191	15.3
5	207	85	45	11	66	16.5	40	36	15	51	12.9	1200	554	107	539	379	16.8
7	228	94	43	13	78	19.6	35	56	22	56	14.0	1323	529	150	644	593	17.3
10	264	109	39	16	100	24.9	29	87	35	65	16.2	1531	485	207	839	974	17.5

TABLE 13-3
New Residential—200 Percent of Straight Line Depreciation (per $1,000)

KEY FACTORS ARE ----

TOTAL INVESTED	MORTGAGE TERMS AMOUNT	% INTR	LIFE	NET SALE PRICE	GROSS OPERATING INCOME	OPERATING EXPENSE	% ANNUAL INFLATION	DEPRECIATION AMOUNT	LIFE	TYPE	TAX RATES INCOME	CAP GAIN
1000	750	8.00	25	940	140	60	0.0	800	30	200%	40%	20%

COMPUTED SUMMARY ----

EQUITY AMOUNT	MORTGAGE TERMS % DEBT MONTHLY	YEARLY		NET SALE PRICE	% NET SALE TO TOTAL	% INCOME TO TOTAL	% EXPENSE TO INCOME	% NET TO TOTAL	% DEPREC TO TOTAL
250	75.0	5.79	69	940	94.0	14.0	42.9	8.0	80.0

COMPUTED RESULTS ----

---- INFLATION OF 0.0 ----

	HOLDING RESULTS BEFORE INCOME TAXES						HOLDING RESULTS AFTER TAXES					OVERALL RESULTS WITH SALE AT YEAR END					
YR	GROSS INCOME	OPERATE EXPENSE	MORTGAGE INTR	MORTGAGE AMORT	CASH FLOW	% RETURN	DEPRECIATION	TAXABLE INCOME	TAXES DUE	CASH FLOW	% RETURN	SALE PRICE	DEBT REPAY	TAXES DUE	CASH FLOW	TOTAL PROFIT	% RETURN
1	140	60	60	10	11	4.2	53	-33	-13	24	9.5	940	740	-1	201	-25	-10.0
2	140	60	59	11	11	4.2	50	-29	-11	22	8.8	940	730	17	193	-11	-2.4
3	140	60	58	12	11	4.2	46	-24	-10	20	8.1	940	718	32	190	6	0.9
5	140	60	56	14	11	4.2	40	-16	-7	17	6.8	940	692	55	193	45	4.0
7	140	60	54	16	11	4.2	35	-9	-4	14	5.6	940	662	73	205	87	5.5
10	140	60	49	20	11	4.2	29	2	1	10	3.9	940	606	89	245	160	6.8

---- INFLATION OF SALE PRICE, INCOME, AND EXPENSE AT 5% ANNUALLY ----

	HOLDING RESULTS BEFORE INCOME TAXES						HOLDING RESULTS AFTER TAXES					OVERALL RESULTS WITH SALE AT YEAR END					
YR	GROSS INCOME	OPERATE EXPENSE	MORTGAGE INTR	MORTGAGE AMORT	CASH FLOW	% RETURN	DEPRECIATION	TAXABLE INCOME	TAXES DUE	CASH FLOW	% RETURN	SALE PRICE	DEBT REPAY	TAXES DUE	CASH FLOW	TOTAL PROFIT	% RETURN
1	140	60	60	10	11	4.2	53	-33	-13	24	9.5	987	740	13	233	7	2.8
2	147	63	59	11	15	5.8	50	-25	-10	24	9.8	1036	730	38	269	67	13.2
3	154	66	58	12	19	7.5	46	-16	-6	25	10.1	1088	718	61	309	132	16.4
5	170	73	56	14	28	11.1	40	1	0	27	11.0	1200	692	107	401	278	18.4
7	188	80	54	16	38	15.1	35	18	7	30	12.2	1323	662	150	511	448	18.8
10	217	93	49	20	55	21.9	29	46	18	36	14.5	1531	606	207	718	757	18.6

TABLE 13-4
New Residential—200 Percent of Straight Line Depreciation (per $1,000)

KEY FACTORS ARE ----

TOTAL INVESTED	MORTGAGE TERMS			OPERATING & INFLATION ASSUMPTIONS				TAX RATES	
	AMOUNT	% INTR	LIFE	NET SALE PRICE	GROSS INCOME	OPERATING EXPENSE	% ANNUAL INFLATION	INCOME	CAP GAIN
1000	750	8.00	25	940	170	70	0.0	40%	20%

			DEPRECIATION		
			AMOUNT	LIFE	TYPE
			800	30	200%

COMPUTED SUMMARY ----

EQUITY AMOUNT	MORTGAGE TERMS			% NET SALE TO TCTAL	% INCOME TO TOTAL	% EXPENSE TO INCCME	% NET TO TOTAL	% DEPREC TO TOTAL
	% DEBT	MONTHLY	YEARLY					
250	75.0	5.79	69	94.0	17.0	41.2	10.0	80.0

COMPUTED RESULTS ----

---- HOLDING RESULTS BEFORE INCOME TAXES ----

YR	GROSS INCOME	OPERATE EXPENSE	MORTGAGE INTR	MORTGAGE AMORT	CASH FLOW	% RETURN
1	170	70	60	10	31	12.2
2	170	70	59	11	31	12.2
3	170	70	58	12	31	12.2
5	170	70	56	14	31	12.2
7	170	70	54	16	31	12.2
10	170	70	49	20	31	12.2

- - - - - INFLATION OF SALE PRICE, INCOME, AND EXPENSE AT 5%

1	170	70	60	10	31	12.2
2	178	73	59	11	36	14.2
3	187	77	58	12	41	16.3
5	207	85	56	14	52	20.8
7	228	94	54	16	65	25.8
10	264	109	49	20	86	34.3

---- HOLDING RESULTS AFTER TAXES ----

YR	DEPRECIATION	TAXABLE INCOME	TAXES DUE	CASH FLOW	% RETURN
1	53	-13	-5	36	14.3
2	50	-9	-3	34	13.6
3	46	-4	-2	32	12.9
5	40	4	1	29	11.6
7	35	11	4	26	10.4
10	29	22	9	22	8.7

ANNUALLY

1	53	-13	-5	36	14.3
2	50	-4	-1	37	14.8
3	46	6	2	38	15.4
5	40	25	10	42	16.8
7	35	45	18	46	18.6
10	29	77	31	55	21.9

---- OVERALL RESULTS WITH SALE AT YEAR END ----

YR	SALE PRICE	DEBT REPAY	TAXES DUE	CASH FLOW	TOTAL PROFIT	% RETURN
1	940	740	-1	201	-13	-5.2
2	940	730	17	193	13	2.7
3	940	718	32	190	42	6.1
5	940	692	55	193	105	9.3
7	940	662	73	205	171	10.7
10	940	606	89	245	280	11.9

ANNUALLY

1	987	740	13	233	19	7.7
2	1036	730	38	269	92	18.0
3	1088	718	61	309	170	21.1
5	1200	692	107	401	344	22.9
7	1323	662	150	511	545	23.0
10	1531	606	207	718	908	22.6

TABLE 13-5
New Residential—200 Percent of Straight Line Depreciation (per $1,000)

KEY FACTORS ARE ---

TOTAL INVESTED	----MORTGAGE TERMS----			----OPERATING & INFLATION ASSUMPTIONS----				----DEPRECIATION----			----TAX RATES----	
	AMOUNT	% INTR	LIFE	NET SALE PRICE	GROSS INCOME	OPERATING EXPENSE	% ANNUAL INFLATION	AMOUNT	LIFE	TYPE	INCOME	CAP GAIN
1000	750	10.00	25	940	170	70	0.0	800	30	200%	40%	20%

COMPUTED SUMMARY ---

EQUITY AMOUNT	----MORTGAGE TERMS----			% NET SALE TO TOTAL	% INCOME TO TOTAL	% EXPENSE TO INCOME	% NET TO TOTAL	% DEPREC TO TOTAL
	% DEBT	MONTHLY	YEARLY					
250	75.0	6.82	82	94.0	17.0	41.2	10.0	80.0

COMPUTED RESULTS ---

YR	GROSS INCOME	OPERATE EXPENSE	INTR	AMORT	CASH FLOW	% RE TURN	DEPREC IATION	TAXABLE INCOME	TAXES DUE	CASH FLOW	% RE TURN	SALE PRICE	DEBT REPAY	TAXES DUE	CASH FLOW	TOTAL PROFIT	% RE TURN
---	HOLDING RESULTS BEFORE INCOME TAXES---						----HOLDING RESULTS AFTER TAXES----					----OVERALL RESULTS WITH SALE AT YEAR END---					
- - - -	I N F L A T I O N	O F						S A L E	P R I C E ,	I N C O M E ,	A N D	E X P E N S E	A T	5 %	A N N U A L L Y - - - - -		
1	170	70	75	7	18	7.3	53	-28	-11	29	11.8	940	743	-1	198	-22	-8.8
2	170	70	74	8	18	7.3	50	-24	-9	28	11.1	940	735	17	188	-5	-1.1
3	170	70	73	9	18	7.3	46	-20	-8	26	10.4	940	726	32	182	15	2.2
5	170	70	71	11	18	7.3	40	-12	-5	23	9.2	940	706	55	179	60	5.4
7	170	70	69	13	18	7.3	35	-4	-2	20	7.9	940	682	73	185	107	7.0
10	170	70	64	17	18	7.3	29	7	3	15	6.2	940	634	89	217	189	8.4
1	170	70	75	7	18	7.3	53	-28	-11	29	11.8	987	743	13	231	10	4.0
2	178	73	74	8	23	9.3	50	-19	-7	31	12.3	1036	735	38	263	74	14.5
3	187	77	73	9	28	11.4	46	-9	-4	32	12.9	1088	726	61	300	143	17.9
5	207	85	71	11	40	15.9	40	10	4	36	14.3	1200	706	107	387	299	20.1
7	228	94	69	13	52	20.9	35	30	12	40	16.1	1323	682	150	491	482	20.6
10	264	109	64	17	73	29.3	29	62	25	49	19.4	1531	634	207	690	817	20.5

TABLE 13-6
New Residential—200 Percent of Straight Line Depreciation (per $1,000)

KEY FACTORS ARE ----

	TOTAL INVESTED	----MORTGAGE TERMS----			----OPERATING & INFLATION ASSUMPTIONS----				----DEPRECIATION----			----TAX RATES----	
		AMOUNT	% INTR	LIFE	NET SALE PRICE	GROSS INCOME	OPERATING EXPENSE	% ANNUAL INFLATION	AMOUNT	LIFE	TYPE	INCOME	CAP GAIN
	1000	750	10.00	25	940	200	80	0.0	800	30	200%	40%	20%

COMPUTED SUMMARY ----

EQUITY AMOUNT	----MORTGAGE TERMS----			% NET SALE TO TOTAL	% INCOME TO TOTAL	% EXPENSE TO INCOME	% NET TO TOTAL	% DEPREC TO TOTAL
	% DEBT	MONTHLY	YEARLY					
250	75.0	6.82	82	94.0	20.0	40.0	12.0	80.0

COMPUTED RESULTS ----

	----HOLDING RESULTS BEFORE INCOME TAXES----					----HOLDING RESULTS AFTER TAXES----					----OVERALL RESULTS WITH SALE AT YEAR END----					
YR	GROSS INCOME	OPERATE EXPENSE	MORTGAGE INTR	MORTGAGE AMORT	CASH FLOW	%RE TURN	DEPREC IATION	TAXABLE INCOME	TAXES DUE	CASH FLOW	%RE TURN	SALE PRICE	DEBT REPAY	TAXES DUE	CASH FLOW	TOTAL PROFIT	%RE TURN

---- INFLATION OF SALE PRICE, INCOME, AND EXPENSE AT 0% ----

YR	GROSS INCOME	OPERATE EXPENSE	INTR	AMORT	CASH FLOW	%RE TURN	DEPREC IATION	TAXABLE INCOME	TAXES DUE	CASH FLOW	%RE TURN	SALE PRICE	DEBT REPAY	TAXES DUE	CASH FLOW	TOTAL PROFIT	%RE TURN
1	200	80	75	7	38	15.3	53	-8	-3	41	16.6	940	743	-1	198	-10	-4.1
2	200	80	74	8	38	15.3	50	-4	-1	40	15.9	940	735	17	188	19	4.0
3	200	80	73	9	38	15.3	46	0	0	38	15.2	940	726	32	182	51	7.5
5	200	80	71	11	38	15.3	40	8	3	35	14.0	940	706	55	179	120	10.8
7	200	80	69	13	38	15.3	35	16	6	32	12.7	940	682	73	185	191	12.4
10	200	80	64	17	38	15.3	29	27	11	27	11.0	940	634	89	217	309	13.6

---- INFLATION OF SALE PRICE, INCOME, AND EXPENSE AT 5% ANNUALLY ----

YR	GROSS INCOME	OPERATE EXPENSE	INTR	AMORT	CASH FLOW	%RE TURN	DEPREC IATION	TAXABLE INCOME	TAXES DUE	CASH FLOW	%RE TURN	SALE PRICE	DEBT REPAY	TAXES DUE	CASH FLOW	TOTAL PROFIT	%RE TURN
1	200	80	75	7	38	15.3	53	-8	-3	41	16.6	987	743	13	231	22	8.8
2	210	84	74	8	44	17.7	50	2	1	43	17.3	1036	735	38	263	98	19.4
3	220	88	73	9	51	20.2	46	13	5	45	18.2	1088	726	61	300	180	22.6
5	243	97	71	11	64	25.6	40	34	14	50	20.2	1200	706	107	387	365	24.6
7	268	107	69	13	79	31.6	35	57	23	56	22.5	1323	682	150	491	579	24.9
10	310	124	64	17	104	41.8	29	93	37	67	26.9	1531	634	207	690	968	24.6

TABLE 13-7
New Residential—200 Percent of Straight Line Depreciation (per $1,000)

KEY FACTORS ARE ---

TOTAL INVESTED	---MORTGAGE TERMS---			---OPERATING & INFLATION ASSUMPTIONS---				---DEPRECIATION---			---TAX RATES---	
	AMOUNT	% INTR	LIFE	NET SALE PRICE	GROSS INCOME	OPERATING EXPENSE	% ANNUAL INFLATION	AMOUNT	LIFE	TYPE	INCOME	CAP GAIN
1000	900	10.00	25	940	170	70	0.0	800	30	200%	40%	20%

COMPUTED SUMMARY ---

EQUITY AMOUNT	---MORTGAGE TERMS---			% NET SALE TO TOTAL	% INCOME TO TOTAL	% EXPENSE TO INCOME	% NET TO TOTAL	% DEPREC TO TOTAL
	% DEBT	MONTHLY	YEARLY					
100	90.0	8.18	98	94.0	17.0	41.2	10.0	80.0

COMPUTED RESULTS ---

YR	---HOLDING RESULTS BEFORE INCOME TAXES---						---HOLDING RESULTS AFTER TAXES---					---OVERALL RESULTS WITH SALE AT YEAR END---					
	GROSS INCOME	OPERATE EXPENSE	MORTGAGE INTR	AMORT	CASH FLOW	% RE TURN	DEPREC IATION	TAXABLE INCOME	TAXES DUE	CASH FLOW	% RE TURN	SALE PRICE	DEBT REPAY	TAXES DUE	CASH FLOW	TOTAL PROFIT	% RE TURN
1	170	70	90	5	2	1.9	53	-43	-17	19	19.0	940	891	-1	50	-31	-31.1
2	170	70	89	5	2	1.9	50	-39	-15	17	17.3	940	882	17	41	-23	-13.8
3	170	70	88	10	2	1.9	46	-34	-14	16	15.5	940	872	32	37	-12	-5.0
5	170	70	85	13	2	1.9	40	-26	-10	12	12.2	940	847	55	38	16	4.3
7	170	70	83	15	2	1.9	35	-18	-7	9	9.0	940	818	73	49	46	8.9
10	170	70	77	21	2	1.9	29	-6	-2	4	4.2	940	761	89	90	105	12.5
- - - - I N F L A T I O N O F							SALE PRICE, INCOME, AND EXPENSE				A T	5%		A N N U A L L Y		- - - - -
1	170	70	90	5	2	1.9	53	-43	-17	19	19.0	987	891	13	82	1	1.2
2	178	73	89	5	7	6.9	50	-34	-13	20	20.3	1036	882	38	116	56	26.8
3	187	77	88	10	12	12.1	46	-24	-10	22	21.7	1088	872	61	155	116	33.5
5	207	85	85	13	23	23.4	40	-4	-2	25	25.2	1200	847	107	246	255	35.5
7	228	94	83	15	36	35.9	35	16	6	29	29.4	1323	818	150	355	421	34.5
10	264	109	77	21	57	57.0	29	49	20	37	37.3	1531	761	207	563	733	32.5

TABLE 13-8
New Residential—200 Percent of Straight Line Depreciation (per $1,000)

KEY FACTORS ARE ---

TOTAL INVESTED	---MORTGAGE TERMS--- AMOUNT	% INTR	LIFE	---OPERATING & INFLATION ASSUMPTIONS--- NET SALE PRICE	GROSS INCOME	OPERATING EXPENSE	% ANNUAL INFLATION	---DEPRECIATION--- AMOUNT	LIFE	TYPE	---TAX RATES--- INCOME	CAP GAIN
1000	900	10.00	25	940	200	80	0.0	800	30	200%	40%	20%

COMPUTED SUMMARY ---

EQUITY AMOUNT	---MORTGAGE TERMS--- % DEBT	MONTHLY	YEARLY	% NET SALE TO TOTAL	% INCOME TO TOTAL	% EXPENSE TO INCOME	% NET TO TOTAL	% DEPREC TO TOTAL
100	90.0	8.18	98	94.0	20.0	40.0	12.0	80.0

COMPUTED RESULTS ---

	---HOLDING RESULTS BEFORE INCOME TAXES---		---MORTGAGE---				---HOLDING RESULTS AFTER TAXES---					---OVERALL RESULTS WITH SALE AT YEAR END---					
YR	GROSS INCOME	OPERATE EXPENSE	INTR	AMORT	CASH FLOW	% RETURN	DEPRECIATION	TAXABLE INCOME	TAXES DUE	CASH FLOW	% RETURN	SALE PRICE	DEBT REPAY	TAXES DUE	CASH FLOW	TOTAL PROFIT	% RETURN
1	200	80	90	5	22	21.9	53	-23	-9	31	31.0	940	891	-1	50	-19	-19.1
2	200	80	89	5	22	21.9	50	-19	-7	29	29.3	940	882	17	41	1	0.6
3	200	80	88	10	22	21.9	46	-14	-6	28	27.5	940	872	32	37	24	10.3
5	200	80	85	13	22	21.9	40	-6	-2	24	24.2	940	847	55	38	76	19.8
7	200	80	83	15	22	21.9	35	2	1	21	21.0	940	818	73	49	130	23.8
10	200	80	77	21	22	21.9	29	14	6	16	16.2	940	761	89	90	225	26.1

- - - - INFLATION OF 5% ANNUALLY - - - - SALE PRICE, INCOME, AND EXPENSE AT - - - -

YR	GROSS INCOME	OPERATE EXPENSE	INTR	AMORT	CASH FLOW	% RETURN	DEPRECIATION	TAXABLE INCOME	TAXES DUE	CASH FLOW	% RETURN	SALE PRICE	DEBT REPAY	TAXES DUE	CASH FLOW	TOTAL PROFIT	% RETURN
1	200	80	90	5	22	21.9	53	-23	-9	31	31.0	987	891	13	82	13	13.2
2	210	84	89	9	28	27.9	50	-13	-5	33	32.9	1036	882	38	116	80	38.7
3	220	88	88	10	34	34.2	46	-2	-1	35	34.9	1088	872	61	155	154	44.6
5	243	97	85	13	48	47.7	40	20	8	40	39.7	1200	847	107	246	321	45.6
7	268	107	83	15	63	62.7	35	43	17	46	45.5	1323	818	150	355	519	44.0
10	310	124	77	21	88	88.0	29	80	32	56	55.9	1531	761	207	563	884	41.8

14

New Commercial Property

This chapter presents eight reference tables detailing the profitability of *new commercial property*, which qualifies for *150 percent of straight line depreciation*. Below is an index to this chapter's specific tables, showing their key factor values and summarized results.

Percent Mortgaged	Percent Mortgage Interest Rate	Percent Net Income to Total Invested	Percent Year 5 Rates of Return		Page Number of Table
			0% Inflation	5% Inflation	
60	8	8	4.0	13.4	186
60	8	10	7.1	16.3	187
75	8	8	3.5	17.5	188
75	8	10	8.5	21.9	189
75	10	10	4.8	19.1	190
75	10	12	10.0	23.5	191
90	10	10	2.8	32.7	192
90	10	12	16.7	42.2	193

TABLE 14-1
New Commercial—150 Percent of Straight Line Depreciation (per $1,000)

KEY FACTORS ARE ---

TOTAL INVESTED	----MORTGAGE TERMS---- AMOUNT	% INTR	LIFE	----OPERATING & INFLATION ASSUMPTIONS---- NET SALE PRICE	GROSS INCOME	OPERATING EXPENSE	% ANNUAL INFLATION	----DEPRECIATION---- AMOUNT	LIFE	TYPE	----TAX RATES---- INCOME	CAP GAIN
1000	600	8.00	25	940	140	60	0.0	800	35	150%	40%	20%

COMPUTED SUMMARY ---

EQUITY AMOUNT	----MORTGAGE TERMS---- % DEBT	MCNTHLY	YEARLY	% NET SALE TC TCTAL	% INCOME TO TOTAL	% EXPENSE TO INCOME	% NET TO TOTAL	% DEPREC TO TOTAL
400	60.0	4.63	56	94.0	14.0	42.9	8.0	80.0

COMPUTED RESULTS ---

YR	----HOLDING RESULTS BEFORE INCOME TAXES---- GROSS INCOME	OPERATE EXPENSE	--MORTGAGE-- INTR	AMORT	CASH FLOW	% RE TURN	----HOLDING RESULTS AFTER TAXES---- DEPREC IATION	TAXABLE INCOME	TAXES DUE	CASH FLOW	% RE TURN	----OVERALL RESULTS WITH SALE AT YEAR END---- SALE PRICE	DEBT REPAY	TAXES DUE	CASH FLOW	TOTAL PROFIT	% RE TURN
1	140	60	48	8	24	6.1	34	-2	-1	25	6.3	940	592	-5	353	-22	-5.4
2	140	60	47	9	24	6.1	33	0	0	24	6.1	940	584	3	354	3	0.4
3	140	60	46	9	24	6.1	31	2	1	24	5.9	940	574	14	352	25	2.2
5	140	60	45	11	24	6.1	29	6	3	22	5.5	940	554	28	358	76	4.0
7	140	60	43	13	24	6.1	26	11	4	20	5.0	940	529	41	370	129	4.8
10	140	60	39	16	24	6.1	23	17	7	17	4.4	940	485	56	400	214	5.4

- - - I N F L A T I C N   O F   S A L E   P R I C E ,   I N C O M E ,   A N D   E X P E N S E   A T   5 %   A N N U A L L Y - - - -

1	140	60	48	8	24	6.1	34	-2	-1	25	6.3	987	592	7	388	14	3.4
2	147	63	47	9	28	7.1	33	4	2	27	6.7	1036	584	25	428	80	9.8
3	154	66	46	9	33	8.2	31	10	4	28	7.1	1088	574	43	470	151	11.9
5	170	73	45	11	42	10.4	29	24	9	32	8.0	1200	554	80	566	309	13.4
7	188	80	43	13	52	12.9	26	38	15	36	9.1	1323	529	117	676	490	13.9
10	217	93	39	16	69	17.1	23	62	25	44	11.0	1531	485	174	873	810	14.0

TABLE 14-2
New Commercial—150 Percent of Straight Line Depreciation (per $1,000)

KEY FACTORS ARE ---

TOTAL INVESTED	----MORTGAGE TERMS----			----OPERATING & INFLATION ASSUMPTIONS----				----DEPRECIATION----			----TAX RATES----	
	AMOUNT	% INTR	LIFE	NET SALE PRICE	GROSS INCOME	OPERATING EXPENSE	% ANNUAL INFLATION	AMOUNT	LIFE	TYPE	INCOME	CAP GAIN
1000	600	8.00	25	940	170	70	0.0	800	35	150%	40%	20%

COMPUTED SUMMARY ---

EQUITY AMOUNT	----MORTGAGE TERMS----			% NET SALE TO TOTAL	% INCOME TO TOTAL	% EXPENSE TO INCOME	% NET TO TOTAL	% DEPREC TO TOTAL
	% DEBT	MONTHLY	YEARLY					
400	60.0	4.63	56	94.0	17.0	41.2	10.0	80.0

COMPUTED RESULTS ---

----HOLDING RESULTS BEFORE INCOME TAXES----

YR	GROSS INCOME	OPERATE EXPENSE	----MORTGAGE---- INTR	----MORTGAGE---- AMORT	CASH FLOW	% RETURN
1	170	70	48	8	44	11.1
2	170	70	47	9	44	11.1
3	170	70	46	9	44	11.1
5	170	70	45	11	44	11.1
7	170	70	43	13	44	11.1
10	170	70	39	16	44	11.1
- - - - INFLATION OF SALE PRICE, INCOME, AND EXPENSE AT 5% ANNUALLY - - - -						
1	170	70	48	8	44	11.1
2	178	73	47	9	49	12.4
3	187	77	46	9	55	13.7
5	207	85	45	11	66	16.5
7	228	94	43	13	78	19.6
10	264	109	39	16	100	24.9

----HOLDING RESULTS AFTER TAXES----

YR	DEPRECIATION	TAXABLE INCOME	TAXES DUE	CASH FLOW	% RETURN
1	34	18	7	37	9.3
2	33	20	8	36	9.1
3	31	22	9	36	8.9
5	29	26	11	34	8.5
7	26	31	12	32	8.0
10	23	37	15	29	7.4
- - - - INFLATION OF SALE PRICE, INCOME, AND EXPENSE AT 5% ANNUALLY - - - -					
1	34	18	7	37	9.3
2	33	25	10	39	9.8
3	31	32	13	42	10.4
5	29	48	19	47	11.7
7	26	65	26	53	13.1
10	23	93	37	63	15.6

----OVERALL RESULTS WITH SALE AT YEAR END----

YR	SALE PRICE	DEBT REPAY	TAXES DUE	CASH FLOW	TOTAL PROFIT	% RETURN
1	940	592	-5	353	-10	-2.4
2	940	584	3	354	27	3.5
3	940	574	14	352	61	5.3
5	940	554	28	358	136	7.1
7	940	529	41	370	213	7.9
10	940	485	56	400	334	8.5
- - - - INFLATION OF SALE PRICE, INCOME, AND EXPENSE AT 5% ANNUALLY - - - -						
1	987	592	7	388	26	6.4
2	1036	584	25	428	104	12.8
3	1088	574	43	470	189	14.9
5	1200	554	80	566	375	16.3
7	1323	529	117	676	588	16.7
10	1531	485	174	873	961	16.7

TABLE 14-3
New Commercial—150 Percent of Straight Line Depreciation (per $1,000)

KEY FACTORS ARE —

TOTAL INVESTED	MORTGAGE TERMS			OPERATING & INFLATION ASSUMPTIONS				DEPRECIATION			TAX RATES	
	AMOUNT	% INTR	LIFE	NET SALE PRICE	GROSS INCOME	OPERATING EXPENSE	% ANNUAL INFLATION	AMOUNT	LIFE	TYPE	INCOME	CAP GAIN
1000	750	8.00	25	940	140	60	0.0	800	35	150%	40%	20%

COMPUTED SUMMARY —

EQUITY AMOUNT	MORTGAGE TERMS			% NET SALE TO TOTAL	% INCOME TO TOTAL	% EXPENSE TO INCOME	% NET TO TOTAL	% DEPREC TO TOTAL
	% DEBT	MONTHLY	YEARLY					
250	75.0	5.79	69	94.0	14.0	42.9	8.0	80.0

COMPUTED RESULTS —

HOLDING RESULTS BEFORE INCOME TAXES / HOLDING RESULTS AFTER TAXES / OVERALL RESULTS WITH SALE AT YEAR END

YR	GROSS INCOME	OPERATE EXPENSE	MORTGAGE INTR	MORTGAGE AMORT	CASH FLOW	% RETURN	DEPRECIATION	TAXABLE INCOME	TAXES DUE	CASH FLOW	% RETURN	SALE PRICE	DEBT REPAY	TAXES DUE	CASH FLOW	TOTAL PROFIT	% RETURN
1	140	60	60	10	11	4.2	34	-14	-6	16	6.4	940	740	-5	205	-29	-11.6
2	140	60	59	11	11	4.2	33	-12	-5	15	6.1	940	730	3	208	-11	-2.3
3	140	60	58	12	11	4.2	31	-9	-4	14	5.7	940	718	14	208	4	0.5
5	140	60	56	14	11	4.2	29	-5	-2	12	5.0	940	692	28	220	41	3.5
7	140	60	54	16	11	4.2	26	0	0	11	4.2	940	662	41	238	81	4.8
10	140	60	49	20	11	4.2	23	8	3	8	3.0	940	606	56	278	148	5.8

- - - INFLATION OF SALE PRICE, INCOME, AND EXPENSE AT 5% - - - / - - - - ANNUALLY - - - -

YR	GROSS INCOME	OPERATE EXPENSE	MORTGAGE INTR	MORTGAGE AMORT	CASH FLOW	% RETURN	DEPRECIATION	TAXABLE INCOME	TAXES DUE	CASH FLOW	% RETURN	SALE PRICE	DEBT REPAY	TAXES DUE	CASH FLOW	TOTAL PROFIT	% RETURN
1	140	60	60	10	11	4.2	34	-14	-6	16	6.4	587	740	7	240	6	2.5
2	147	63	59	11	15	5.8	33	-8	-3	18	7.0	1036	730	25	282	66	12.7
3	154	66	58	12	19	7.5	31	-1	0	19	7.7	1088	718	43	327	130	15.8
5	170	73	56	14	28	11.1	29	13	5	23	9.1	1200	692	80	428	274	17.5
7	188	80	54	16	38	15.1	26	27	11	27	10.7	1323	662	117	544	442	17.8
10	217	93	49	20	55	21.9	23	52	21	34	13.6	1531	606	174	751	744	17.5

TABLE 14-4
New Commercial—150 Percent of Straight Line Depreciation (per $1,000)

KEY FACTORS ARE ----

TOTAL INVESTED	MORTGAGE TERMS			NET SALE PRICE	GROSS INCOME	OPERATING EXPENSE	% ANNUAL INFLATION	TAX RATES		DEPRECIATION		
	AMOUNT	% INTR	LIFE					INCOME	CAP GAIN	AMOUNT	LIFE	TYPE
1000	750	8.00	25	940	170	70	0.0	40%	20%	800	35	150%

COMPUTED SUMMARY ----

EQUITY AMOUNT	MORTGAGE TERMS			% NET SALE TO TOTAL	% INCOME TO TOTAL	% EXPENSE TO INCOME	% NET TO INCOME	% DEPREC TO TOTAL
	% DEBT	MONTHLY	YEARLY					
250	75.0	5.79	69	94.0	17.0	41.2	10.0	80.0

COMPUTED RESULTS ----

YR	HOLDING RESULTS BEFORE INCOME TAXES						HOLDING RESULTS AFTER TAXES					OVERALL RESULTS WITH SALE AT YEAR END					
	GROSS INCOME	OPERATE EXPENSE	MORTGAGE INTR	MORTGAGE AMORT	CASH FLOW	% RE TURN	DEPREC IATION	TAXABLE INCOME	TAXES DUE	CASH FLOW	% RE TURN	SALE PRICE	DEBT REPAY	TAXES DUE	CASH FLOW	TOTAL PROFIT	% RE TURN
1	170	70	60	10	31	12.2	34	6	2	28	11.2	940	740	-5	205	-17	-6.8
2	170	70	59	11	31	12.2	33	8	3	27	10.9	940	730	3	208	13	2.7
3	170	70	58	12	31	12.2	31	11	4	26	10.5	940	718	14	208	40	5.6
5	170	70	56	14	31	12.2	29	15	6	24	9.8	940	692	28	220	101	8.5
7	170	70	54	16	31	12.2	26	20	8	23	9.0	940	662	41	238	165	9.8
10	170	70	49	20	31	12.2	23	28	11	20	7.8	940	606	56	278	268	10.6

---- INFLATION OF SALE PRICE, INCOME, AND EXPENSE AT 5% ANNUALLY ----

YR	GROSS INCOME	OPERATE EXPENSE	MORTGAGE INTR	MORTGAGE AMORT	CASH FLOW	% RE TURN	DEPREC IATION	TAXABLE INCOME	TAXES DUE	CASH FLOW	% RE TURN	SALE PRICE	DEBT REPAY	TAXES DUE	CASH FLOW	TOTAL PROFIT	% RE TURN
1	170	70	60	10	31	12.2	34	6	2	28	11.2	987	740	7	240	18	7.3
2	178	73	59	11	36	14.2	33	13	5	30	12.1	1036	730	25	282	90	17.5
3	187	77	58	12	41	16.3	31	21	8	32	13.0	1088	718	43	327	168	20.4
5	207	85	56	14	52	20.8	29	37	15	37	14.9	1200	692	80	428	341	21.9
7	228	94	54	16	65	25.8	26	54	22	43	17.2	1323	662	117	544	540	21.9
10	264	109	49	20	86	34.3	23	83	33	53	21.0	1531	606	174	751	895	21.4

TABLE 14-5
New Commercial—150 Percent of Straight Line Depreciation (per $1,000)

KEY FACTCRS ARE ---

TOTAL INVESTED	MORTGAGE TERMS--- AMOUNT	% INTR	LIFE	OPERATING & INFLATION ASSUMPTIONS---- NET SALE PRICE	GROSS INCOME	OPERATING EXPENSE	% ANNUAL INFLATION	DEPRECIATION---- AMOUNT	LIFE	TYPE	TAX RATES---- INCOME	CAP GAIN
1000	750	10.00	25	940	170	70	0.0	800	35	150%	40%	20%

CCMPUTED SUMMARY ---

EQUITY AMCUNT	MORTGAGE TERMS--- % DEBT	MCNTHLY	YEARLY	% NET SALE TC TOTAL	% INCOME TO TOTAL	% EXPENSE TO INCOME	% NET TO TOTAL	% DEPREC TO TOTAL
250	75.0	6.82	82	94.0	17.0	41.2	10.0	80.0

CCMPUTED RESULTS ---

	HOLDING RESULTS BEFORE INCCME TAXES----						HOLDING RESULTS AFTER TAXES---					OVERALL RESULTS WITH SALE AT YEAR END---					
YR	GROSS INCOME	OPERATE EXPENSE	MORTGAGE-- INTR	AMORT	CASH FLOW	% RETURN	DEPRECIATION	TAXABLE INCOME	TAXES DUE	CASH FLOW	% RETURN	SALE PRICE	DEBT REPAY	TAXES DUE	CASH FLOW	TOTAL PROFIT	% RETURN
1	170	70	75	7	18	7.3	34	-9	-4	22	8.7	940	743	-5	202	-26	-10.4
2	170	70	74	8	18	7.3	33	-7	-3	21	8.4	940	735	3	202	-5	-1.1
3	170	70	73	9	18	7.3	31	-5	-2	20	8.0	940	726	14	200	13	1.8
5	170	70	71	11	18	7.3	29	0	0	18	7.3	940	706	28	206	56	4.8
7	170	70	69	13	18	7.3	26	5	2	16	6.5	940	682	41	218	102	6.2
10	170	70	64	17	18	7.3	23	13	5	13	5.3	940	634	56	250	177	7.3

- - - - I N F L A T I C N   O F   SALE PRICE, INCCME, ANC EXPENSE   A T   5%   A N N U A L L Y - - - -

YR	GROSS INCOME	OPERATE EXPENSE	INTR	AMORT	CASH FLOW	% RETURN	DEPREC IATICN	TAXABLE INCOME	TAXES DUE	CASH FLOW	% RETURN	SALE PRICE	DEBT REPAY	TAXES DUE	CASH FLOW	TOTAL PROFIT	% RETURN
1	170	70	75	7	18	7.3	34	-9	-4	22	8.7	987	743	7	238	9	3.7
2	178	73	74	8	23	9.3	33	-2	-1	24	9.6	1036	735	25	276	72	14.0
3	187	77	73	9	28	11.4	31	6	2	26	10.5	1088	726	43	318	140	17.2
5	2C7	85	71	11	40	15.9	29	22	9	31	12.5	1200	706	80	413	295	19.1
7	228	94	69	13	52	20.9	26	39	16	37	14.7	1323	682	117	524	476	19.5
10	264	109	64	17	73	29.3	23	68	27	46	18.5	1531	634	174	723	804	19.3

TABLE 14-6
New Commercial—150 Percent of Straight Line Depreciation (per $1,000)

KEY FACTORS ARE ----

TOTAL INVESTED	----MORTGAGE TERMS---- AMOUNT	% INTR	LIFE	----OPERATING & INFLATION ASSUMPTIONS---- NET SALE PRICE	GROSS INCOME	OPERATING EXPENSE	% ANNUAL INFLATION	----TAX RATES---- INCOME	CAP GAIN
1000	750	10.00	25	940	200	80	0.0	40%	20%

----DEPRECIATION---- AMOUNT	LIFE	TYPE
800	35	150%

COMPUTED SUMMARY ----

EQUITY AMOUNT	----MORTGAGE TERMS---- % DEBT	MONTHLY	YEARLY	% NET SALE TO TOTAL	% INCOME TO TOTAL	% EXPENSE TO INCOME	% NET TO TOTAL	% DEPREC TO TOTAL
250	75.0	6.82	82	94.0	20.0	40.0	12.0	80.0

COMPUTED RESULTS ----

HOLDING RESULTS BEFORE INCOME TAXES

YR	GROSS INCOME	OPERATE EXPENSE	----MORTGAGE---- INTR	AMORT	CASH FLOW	% RETURN
1	200	80	75	7	38	15.3
2	200	80	74	8	38	15.3
3	200	80	73	9	38	15.3
5	200	80	71	11	38	15.3
7	200	80	69	13	38	15.3
10	200	80	64	17	38	15.3
- - - - I N F L A T I O N O F S A L E P R I C E , I N C O M E , A N D E X P E N S E A T 5% - - - -						
1	200	80	75	7	38	15.3
2	210	84	74	8	44	17.7
3	220	88	73	9	51	20.2
5	243	97	71	11	64	25.6
7	268	107	69	13	79	31.6
10	310	124	64	17	104	41.8

HOLDING RESULTS AFTER TAXES

YR	DEPREC IATION	TAXABLE INCOME	TAXES DUE	CASH FLOW	% RETURN
1	34	11	4	34	13.5
2	33	13	5	33	13.2
3	31	15	6	32	12.8
5	29	20	8	30	12.1
7	26	25	10	28	11.3
10	23	33	13	25	10.1
A N N U A L L Y - - - -					
1	34	11	4	34	13.5
2	33	19	8	37	14.6
3	31	28	11	39	15.8
5	29	46	18	46	18.3
7	26	66	26	53	21.1
10	23	99	39	65	26.0

OVERALL RESULTS WITH SALE AT YEAR END----

YR	SALE PRICE	DEBT REPAY	TAXES DUE	CASH FLOW	TOTAL PROFIT	% RETURN
1	940	743	-5	202	-14	-5.6
2	940	735	3	202	19	4.0
3	940	726	14	200	49	6.9
5	940	706	28	206	116	10.0
7	940	682	41	218	186	11.3
10	940	634	56	250	297	12.2
A N N U A L L Y - - - -						
1	987	743	7	238	21	8.5
2	1036	735	25	276	97	18.8
3	1088	726	43	318	178	21.9
5	1200	706	80	413	361	23.5
7	1323	682	117	524	574	23.7
10	1531	634	174	723	955	23.3

TABLE 14-7
New Commercial—150 Percent of Straight Line Depreciation (per $1,000)

KEY FACTCRS ARE ---

TOTAL INVESTED	----MORTGAGE TERMS----			----OPERATING & INFLATION ASSUMPTIONS----				----DEPRECIATION----			----TAX RATES----	
	AMOUNT	% INTR	LIFE	NET SALE PRICE	GROSS INCOME	OPERATING EXPENSE	% ANNUAL INFLATION	AMOUNT	LIFE	TYPE	INCOME	CAP GAIN
1000	900	10.00	25	940	170	70	0.0	800	35	150%	40%	20%

COMPUTED SUMMARY ---

EQUITY AMCUNT	----MORTGAGE TERMS----		% NET SALE TO TCTAL	% INCOME TO TOTAL	% EXPENSE TO INCCME	% NET TO TOTAL	% DEPREC TO TOTAL
	% DEBT	MONTHLY YEARLY					
100	90.0	8.18	98	94.0	17.0	41.2	10.0	80.0

COMPUTED RESULTS ---

----HOLDING RESULTS BEFORE INCCME TAXES----

YR	GRCSS INCOME	OPERATE EXPENSE	----MORTGAGE---- INTR	----MORTGAGE---- AMORT	CASH FLOW	% RETURN
1	170	70	90	9	2	1.9
2	170	70	89	9	2	1.9
3	170	70	88	10	2	1.9
5	170	70	85	13	2	1.9
7	170	70	83	15	2	1.9
10	170	70	77	21	2	1.9

- - - - I N F L A T I C N   O F   SALE PRICE, INCOME, ANC EXPENSE A T 5%

1	17C	70	90	9	2	1.9
2	178	73	89	9	7	6.9
3	187	77	88	10	12	12.1
5	2C7	85	85	13	23	23.4
7	228	94	83	15	36	35.9
10	264	109	77	21	57	57.0

----HOLDING RESULTS AFTER TAXES----

DEPREC IATION	TAXABLE INCCME	TAXES DUE	CASH FLOW	% RE TURN
34	-24	-1C	11	11.4
33	-22	-9	10	10.5
31	-19	-8	10	9.5
29	-14	-6	8	7.5
26	-9	-4	5	5.5
23	0	0	2	2.0

(Inflation of 5%)

34	-24	-1C	11	11.4
33	-17	-7	13	13.5
31	-9	-4	16	15.7
29	7	3	20	20.5
26	25	10	26	25.9
23	55	22	35	35.1

----OVERALL RESULTS WITH SALE AT YEAR END----

SALE PRICE	DEBT REPAY	TAXES DUE	CASH FLOW	TOTAL PROFIT	% RE TURN
940	891	-5	54	-35	-34.9
940	882	3	55	-23	-13.1
940	872	14	55	-14	-5.6
940	847	28	64	12	2.8
940	818	41	82	41	6.6
940	761	56	123	92	9.2

A N N U A L L Y (at 5%)

987	891	7	89	0	0.4
1036	882	25	129	54	25.3
1088	872	43	173	114	31.3
1200	847	80	272	251	32.7
1323	818	117	388	416	31.5
1531	761	174	596	720	29.4

TABLE 14-8
New Commercial—150 Percent of Straight Line Depreciation (per $1,000)

KEY FACTORS ARE ----

TOTAL INVESTED	MORTGAGE TERMS AMOUNT	% INTR	LIFE	NET SALE PRICE	GROSS INCOME	OPERATING EXPENSE	% ANNUAL INFLATION	DEPRECIATION AMOUNT	LIFE	TYPE	TAX RATES INCOME	CAP GAIN
1000	900	10.00	25	940	200	80	0.0	800	35	150%	40%	20%

COMPUTED SUMMARY ----

EQUITY AMOUNT	MORTGAGE TERMS % DEBT	MONTHLY	YEARLY	% NET SALE TO TOTAL	% INCOME TO TOTAL	% EXPENSE TO INCOME	% NET TO TOTAL	% DEPREC TO TOTAL
100	90.0	8.18	98	94.0	20.0	40.0	12.0	80.0

COMPUTED RESULTS ----

YR	HOLDING RESULTS BEFORE INCOME TAXES GROSS INCOME	OPERATE EXPENSE	MORTGAGE INTR	AMORT	CASH FLOW	% RE TURN	HOLDING RESULTS AFTER TAXES DEPREC IATION	TAXABLE INCOME	TAXES DUE	CASH FLOW	% RE TURN	OVERALL RESULTS WITH SALE AT YEAR END SALE PRICE	DEBT REPAY	TAXES DUE	CASH FLOW	TOTAL PROFIT	% RE TURN
1	200	80	90	5	22	21.9	34	-4	-2	23	23.4	940	891	-5	54	-23	-22.9
2	200	80	89	9	22	21.9	33	-2	-1	22	22.5	940	882	3	55	1	0.6
3	200	80	88	10	22	21.9	31	1	0	22	21.5	940	872	14	55	22	8.6
5	200	80	85	13	22	21.9	29	6	2	20	19.5	940	847	28	64	72	16.7
7	200	80	83	15	22	21.9	26	11	4	17	17.5	940	818	41	82	125	19.8
10	200	80	77	21	22	21.9	23	20	8	14	14.0	940	761	56	123	212	21.3

- - - - I N F L A T I O N   A T   5 %   O F   S A L E   P R I C E ,   I N C O M E ,   A N D   E X P E N S E - - - - A N N U A L L Y - - - -

YR	GROSS INCOME	OPERATE EXPENSE	INTR	AMORT	CASH FLOW	% RE TURN	DEPREC IATION	TAXABLE INCOME	TAXES DUE	CASH FLOW	% RE TURN	SALE PRICE	DEBT REPAY	TAXES DUE	CASH FLOW	TOTAL PROFIT	% RE TURN
1	200	80	90	5	22	21.9	34	-4	-2	23	23.4	987	891	7	89	12	12.4
2	210	84	89	9	28	27.9	33	4	2	26	26.1	1036	882	25	129	79	36.9
3	220	88	88	10	34	34.2	31	13	5	29	28.9	1088	872	43	173	152	42.0
5	243	97	85	13	48	47.7	29	32	13	35	35.1	1200	847	80	272	318	42.2
7	268	107	83	15	63	62.7	26	52	21	42	42.0	1323	818	117	388	513	40.4
10	310	124	77	21	88	88.0	23	86	34	54	53.7	1531	761	174	595	871	37.9

15

Used Residential Property

This chapter presents eight reference tables detailing the profitability of *used residential property*, which qualifies for *125 percent of straight line depreciation*. Below is an index to this chapter's specific tables, showing their key factor values and summarized results.

Percent Mortgaged	Percent Mortgage Interest Rate	Percent Net Income to Total Invested	Percent Year 5 Rates of Return		Page Number of Table
			0% Inflation	5% Inflation	
60	8	8	4.5	13.8	196
60	8	10	7.6	16.7	197
75	8	8	4.3	18.2	198
75	8	10	9.3	22.5	199
75	10	10	5.6	19.8	200
75	10	12	10.8	24.2	201
90	10	10	5.0	34.1	202
90	10	12	18.9	43.7	203

TABLE 15-1
Used Residential—125 Percent of Straight Line Depreciation (per $1,000)

KEY FACTORS ARE ----

TOTAL INVESTED	----MORTGAGE TERMS----			----OPERATING & INFLATION ASSUMPTIONS----				----DEPRECIATION----			----TAX RATES----	
	AMOUNT	% INTR	LIFE	NET SALE PRICE	GROSS INCOME	OPERATING EXPENSE	% ANNUAL INFLATION	AMOUNT	LIFE	TYPE	INCOME	CAP GAIN
1000	600	8.00	25	940	140	60	0.0	800	25	125%	40%	20%

COMPUTED SUMMARY ----

EQUITY AMOUNT	----MORTGAGE TERMS----			% NET SALE TO TOTAL	% INCOME TO TOTAL	% EXPENSE TO INCOME	% NET TO TOTAL	% DEPREC TO TOTAL
	% DEBT	MONTHLY	YEARLY					
400	60.0	4.63	56	94.0	14.0	42.9	8.0	80.0

COMPUTED RESULTS ----

	----HOLDING RESULTS BEFORE INCOME TAXES----						----HOLDING RESULTS AFTER TAXES----					----OVERALL RESULTS WITH SALE AT YEAR END----					
	GROSS	OPERATE	--MORTGAGE--		CASH	% RE	DEPREC	TAXABLE	TAXES	CASH	% RE	SALE	DEBT	TAXES	CASH	TOTAL	% RE
YR	INCOME	EXPENSE	INTR	AMORT	FLOW	TURN	IATION	INCOME	DUE	FLOW	TURN	PRICE	REPAY	DUE	FLOW	PROFIT	TURN
1	140	60	48	8	24	6.1	40	-8	-3	28	6.9	940	592	-4	352	-21	-5.2
2	140	60	47	9	24	6.1	38	-5	-2	26	6.6	940	584	6	350	4	0.5
3	140	60	46	9	24	6.1	36	-2	-1	25	6.4	940	574	14	351	31	2.7
5	140	60	45	11	24	6.1	33	3	1	23	5.8	940	554	28	358	85	4.5
7	140	60	43	13	24	6.1	31	6	2	22	5.5	940	529	40	370	142	5.3
10	140	60	39	16	24	6.1	31	10	4	21	5.2	940	485	58	398	232	5.9

- - - - INFLATION OF SALE PRICE, INCOME, AND EXPENSE AT 5% ANNUALLY - - - -

YR	GROSS INCOME	OPERATE EXPENSE	INTR	AMORT	CASH FLOW	% RE TURN	DEPREC IATION	TAXABLE INCOME	TAXES DUE	CASH FLOW	% RE TURN	SALE PRICE	DEBT REPAY	TAXES DUE	CASH FLOW	TOTAL PROFIT	% RE TURN
1	140	60	48	8	24	6.1	40	-8	-3	28	6.9	987	592	7	388	15	3.8
2	147	63	47	9	28	7.1	38	-1	0	29	7.2	1036	584	26	427	83	10.3
3	154	66	46	9	33	8.2	36	6	2	30	7.6	1088	574	44	470	156	12.3
5	170	73	45	11	42	10.4	33	20	8	34	8.4	1200	554	80	566	318	13.8
7	188	80	43	13	52	12.9	31	33	13	38	9.6	1323	529	117	677	503	14.2
10	217	93	39	16	69	17.1	31	54	21	47	11.8	1531	485	176	871	829	14.4

TABLE 15-2
Used Residential—125 Percent of Straight Line Depreciation (per $1,000)

KEY FACTORS ARE ——

TOTAL INVESTED	---MORTGAGE TERMS---			---OPERATING & INFLATION ASSUMPTIONS---				---DEPRECIATION---			---TAX RATES---	
	AMOUNT	% INTR	LIFE	NET SALE PRICE	GROSS INCOME	OPERATING EXPENSE	% ANNUAL INFLATION	AMOUNT	LIFE	TYPE	INCOME	CAP GAIN
1000	600	8.00	25	540	170	70	0.0	800	25	125%	40%	20%

COMPUTED SUMMARY ——

EQUITY AMOUNT	---MORTGAGE TERMS---			% NET SALE TO TOTAL	% INCOME TO TOTAL	% EXPENSE TO INCOME	% NET TO TOTAL	% DEPREC TO TOTAL
	% DEBT	MONTHLY	YEARLY					
400	60.0	4.63	56	94.0	17.0	41.2	10.0	80.0

COMPUTED RESULTS ——

YR	---HOLDING RESULTS BEFORE INCOME TAXES---						---HOLDING RESULTS AFTER TAXES---					---OVERALL RESULTS WITH SALE AT YEAR END---					
	GROSS INCOME	OPERATE EXPENSE	MORTGAGE INTR	AMORT	CASH FLOW	% RE TURN	DEPRECIATION	TAXABLE INCOME	TAXES DUE	CASH FLOW	% RE TURN	SALE PRICE	DEBT REPAY	TAXES DUE	CASH FLOW	TOTAL PROFIT	% RE TURN
1	170	70	48	8	44	11.1	40	12	5	40	9.9	940	592	-4	352	-9	-2.2
2	170	70	47	9	44	11.1	38	15	6	38	9.6	940	584	6	350	28	3.6
3	170	70	46	9	44	11.1	36	18	7	37	9.4	940	574	14	351	67	5.8
5	170	70	45	11	44	11.1	33	23	9	35	8.8	940	554	28	358	145	7.6
7	170	70	43	13	44	11.1	31	26	10	34	8.5	940	529	40	370	226	8.4
10	170	70	39	16	44	11.1	31	30	12	33	8.2	940	485	58	398	352	9.0

- - - - - INFLATION OF SALE PRICE, INCOME, AND EXPENSE AT 5% ANNUALLY - - - - -

YR	GROSS INCOME	OPERATE EXPENSE	MORTGAGE INTR	AMORT	CASH FLOW	% RE TURN	DEPRECIATION	TAXABLE INCOME	TAXES DUE	CASH FLOW	% RE TURN	SALE PRICE	DEBT REPAY	TAXES DUE	CASH FLOW	TOTAL PROFIT	% RE TURN
1	170	70	48	8	44	11.1	40	12	5	40	9.9	987	592	7	388	27	6.8
2	178	73	47	9	49	12.4	38	20	8	41	10.4	1036	584	26	427	108	13.3
3	187	77	46	9	55	13.7	36	28	11	44	10.9	1088	574	44	470	194	15.3
5	207	85	45	11	66	16.5	33	44	18	48	12.1	1200	554	80	566	384	16.7
7	228	94	43	13	78	19.6	31	60	24	54	13.6	1323	529	117	677	601	17.1
10	264	109	39	16	100	24.9	31	85	34	66	16.4	1531	485	176	871	980	17.1

TABLE 15-3
Used Residential—125 Percent of Straight Line Depreciation (per $1,000)

KEY FACTORS ARE ---

TOTAL INVESTED	---MORTGAGE TERMS---			---OPERATING & INFLATION ASSUMPTIONS---				---DEPRECIATION---			---TAX RATES---	
	AMOUNT	% INTR	LIFE	NET SALE PRICE	GROSS INCOME	OPERATING EXPENSE	% ANNUAL INFLATION	AMOUNT	LIFE	TYPE	INCOME	CAP GAIN
1000	750	8.00	25	940	140	60	0.0	800	25	125%	40%	20%

COMPUTED SUMMARY ---

EQUITY AMOUNT	---MORTGAGE TERMS---			% NET SALE TO TOTAL	% INCOME TO TOTAL	% EXPENSE TO INCOME	% NET TO TOTAL	% DEPREC TO TOTAL
	% DEBT	MONTHLY	YEARLY					
250	75.0	5.79	69	94.0	14.0	42.9	8.0	80.0

COMPUTED RESULTS ---

YR	---HOLDING RESULTS BEFORE INCOME TAXES---						---HOLDING RESULTS AFTER TAXES---					---OVERALL RESULTS WITH SALE AT YEAR END---					
	GROSS INCOME	OPERATE EXPENSE	MORTGAGE INTR	AMORT	CASH FLOW	% RETURN	DEPRECIATION	TAXABLE INCOME	TAXES DUE	CASH FLOW	% RETURN	SALE PRICE	DEBT REPAY	TAXES DUE	CASH FLOW	TOTAL PROFIT	% RETURN
1	140	60	60	10	11	4.2	40	-20	-8	18	7.4	940	740	-4	204	-28	-11.1
2	140	60	59	11	11	4.2	38	-17	-7	17	6.9	940	730	6	204	-10	-2.2
3	140	60	58	12	11	4.2	36	-14	-6	16	6.5	940	718	14	208	9	1.3
5	140	60	56	14	11	4.2	33	-9	-3	14	5.6	940	692	28	220	50	4.3
7	140	60	54	16	11	4.2	31	-5	-2	12	4.9	940	662	40	238	94	5.6
10	140	60	49	20	11	4.2	31	0	0	11	4.3	940	606	58	277	166	6.6

- - - - INFLATION OF SALE PRICE, INCOME, AND EXPENSE AT 5% ANNUALLY - - - - -

YR	GROSS INCOME	OPERATE EXPENSE	MORTGAGE INTR	AMORT	CASH FLOW	% RETURN	DEPRECIATION	TAXABLE INCOME	TAXES DUE	CASH FLOW	% RETURN	SALE PRICE	DEBT REPAY	TAXES DUE	CASH FLOW	TOTAL PROFIT	% RETURN
1	140	60	60	10	11	4.2	40	-20	-8	18	7.4	987	740	7	240	8	3.3
2	147	63	59	11	15	5.8	38	-13	-5	20	7.9	1036	730	26	281	69	13.4
3	154	66	58	12	19	7.5	36	-6	-2	21	8.4	1088	718	44	326	135	16.5
5	170	73	56	14	28	11.1	33	9	3	24	9.7	1200	692	80	427	283	18.2
7	188	80	54	16	38	15.1	31	23	9	29	11.5	1323	662	117	544	455	18.3
10	217	93	49	20	55	21.9	31	44	18	37	14.8	1531	606	176	750	763	18.0

TABLE 15-4
Used Residential— 125 Percent of Straight Line Depreciation (per $1,000)

KEY FACTORS ARE ---

TOTAL INVESTED	MORTGAGE TERMS AMOUNT	% INTR	LIFE	NET SALE PRICE	GROSS INCOME	OPERATING EXPENSE	% ANNUAL INFLATION	DEPRECIATION AMOUNT	LIFE	TYPE	TAX RATES INCOME	CAP GAIN
1000	750	8.00	25	940	170	70	0.0	800	25	125%	40%	20%

COMPUTED SUMMARY ---

EQUITY AMOUNT	MORTGAGE TERMS % DEBT	MONTHLY	YEARLY	% NET SALE TO TOTAL	% INCOME TO TOTAL	% EXPENSE TO INCOME	% NET TO TOTAL	% DEPREC TO TOTAL
250	75.0	5.79	69	94.0	17.0	41.2	10.0	80.0

COMPUTED RESULTS ---

	HOLDING RESULTS BEFORE INCOME TAXES						HOLDING RESULTS AFTER TAXES					OVERALL RESULTS WITH SALE AT YEAR END					
YR	GROSS INCOME	OPERATE EXPENSE	MORTGAGE INTR	AMORT	CASH FLOW	%RE TURN	DEPRECIATION	TAXABLE INCOME	TAXES DUE	CASH FLOW	%RE TURN	SALE PRICE	DEBT REPAY	TAXES DUE	CASH FLOW	TOTAL PROFIT	%RE TURN
1	170	70	60	10	31	12.2	40	0	0	30	12.2	940	740	-4	204	-16	-6.3
2	170	70	59	11	31	12.2	38	3	1	29	11.7	940	730	6	204	14	2.9
3	170	70	58	12	31	12.2	36	6	2	28	11.3	940	718	14	208	45	6.4
5	170	70	56	14	31	12.2	33	11	5	26	10.4	940	692	28	220	110	9.3
7	170	70	54	16	31	12.2	31	15	6	24	9.7	940	662	40	238	178	10.5
10	170	70	49	20	31	12.2	31	20	8	23	9.1	940	606	58	277	286	11.3

- - - - I N F L A T I O N O F S A L E P R I C E, I N C O M E, A N D E X P E N S E A T 5% A N N U A L L Y - - - -

	HOLDING RESULTS BEFORE INCOME TAXES						HOLDING RESULTS AFTER TAXES					OVERALL RESULTS WITH SALE AT YEAR END					
YR	GROSS INCOME	OPERATE EXPENSE	MORTGAGE INTR	AMORT	CASH FLOW	%RE TURN	DEPRECIATION	TAXABLE INCOME	TAXES DUE	CASH FLOW	%RE TURN	SALE PRICE	DEBT REPAY	TAXES DUE	CASH FLOW	TOTAL PROFIT	%RE TURN
1	170	70	60	10	31	12.2	40	0	0	30	12.2	987	740	7	240	20	8.1
2	178	73	59	11	36	14.2	38	8	3	32	12.9	1036	730	26	281	94	18.2
3	187	77	58	12	41	16.3	36	16	6	34	13.7	1088	718	44	326	173	21.1
5	207	85	56	14	52	20.8	33	33	13	39	15.6	1200	692	80	427	350	22.5
7	228	94	54	16	65	25.8	31	49	20	45	17.9	1323	662	117	544	553	22.5
10	264	109	49	20	86	34.3	31	75	30	56	22.3	1531	606	176	750	914	21.9

TABLE 15-5
Used Residential — 125 Percent of Straight Line Depreciation (per $1,000)

KEY FACTORS ARE ---

TOTAL INVESTED	MORTGAGE TERMS---			OPERATING & INFLATION ASSUMPTIONS---				DEPRECIATION---			TAX RATES---	
	AMOUNT	% INTR	LIFE	NET SALE PRICE	GROSS INCOME	OPERATING EXPENSE	% ANNUAL INFLATION	AMOUNT	LIFE	TYPE	INCOME	CAP GAIN
1000	750	10.00	25	940	170	70	0.0	800	25	125%	40%	20%

COMPUTED SUMMARY ---

EQUITY AMOUNT	MORTGAGE TERMS---			NET SALE PRICE	% NET SALE TO TOTAL	% INCOME TO TOTAL	% EXPENSE TO INCOME	% NET TO TOTAL	% DEPREC TO TOTAL
	% DEBT	MONTHLY	YEARLY						
250	75.0	6.82	82	940	94.0	17.0	41.2	10.0	80.0

COMPUTED RESULTS ---

HOLDING RESULTS BEFORE INCOME TAXES --- | HOLDING RESULTS AFTER TAXES --- | OVERALL RESULTS WITH SALE AT YEAR END ---

YR	GROSS INCOME	OPERATE EXPENSE	MORTGAGE— INTR	MORTGAGE— AMORT	CASH FLOW	% RE TURN	DEPREC IATION	TAXABLE INCOME	TAXES DUE	CASH FLOW	% RE TURN	SALE PRICE	DEBT REPAY	TAXES DUE	CASH FLOW	TOTAL PROFIT	% RE TURN
1	170	70	75	7	18	7.3	40	-15	-6	24	9.6	940	743	-4	201	-25	-9.9
2	170	70	74	8	18	7.3	38	-12	-5	23	9.2	940	735	6	199	-4	-0.9
3	170	70	73	9	18	7.3	36	-9	-4	22	8.8	940	726	14	199	18	2.6
5	170	70	71	11	18	7.3	33	-4	-2	20	7.9	940	706	28	205	65	5.6
7	170	70	69	13	18	7.3	31	0	0	18	7.3	940	682	40	218	114	7.0
10	170	70	64	17	18	7.3	31	5	2	16	6.5	940	634	58	248	195	8.1

- - - - INFLATION OF SALE PRICE, INCOME, AND EXPENSE AT 5% ANNUALLY - - - -

YR	GROSS INCOME	OPERATE EXPENSE	MORTGAGE— INTR	MORTGAGE— AMORT	CASH FLOW	% RE TURN	DEPREC IATION	TAXABLE INCOME	TAXES DUE	CASH FLOW	% RE TURN	SALE PRICE	DEBT REPAY	TAXES DUE	CASH FLOW	TOTAL PROFIT	% RE TURN
1	170	70	75	7	18	7.3	40	-15	-6	24	9.6	987	743	7	237	11	4.5
2	178	73	74	8	23	9.3	38	-7	-3	26	10.4	1036	735	26	276	76	14.8
3	187	77	73	9	28	11.4	36	1	0	28	11.2	1088	726	44	318	146	17.9
5	207	85	71	11	40	15.9	33	18	7	33	13.1	1200	706	80	413	304	19.8
7	228	94	69	13	52	20.9	31	34	14	39	15.4	1323	682	117	524	489	20.1
10	264	109	64	17	73	29.3	31	60	24	49	19.8	1531	634	176	721	823	19.8

TABLE 15-6
Used Residential—125 Percent of Straight Line Depreciation (per $1,000)

KEY FACTORS ARE ---

TOTAL INVESTED	MORTGAGE TERMS			OPERATING & INFLATION ASSUMPTIONS				DEPRECIATION			TAX RATES	
	AMOUNT	% INTR	LIFE	NET SALE PRICE	GROSS INCOME	OPERATING EXPENSE	% ANNUAL INFLATION	AMOUNT	LIFE	TYPE	INCOME	CAP GAIN
1000	750	10.00	25	940	200	80	0.0	800	25	125%	40%	20%

COMPUTED SUMMARY ---

EQUITY AMOUNT	MORTGAGE TERMS			% NET SALE TO TOTAL	% INCOME TO TOTAL	% EXPENSE TO INCOME	% NET TO TOTAL	% DEPREC TO TOTAL
	% DEBT	MONTHLY	YEARLY					
250	75.0	6.82	82	94.0	20.0	40.0	12.0	80.0

COMPUTED RESULTS ---

YR	HOLDING RESULTS BEFORE INCOME TAXES						HOLDING RESULTS AFTER TAXES					OVERALL RESULTS WITH SALE AT YEAR END					
	GROSS INCOME	OPERATE EXPENSE	MORTGAGE INTR	MORTGAGE AMORT	CASH FLOW	% RE TURN	DEPRECIATION	TAXABLE INCOME	TAXES DUE	CASH FLOW	% RE TURN	SALE PRICE	DEBT REPAY	TAXES DUE	CASH FLOW	TOTAL PROFIT	% RE TURN
1	200	80	75	7	38	15.3	40	5	2	36	14.4	940	743	-4	201	-13	-5.1
2	200	80	74	8	38	15.3	38	8	3	35	14.0	940	735	6	199	20	4.1
3	200	80	73	9	38	15.3	36	11	4	34	13.6	940	726	14	199	54	7.7
5	200	80	71	11	38	15.3	33	16	6	32	12.7	940	706	28	205	125	10.8
7	200	80	69	13	38	15.3	31	20	8	30	12.1	940	682	40	218	198	12.1
10	200	80	64	17	38	15.3	31	25	10	28	11.3	940	634	58	248	315	13.0

- - - - INFLATION OF SALE PRICE, INCOME, AND EXPENSE AT 5% ANNUALLY - - - -

YR	GROSS INCOME	OPERATE EXPENSE	MORTGAGE INTR	MORTGAGE AMORT	CASH FLOW	% RE TURN	DEPRECIATION	TAXABLE INCOME	TAXES DUE	CASH FLOW	% RE TURN	SALE PRICE	DEBT REPAY	TAXES DUE	CASH FLOW	TOTAL PROFIT	% RE TURN
1	200	80	75	7	38	15.3	40	5	2	36	14.4	587	743	7	237	23	9.3
2	210	84	74	8	44	17.7	38	14	6	39	15.4	1036	735	26	276	100	19.6
3	220	88	73	9	51	20.2	36	23	9	41	16.5	1088	726	44	318	184	22.6
5	243	97	71	11	64	25.6	33	42	17	47	18.9	1200	706	80	413	371	24.2
7	268	107	69	13	79	31.6	31	61	24	55	21.9	1323	682	117	524	587	24.3
10	310	124	64	17	104	41.8	31	91	36	68	27.2	1531	634	176	721	974	23.9

TABLE 15-7
Used Residential—125 Percent of Straight Line Depreciation (per $1,000)

KEY FACTORS ARE ----

TOTAL INVESTED	---MORTGAGE TERMS--- AMOUNT	% INTR	LIFE	---OPERATING & INFLATION ASSUMPTIONS--- NET SALE PRICE	GROSS INCOME	OPERATING EXPENSE	% ANNUAL INFLATION	---DEPRECIATION--- AMOUNT	LIFE	TYPE	---TAX RATES--- INCOME	CAP GAIN
1000	900	10.00	25	940	170	70	0.0	800	25	125%	40%	20%

COMPUTED SUMMARY ----

EQUITY AMOUNT	---MORTGAGE TERMS--- % DEBT	MONTHLY	YEARLY	% NET SALE TO TOTAL	% INCOME TO TOTAL	% EXPENSE TO INCOME	% NET TO TOTAL	% DEPREC TO TOTAL
100	90.0	8.18	98	94.0	17.0	41.2	10.0	80.0

COMPUTED RESULTS ----

YR	---HOLDING RESULTS BEFORE INCOME TAXES--- GROSS INCOME	OPERATE EXPENSE	MORTGAGE INTR	AMORT	CASH FLOW	% RETURN	---HOLDING RESULTS AFTER TAXES--- DEPRECIATION	TAXABLE INCOME	TAXES DUE	CASH FLOW	% RETURN	---OVERALL RESULTS WITH SALE AT YEAR END--- SALE PRICE	DEBT REPAY	TAXES DUE	CASH FLOW	TOTAL PROFIT	% RETURN
1	170	70	90	9	2	1.9	40	-30	-12	14	13.7	940	891	-4	53	-34	-33.8
2	170	70	89	9	2	1.9	38	-27	-11	13	12.6	940	882	6	52	-22	-12.8
3	170	70	88	10	2	1.9	36	-24	-10	11	11.4	940	872	14	54	-8	-3.4
5	170	70	85	13	2	1.9	33	-18	-7	9	9.1	940	847	28	64	21	5.0
7	170	70	83	15	2	1.9	31	-14	-5	7	7.3	940	818	40	82	54	8.7
10	170	70	77	21	2	1.9	31	-8	-3	5	5.1	940	761	58	121	111	11.1

- - - - INFLATION OF 5% ANNUALLY - - - - SALE PRICE, INCOME, AND EXPENSE AT 5%

YR	GROSS INCOME	OPERATE EXPENSE	INTR	AMORT	CASH FLOW	% RETURN	DEPRECIATION	TAXABLE INCOME	TAXES DUE	CASH FLOW	% RETURN	SALE PRICE	DEBT REPAY	TAXES DUE	CASH FLOW	TOTAL PROFIT	% RETURN
1	170	70	90	9	2	1.9	40	-30	-12	14	13.7	987	891	7	89	2	2.2
2	178	73	89	9	7	6.9	38	-22	-9	16	15.6	1036	882	26	129	58	27.1
3	187	77	88	10	12	12.1	36	-14	-5	18	17.5	1088	872	44	172	119	32.9
5	207	85	85	13	23	23.4	33	4	1	22	22.0	1200	847	80	272	260	34.1
7	228	94	83	15	36	35.9	31	20	8	28	27.7	1323	818	117	388	429	32.7
10	264	109	77	21	57	57.0	31	47	19	38	38.2	1531	761	176	594	739	30.6

TABLE 15-8
Used Residential—125 Percent of Straight Line Depreciation (per $1,000)

KEY FACTORS ARE ---

TOTAL INVESTED	---MORTGAGE TERMS---			---OPERATING & INFLATION ASSUMPTIONS---				---DEPRECIATION---			---TAX RATES---	
	AMOUNT	% INTR	LIFE	NET SALE PRICE	GROSS INCOME	OPERATING EXPENSE	% ANNUAL INFLATION	AMOUNT	LIFE	TYPE	INCOME	CAP GAIN
1000	900	10.00	25	940	200	80	0.0	800	25	125%	40%	20%

COMPUTED SUMMARY ---

EQUITY AMOUNT	---MORTGAGE TERMS---			% NET SALE TO TOTAL	% INCOME TO TOTAL	% EXPENSE TO INCOME	% NET TO TOTAL	% DEPREC TO TOTAL
	% DEBT	MONTHLY	YEARLY					
100	90.0	8.18	98	94.0	20.0	40.0	12.0	80.0

COMPUTED RESULTS ---

YR	---HOLDING RESULTS BEFORE INCOME TAXES---						---HOLDING RESULTS AFTER TAXES---				
	GROSS INCOME	OPERATE EXPENSE	--MORTGAGE-- INTR	AMORT	CASH FLOW	% RE TURN	DEPRECIATION	TAXABLE INCOME	TAXES DUE	CASH FLOW	% RE TURN
1	200	80	90	5	22	21.9	40	-10	-4	26	25.7
2	200	80	89	9	22	21.9	38	-7	-3	25	24.6
3	200	80	88	10	22	21.9	36	-4	-2	23	23.4
5	200	80	85	13	22	21.9	33	2	1	21	21.1
7	200	80	83	15	22	21.9	31	6	3	19	19.3
10	200	80	77	21	22	21.9	31	12	5	17	17.1

- - - - I N F L A T I O N   O F   S A L E   P R I C E,   I N C O M E,   A N D   E X P E N S E   A T   5%   A N N U A L L Y - - -

YR	GROSS INCOME	OPERATE EXPENSE	--MORTGAGE-- INTR	AMORT	CASH FLOW	% RE TURN	DEPRECIATION	TAXABLE INCOME	TAXES DUE	CASH FLOW	% RE TURN
1	200	80	90	5	22	21.9	40	-10	-4	26	25.7
2	210	84	89	9	28	27.9	38	-1	0	28	28.2
3	220	88	88	10	34	34.2	36	8	3	31	30.8
5	243	97	85	13	48	47.7	33	28	11	37	36.6
7	268	107	83	15	63	62.7	31	47	19	44	43.8
10	310	124	77	21	88	88.0	31	78	31	57	56.8

YR	---OVERALL RESULTS WITH SALE AT YEAR END---					
	SALE PRICE	DEBT REPAY	TAXES DUE	CASH FLOW	TOTAL PROFIT	% RE TURN
1	940	891	-4	53	-22	-21.8
2	940	882	6	52	2	1.0
3	940	872	14	54	28	10.8
5	940	847	28	64	81	18.9
7	940	818	40	82	138	21.8
10	940	761	58	121	231	23.3

- - - - - - A N N U A L L Y - - -   5%

YR	SALE PRICE	DEBT REPAY	TAXES DUE	CASH FLOW	TOTAL PROFIT	% RE TURN
1	987	891	7	89	14	14.2
2	1036	882	26	129	82	38.7
3	1088	872	44	172	157	43.7
5	1200	847	80	272	327	43.7
7	1323	818	117	388	526	41.8
10	1531	761	176	594	890	39.2

16

Used Commercial Property

This chapter presents eight reference tables detailing the profitability of *used commercial property* (or used residential having a remaining life of less than twenty years), which qualifies for *100 percent of straight line depreciation.* Below is an index to this chapter's specific tables, showing their key factor values and summarized results.

Percent Mortgaged	Percent Mortgage Interest Rate	Percent Net Income to Total Invested	Percent Year 5 Rates of Return		Page Number of Table
			0% Inflation	5% Inflation	
60	8	8	4.4	13.7	206
60	8	10	7.5	16.6	207
75	8	8	4.2	17.9	208
75	8	10	9.1	22.2	209
75	10	10	5.5	19.5	210
75	10	12	10.6	23.9	211
90	10	10	4.8	33.2	212
90	10	12	18.0	42.6	213

TABLE 16-1
Used Commercial—100 Percent (Straight Line) Depreciation (per $1,000)

KEY FACTORS ARE ----

TOTAL INVESTED	----MORTGAGE TERMS----			----OPERATING & INFLATION ASSUMPTIONS----				----DEPRECIATION----			----TAX RATES----	
	AMOUNT	% INTR	LIFE	NET SALE PRICE	GROSS INCOME	OPERATING EXPENSE	% ANNUAL INFLATION	AMOUNT	LIFE	TYPE	INCOME	CAP GAIN
1000	600	8.00	25	940	140	60	0.0	800	25	100%	40%	20%

COMPUTED SUMMARY ----

EQUITY AMOUNT	----MORTGAGE----		
	% DEBT	MONTHLY	YEARLY
400	60.0	4.63	56

% NET SALE TO TOTAL	% INCOME TO TOTAL	% EXPENSE TO INCOME	% NET TO TOTAL	% DEPREC TO TOTAL
94.0	14.0	42.9	8.0	80.0

COMPUTED RESULTS ----

---- INFLATION OF 0 ----

YR	----HOLDING RESULTS BEFORE INCOME TAXES----						----HOLDING RESULTS AFTER TAXES----					----OVERALL RESULTS WITH SALE AT YEAR END----					
	GROSS INCOME	OPERATE EXPENSE	MORTGAGE— INTR	AMORT	CASH FLOW	% RE TURN	DEPREC IATION	TAXABLE INCOME	TAXES DUE	CASH FLOW	% RE TURN	SALE PRICE	DEBT REPAY	TAXES DUE	TOTAL PROFIT	CASH FLOW	% RE TURN
1	140	60	48	8	24	6.1	32	0	0	24	6.1	940	592	-6	-22	353	-5.6
2	140	60	47	9	24	6.1	32	1	0	24	6.0	940	584	1	4	356	0.5
3	140	60	46	9	24	6.1	32	2	1	24	5.9	940	574	7	31	358	2.6
5	140	60	45	11	24	6.1	32	3	1	23	5.8	940	554	20	85	366	4.4
7	140	60	43	13	24	6.1	32	5	2	22	5.6	940	529	33	142	378	5.2
10	140	60	39	16	24	6.1	32	9	3	21	5.3	940	485	52	232	403	5.8

- - - - INFLATION OF SALE PRICE, INCOME, AND EXPENSE AT 5% ANNUALLY - - - -

YR	GROSS INCOME	OPERATE EXPENSE	MORTGAGE— INTR	AMORT	CASH FLOW	% RE TURN	DEPREC IATION	TAXABLE INCOME	TAXES DUE	CASH FLOW	% RE TURN	SALE PRICE	DEBT REPAY	TAXES DUE	TOTAL PROFIT	CASH FLOW	% RE TURN
1	140	60	48	8	24	6.1	32	0	0	24	6.1	987	592	4	15	391	3.8
2	147	63	47	9	28	7.1	32	5	2	26	6.6	1036	584	20	83	433	10.2
3	154	66	46	9	33	8.2	32	10	4	29	7.2	1088	574	37	156	477	12.3
5	170	73	45	11	42	10.4	32	20	8	33	8.4	1200	554	72	318	574	13.7
7	188	80	43	13	52	12.9	32	32	13	39	9.7	1323	529	109	503	684	14.1
10	217	93	39	16	69	17.1	32	53	21	47	11.9	1531	485	170	828	876	14.2

TABLE 16-2
Used Commercial— 100 Percent (Straight Line) Depreciation (per $1,000)

KEY FACTORS ARE ----

TOTAL INVESTED	----MORTGAGE TERMS----			----OPERATING & INFLATION ASSUMPTIONS----				----DEPRECIATION----			----TAX RATES----	
	AMOUNT	% INTR	LIFE	NET SALE PRICE	GROSS INCOME	OPERATING EXPENSE	% ANNUAL INFLATION	AMOUNT	LIFE	TYPE	INCOME	CAP GAIN
1000	600	8.00	25	940	170	70	0.0	800	25	100%	40%	20%

COMPUTED SUMMARY ----

EQUITY AMOUNT	----MORTGAGE TERMS----			% NET SALE TO TOTAL	% NET INCOME TO TOTAL	% EXPENSE TO INCOME	% NET TO TOTAL	% DEPREC TO TOTAL
	% DEBT	MONTHLY	YEARLY					
400	60.0	4.63	56	94.0	17.0	41.2	10.0	80.0

COMPUTED RESULTS ----

YR	----HOLDING RESULTS BEFORE INCOME TAXES----						----HOLDING RESULTS AFTER TAXES----					----OVERALL RESULTS WITH SALE AT YEAR END----					
	GROSS INCOME	OPERATE EXPENSE	MORTGAGE INTR	AMORT	CASH FLOW	% RETURN	DEPRECIATION	TAXABLE INCOME	TAXES DUE	CASH FLOW	% RETURN	SALE PRICE	DEBT REPAY	TAXES DUE	CASH FLOW	TOTAL PROFIT	% RETURN
1	170	70	48	8	44	11.1	32	20	8	36	9.1	940	592	-6	353	-10	-2.6
2	170	70	47	9	44	11.1	32	21	8	36	9.0	940	584	1	356	28	3.6
3	170	70	46	9	44	11.1	32	22	9	36	8.9	940	574	7	358	67	5.7
5	170	70	45	11	44	11.1	32	23	9	35	8.8	940	554	20	366	145	7.5
7	170	70	43	13	44	11.1	32	25	10	34	8.6	940	529	33	378	226	8.3
10	170	70	39	16	44	11.1	32	29	11	33	8.3	940	485	52	403	352	8.8

---- INFLATION OF SALE PRICE, INCOME, AND EXPENSE AT 5% ANNUALLY ----

YR	GROSS INCOME	OPERATE EXPENSE	INTR	AMORT	CASH FLOW	% RETURN	DEPRECIATION	TAXABLE INCOME	TAXES DUE	CASH FLOW	% RETURN	SALE PRICE	DEBT REPAY	TAXES DUE	CASH FLOW	TOTAL PROFIT	% RETURN
1	170	70	48	8	44	11.1	32	20	8	36	9.1	987	592	4	391	27	6.8
2	178	73	47	9	49	12.4	32	26	10	39	9.8	1036	584	20	433	108	13.2
3	187	77	46	9	55	13.7	32	32	13	42	10.5	1088	574	37	477	194	15.2
5	207	85	45	11	66	16.5	32	45	18	48	12.0	1200	554	72	574	384	16.6
7	228	94	43	13	78	19.6	32	59	24	55	13.7	1323	529	109	684	601	16.9
10	264	109	39	16	100	24.9	32	84	33	66	16.5	1531	485	170	876	979	16.9

TABLE 16-3
Used Commercial—100 Percent (Straight Line) Depreciation (per $1,000)

KEY FACTORS ARE ---

TOTAL INVESTED	---MORTGAGE TERMS--- AMOUNT	% INTR	LIFE
1000	750	8.00	25

---OPERATING & INFLATION ASSUMPTIONS--- NET SALE PRICE	GROSS INCOME	OPERATING EXPENSE	% ANNUAL INFLATION
940	140	60	0.0

---DEPRECIATION--- AMOUNT	LIFE	TYPE
800	25	100%

---TAX RATES--- INCOME	CAP GAIN
40%	20%

COMPUTED SUMMARY ---

EQUITY AMOUNT	---MORTGAGE TERMS--- % DEBT	MONTHLY	YEARLY
250	75.0	5.79	69

% NET SALE TO TOTAL	% INCOME TO TOTAL	% EXPENSE TO INCOME
94.0	14.0	42.9

% DEPREC TO TOTAL	% NET TO TOTAL
80.0	8.0

COMPUTED RESULTS ---

---HOLDING RESULTS BEFORE INCOME TAXES---

YR	GROSS INCOME	OPERATE EXPENSE	---MORTGAGE--- INTR	AMORT	CASH FLOW	% RE TURN
1	140	60	60	10	11	4.2
2	140	60	59	11	11	4.2
3	140	60	58	12	11	4.2
5	140	60	56	14	11	4.2
7	140	60	54	16	11	4.2
10	140	60	49	20	11	4.2

- - - - INFLATION OF SALE PRICE, INCOME, AND EXPENSE AT 5%

YR	GROSS INCOME	OPERATE EXPENSE	---MORTGAGE--- INTR	AMORT	CASH FLOW	% RE TURN
1	140	60	60	10	11	4.2
2	147	63	59	11	15	5.8
3	154	66	58	12	19	7.5
5	170	73	56	14	28	11.1
7	188	80	54	16	38	15.1
10	217	93	49	20	55	21.9

---HOLDING RESULTS AFTER TAXES---

YR	DEPREC IATION	TAXABLE INCOME	TAXES DUE	CASH FLOW	% RE TURN
1	32	-12	-5	15	6.1
2	32	-11	-4	15	5.9
3	32	-10	-4	15	5.8
5	32	-8	-3	14	5.5
7	32	-6	-2	13	5.1
10	32	-1	-1	11	4.4

A N N U A L L Y INCOME, AND EXPENSE AT 5%

YR	DEPREC IATION	TAXABLE INCOME	TAXES DUE	CASH FLOW	% RE TURN
1	32	-12	-5	15	6.1
2	32	-7	-3	17	6.9
3	32	-2	-1	19	7.8
5	32	9	4	24	9.6
7	32	22	9	29	11.6
10	32	43	17	38	15.0

---OVERALL RESULTS WITH SALE AT YEAR END---

YR	SALE PRICE	DEBT REPAY	TAXES DUE	CASH FLOW	TOTAL PROFIT	% RE TURN
1	940	740	-6	205	-29	-11.8
2	940	730	1	210	-10	-2.1
3	940	718	7	215	9	1.3
5	940	692	20	228	50	4.2
7	940	662	33	246	94	5.4
10	940	606	52	282	166	6.4

A N N U A L L Y

YR	SALE PRICE	DEBT REPAY	TAXES DUE	CASH FLOW	TOTAL PROFIT	% RE TURN
1	987	740	4	243	8	3.3
2	1036	730	20	287	69	13.4
3	1088	718	37	333	135	16.3
5	1200	692	72	436	283	17.9
7	1323	662	109	552	455	18.1
10	1531	606	170	755	762	17.7

TABLE 16-4
Used Commercial—100 Percent (Straight Line) Depreciation (per $1,000)

KEY FACTORS ARE ----

	----MORTGAGE TERMS----			----OPERATING & INFLATION ASSUMPTIONS----				----DEPRECIATION----			----TAX RATES----	
TOTAL INVESTED	AMOUNT	% INTR	LIFE	NET SALE PRICE	GROSS INCOME	OPERATING EXPENSE	% ANNUAL INFLATION	AMOUNT	LIFE	TYPE	INCOME	CAP GAIN
1000	750	8.00	25	940	170	70	0.0	800	25	100%	40%	20%

COMPUTED SUMMARY ----

----MORTGAGE TERMS----								
EQUITY AMOUNT	% DEBT	MONTHLY	YEARLY	% NET SALE TO TOTAL	% INCOME TO TOTAL	% EXPENSE TO INCOME	% NET TO INCOME	% DEPREC TO TOTAL
250	75.0	5.79	69	94.0	17.0	41.2	10.0	80.0

COMPUTED RESULTS ----

----HOLDING RESULTS BEFORE INCOME TAXES----

YR	GROSS INCOME	OPERATE EXPENSE	--MORTGAGE-- INTR	AMORT	CASH FLOW	% RETURN
1	170	70	60	10	31	12.2
2	170	70	59	11	31	12.2
3	170	70	58	12	31	12.2
5	170	70	56	14	31	12.2
7	170	70	54	16	31	12.2
10	170	70	49	20	31	12.2

---- INFLATION OF ----

YR	GROSS INCOME	OPERATE EXPENSE	--MORTGAGE-- INTR	AMORT	CASH FLOW	% RETURN
1	170	70	60	10	31	12.2
2	178	73	59	11	36	14.2
3	187	77	58	12	41	16.3
5	207	85	56	14	52	20.8
7	228	94	54	16	65	25.8
10	264	109	49	20	86	34.3

----HOLDING RESULTS AFTER TAXES----

YR	DEPRECIATION	TAXABLE INCOME	TAXES DUE	CASH FLOW	% RETURN
1	32	8	3	27	10.9
2	32	9	4	27	10.7
3	32	10	4	27	10.6
5	32	12	5	26	10.3
7	32	14	6	25	9.9
10	32	19	7	23	9.2

SALE PRICE, INCOME, AND EXPENSE AT ---- INFLATION OF ----

YR	DEPRECIATION	TAXABLE INCOME	TAXES DUE	CASH FLOW	% RETURN
1	32	8	3	27	10.9
2	32	14	6	30	11.9
3	32	20	8	33	13.1
5	32	34	13	39	15.5
7	32	48	19	45	18.1
10	32	74	30	56	22.5

----OVERALL RESULTS WITH SALE AT YEAR END----

YR	SALE PRICE	DEBT REPAY	TAXES DUE	CASH FLOW	TOTAL PROFIT	% RETURN
1	940	740	-6	205	-17	-7.0
2	940	730	1	210	14	2.9
3	940	718	7	215	45	6.3
5	940	692	20	228	110	9.1
7	940	662	33	246	178	10.3
10	940	606	52	282	286	11.1

---- ANNUALLY ---- AT 5%

YR	SALE PRICE	DEBT REPAY	TAXES DUE	CASH FLOW	TOTAL PROFIT	% RETURN
1	987	740	4	243	20	8.1
2	1036	730	20	287	94	18.1
3	1088	718	37	333	173	20.9
5	1200	692	72	436	350	22.2
7	1323	662	109	552	553	22.2
10	1531	606	170	755	913	21.6

TABLE 16-5
Used Commercial — 100 Percent (Straight Line) Depreciation (per $1,000)

KEY FACTORS ARE ---

TOTAL INVESTED	---MORTGAGE TERMS---			---OPERATING & INFLATION ASSUMPTIONS---				---DEPRECIATION---			---TAX RATES---	
	AMOUNT	% INTR	LIFE	NET SALE PRICE	GROSS INCOME	OPERATING EXPENSE	% ANNUAL INFLATION	AMOUNT	LIFE	TYPE	INCOME	CAP GAIN
1000	750	10.00	25	940	170	70	0.0	800	25	100%	40%	20%

CCMPUTED SUMMARY ---

EQUITY AMOUNT	---MORTGAGE TERMS---		% NET SALE TO TCTAL	% INCOME TO TOTAL	% EXPENSE TC INCCME	% NET TO TOTAL	% DEPREC TO TOTAL
	% DEBT MCNTHLY	YEARLY					
250	75.0	6.82	82	94.0	17.0	41.2	10.0	80.0

CCMPUTED RESLLTS ---

YR	---HCLDING RESULTS BEFORE INCOME TAXES---						---HOLDING RESULTS AFTER TAXES---					---OVERALL RESULTS WITH SALE AT YEAR END---					
	GROSS INCOME	OPERATE EXPENSE	--MORTGAGE-- INTR	AMCRT	CASH FLOW	% RE TURN	DEPREC IATION	TAXABLE INCOME	TAXES DUE	CASH FLOW	% RE TURN	SALE PRICE	DEBT REPAY	TAXES DUE	CASH FLOW	TOTAL PROFIT	% RE TURN
1	170	70	75	7	18	7.3	32	-7	-3	21	8.4	940	743	-6	203	-26	-10.5
2	170	70	74	8	18	7.3	32	-6	-2	21	8.2	940	735	1	204	-4	-0.9
3	170	70	73	9	18	7.3	32	-5	-2	20	8.1	940	726	7	206	18	2.6
5	170	70	71	11	18	7.3	32	-3	-1	19	7.8	940	706	20	214	65	5.5
7	170	70	69	13	18	7.3	32	-1	0	19	7.4	940	682	33	226	114	6.8
10	170	70	64	17	18	7.3	32	4	1	17	6.7	940	634	52	254	195	7.9

---- I N F L A T I C N   O F   S A L E   P R I C E ,   I N C O M E ,   A N D   E X P E N S E   A T   5%   A N N U A L L Y - - - -

YR	GROSS INCOME	OPERATE EXPENSE	INTR	AMCRT	CASH FLOW	% RE TURN	DEPREC IATION	TAXABLE INCOME	TAXES DUE	CASH FLOW	% RE TURN	SALE PRICE	DEBT REPAY	TAXES DUE	CASH FLOW	TOTAL PROFIT	% RE TURN
1	170	70	75	7	18	7.3	32	-7	-3	21	8.4	987	743	4	240	11	4.5
2	178	73	74	8	23	9.3	32	-1	0	24	9.4	1036	735	20	281	76	14.7
3	187	77	73	9	28	11.4	32	5	2	26	10.6	1088	726	37	325	146	17.7
5	207	85	71	11	40	15.9	32	18	7	32	13.0	1200	706	72	422	304	19.5
7	228	94	69	13	52	20.9	32	33	13	39	15.6	1323	682	109	532	489	19.8
10	264	109	64	17	73	29.3	32	59	24	50	19.9	1531	634	170	727	822	19.6

TABLE 16-6
Used Commercial—100 Percent (Straight Line) Depreciation (per $1,000)

KEY FACTORS ARE ---

TOTAL INVESTED	MORTGAGE TERMS			OPERATING & INFLATION ASSUMPTIONS				DEPRECIATION			TAX RATES	
	AMOUNT	% INTR	LIFE	NET SALE PRICE	GROSS INCOME	OPERATING EXPENSE	% ANNUAL INFLATION	AMOUNT	LIFE	TYPE	INCOME	CAP GAIN
1000	750	10.00	25	940	200	80	0.0	800	25	100%	40%	20%

COMPUTED SUMMARY ---

EQUITY AMOUNT	MORTGAGE TERMS			NET SALE TO TOTAL	% INCOME TO TOTAL	% EXPENSE TO INCOME	% NET TO TOTAL	% DEPREC TO TOTAL
	% DEBT	MONTHLY	YEARLY					
250	75.0	6.82	82	94.0	20.0	40.0	12.0	80.0

COMPUTED RESULTS ---

	HOLDING RESULTS BEFORE INCOME TAXES						HOLDING RESULTS AFTER TAXES					OVERALL RESULTS WITH SALE AT YEAR END					
YR	GROSS INCOME	OPERATE EXPENSE	MORTGAGE INTR	MORTGAGE AMORT	CASH FLOW	% RETURN	DEPRECIATION	TAXABLE INCOME	TAXES DUE	CASH FLOW	% RETURN	SALE PRICE	DEBT REPAY	TAXES DUE	CASH FLOW	TOTAL PROFIT	% RETURN
1	200	80	75	7	38	15.3	32	13	5	33	13.2	940	743	-6	203	-14	-5.8
2	200	80	74	8	38	15.3	32	14	6	33	13.0	940	735	1	204	20	4.1
3	200	80	73	9	38	15.3	32	15	6	32	12.9	940	726	7	206	54	7.7
5	200	80	71	11	38	15.3	32	17	7	31	12.6	940	706	20	214	125	10.6
7	200	80	69	13	38	15.3	32	19	8	31	12.2	940	682	33	226	198	11.8
10	200	80	64	17	38	15.3	32	24	9	29	11.5	940	634	52	254	315	12.7

- - - - - INFLATION OF 5% ANNUALLY AT SALE PRICE, INCOME, AND EXPENSE - - - - -

	HOLDING RESULTS BEFORE INCOME TAXES						HOLDING RESULTS AFTER TAXES					OVERALL RESULTS WITH SALE AT YEAR END					
YR	GROSS INCOME	OPERATE EXPENSE	MORTGAGE INTR	MORTGAGE AMORT	CASH FLOW	% RETURN	DEPRECIATION	TAXABLE INCOME	TAXES DUE	CASH FLOW	% RETURN	SALE PRICE	DEBT REPAY	TAXES DUE	CASH FLOW	TOTAL PROFIT	% RETURN
1	200	80	75	7	38	15.3	32	13	5	33	13.2	987	743	4	240	23	9.3
2	210	84	74	8	44	17.7	32	20	8	36	14.5	1036	735	20	281	100	19.4
3	220	88	73	9	51	20.2	32	27	11	40	15.9	1088	726	37	325	184	22.4
5	243	97	71	11	64	25.6	32	43	17	47	18.8	1200	706	72	422	371	23.9
7	268	107	69	13	79	31.6	32	60	24	55	22.0	1323	682	109	532	587	23.9
10	310	124	64	17	104	41.8	32	90	36	68	27.4	1531	634	170	727	973	23.5

TABLE 16-7
Used Commercial—100 Percent (Straight Line) Depreciation (per $1,000)

KEY FACTORS ARE ---

TOTAL INVESTED	----MORTGAGE TERMS---- AMOUNT	%INTR	LIFE	----OPERATING & INFLATION ASSUMPTIONS---- NET SALE PRICE	GROSS INCOME	OPERATING EXPENSE	%ANNUAL INFLATION	----DEPRECIATION---- AMOUNT	LIFE	TYPE	----TAX RATES---- INCOME	CAP GAIN
1000	900	10.00	25	940	170	70	0.0	800	25	100%	40%	20%

COMPUTED SUMMARY ---

EQUITY AMOUNT	----MORTGAGE TERMS---- %DEBT	MONTHLY	YEARLY	%NET SALE TO TOTAL	%INCOME TO TOTAL	%EXPENSE TO INCOME	%NET TO TOTAL	%DEPREC TO TOTAL
100	90.0	8.18	98	94.0	17.0	41.2	10.0	80.0

COMPUTED RESULTS ---

YR	----HOLDING RESULTS BEFORE INCOME TAXES---- GROSS INCOME	OPERATE EXPENSE	MORTGAGE INTR	AMORT	CASH FLOW	%RE TURN	----HOLDING RESULTS AFTER TAXES---- DEPREC IATION	TAXABLE INCOME	TAXES DUE	CASH FLOW	%RE TURN
1	170	70	90	9	2	1.9	32	-22	-9	11	10.5
2	170	70	89	9	2	1.9	32	-21	-8	10	10.2
3	170	70	88	10	2	1.9	32	-20	-8	10	9.8
5	170	70	85	13	2	1.9	32	-17	-7	9	8.8
7	170	70	83	15	2	1.9	32	-15	-6	8	7.7
10	170	70	77	21	2	1.9	32	-9	-4	6	5.6

YR	----OVERALL RESULTS WITH SALE AT YEAR END---- SALE PRICE	DEBT REPAY	TAXES DUE	CASH FLOW	TOTAL PROFIT	%RE TURN
1	940	891	-6	54	-35	-35.4
2	940	882	1	57	-22	-12.6
3	940	872	7	61	-8	-3.2
5	940	847	20	73	21	4.8
7	940	818	33	89	54	8.2
10	940	761	52	127	111	10.4

- - - - INFLATION OF SALE PRICE, INCOME, AND EXPENSE AT 5% ANNUALLY - - - -

YR	GROSS INCOME	OPERATE EXPENSE	MORTGAGE INTR	AMORT	CASH FLOW	%RE TURN	DEPREC IATION	TAXABLE INCOME	TAXES DUE	CASH FLOW	%RE TURN
1	170	70	90	9	2	1.9	32	-22	-9	11	10.5
2	178	73	89	9	7	6.9	32	-16	-6	13	13.2
3	187	77	88	10	12	12.1	32	-9	-4	16	15.9
5	207	85	85	13	23	23.4	32	4	2	22	21.8
7	228	94	83	15	36	35.9	32	19	8	28	28.1
10	264	109	77	21	57	57.0	32	46	18	39	38.6

YR	----OVERALL RESULTS WITH SALE AT YEAR END---- SALE PRICE	DEBT REPAY	TAXES DUE	CASH FLOW	TOTAL PROFIT	%RE TURN
1	987	891	4	92	2	2.2
2	1036	882	20	134	58	26.8
3	1088	872	37	180	119	32.3
5	1200	847	72	280	260	33.2
7	1323	818	109	395	429	31.9
10	1531	761	170	600	738	29.7

TABLE 16-8
Used Commercial—100 Percent (Straight Line) Depreciation (per $1,000)

KEY FACTORS ARE ---

TOTAL INVESTED	---MORTGAGE TERMS--- AMOUNT	% INTR	LIFE	NET SALE PRICE	---OPERATING & INFLATION ASSUMPTIONS--- GROSS INCOME	OPERATING EXPENSE	% ANNUAL INFLATION	---DEPRECIATION--- AMOUNT	LIFE	TYPE	---TAX RATES--- INCOME	CAP GAIN
1000	900	10.00	25	940	200	80	0.0	800	25	100%	40%	20%

COMPUTED SUMMARY ---

EQUITY AMOUNT	---MORTGAGE TERMS--- % DEBT	MONTHLY	YEARLY	% NET SALE TO TOTAL	% INCOME TO TOTAL	% EXPENSE TO INCOME	% NET TO TOTAL	% DEPREC TO TOTAL
100	90.0	8.18	98	94.0	20.0	40.0	12.0	80.0

COMPUTED RESULTS ---

	HOLDING RESULTS BEFORE INCOME TAXES						HOLDING RESULTS AFTER TAXES					OVERALL RESULTS WITH SALE AT YEAR END					
YR	GROSS INCOME	OPERATE EXPENSE	MORTGAGE INTR	MORTGAGE AMORT	CASH FLOW	% RETURN	DEPRECIATION	TAXABLE INCOME	TAXES DUE	CASH FLOW	% RETURN	SALE PRICE	DEBT REPAY	TAXES DUE	CASH FLOW	TOTAL PROFIT	% RETURN
1	200	80	90	8	22	21.9	32	-2	-1	23	22.5	940	891	-6	54	-23	-23.4
2	200	80	89	9	22	21.9	32	-1	0	22	22.2	940	882	1	57	2	1.0
3	200	80	88	10	22	21.9	32	0	0	22	21.8	940	872	7	61	28	10.5
5	200	80	85	13	22	21.9	32	3	1	21	20.8	940	847	20	73	81	18.0
7	200	80	83	15	22	21.9	32	5	2	20	19.7	940	818	33	89	138	20.7
10	200	80	77	21	22	21.9	32	11	4	18	17.6	940	761	52	127	231	22.1

- - - - I N F L A T I O N   O F   S A L E   P R I C E ,   I N C O M E ,   A N D   E X P E N S E   A T   5 %   A N N U A L L Y - - - -

	HOLDING RESULTS BEFORE INCOME TAXES						HOLDING RESULTS AFTER TAXES					OVERALL RESULTS WITH SALE AT YEAR END					
YR	GROSS INCOME	OPERATE EXPENSE	MORTGAGE INTR	MORTGAGE AMORT	CASH FLOW	% RETURN	DEPRECIATION	TAXABLE INCOME	TAXES DUE	CASH FLOW	% RETURN	SALE PRICE	DEBT REPAY	TAXES DUE	CASH FLOW	TOTAL PROFIT	% RETURN
1	200	80	90	8	22	21.9	32	-2	-1	23	22.5	987	891	4	92	14	14.2
2	210	84	89	9	28	27.9	32	5	2	26	25.8	1036	882	20	134	82	38.2
3	220	88	88	10	34	34.2	32	13	5	29	29.1	1088	872	37	180	157	42.9
5	243	97	85	13	48	47.7	32	28	11	36	36.4	1200	847	72	280	327	42.6
7	268	107	83	15	63	62.7	32	46	18	44	44.2	1323	818	109	395	526	40.6
10	310	124	77	21	88	88.0	32	77	31	57	57.3	1531	761	170	600	889	38.1

17

Land Investing and Development Property

This chapter presents four reference tables describing land investment and development. Land cannot be depreciated, but does encounter holding costs in pursuit of capital gains. Different leverage levels and appreciation rates are shown. Below is an index to this chapter's specific tables, showing their key factor values and summarized results.

Percent Mortgaged	Percent Mortgage Interest Rate	Percent Year 5 Rates of Return		Page Number of Table
		10% Inflation	15% Inflation	
60..............	8	5.4	13.3	216
60..............	10	4.1	12.2	217
75..............	8	5.6	16.0	218
75..............	10	3.5	14.2	219

TABLE 17-1
Land Investment—No Depreciation (per $1,000)

KEY FACTORS ARE ---

TOTAL INVESTED	---MORTGAGE TERMS--- AMOUNT	% INTR	LIFE
1000	600	8.00	20

---OPERATING & INFLATION ASSUMPTIONS--- NET SALE PRICE	GROSS INCOME	OPERATING EXPENSE	% ANNUAL INFLATION
900	0	20	10.0

---DEPRECIATION--- AMOUNT	LIFE	TYPE
0	0	0%

---TAX RATES--- INCOME	CAP GAIN
40%	20%

COMPUTED SUMMARY ---

EQUITY AMOUNT	---MORTGAGE TERMS--- % DEBT	MONTHLY	YEARLY
400	60.0	5.02	60

% NET SALE TO TOTAL	% INCOME TO TOTAL	% EXPENSE TO INCOME	% NET TO TOTAL	% DEPREC TO TOTAL
90.0	0.0	0.0	-2.0	0.0

COMPUTED RESULTS ---

YR	---HOLDING RESULTS BEFORE INCOME TAXES--- GROSS INCOME	OPERATE EXPENSE	--MORTGAGE-- INTR	AMORT	CASH FLOW	% RE TURN	---HOLDING RESULTS AFTER TAXES--- DEPREC IATION	TAXABLE INCOME	TAXES DUE	CASH FLOW	% RE TURN	---OVERALL RESULTS WITH SALE AT YEAR END--- SALE PRICE	DEBT REPAY	TAXES DUE	CASH FLOW	TOTAL PROFIT	% RE TURN
1	0	20	48	13	-80	-20.1	0	-68	-27	-53	-13.3	990	587	-2	405	-49	-12.1
2	0	22	46	14	-82	-20.6	0	-68	-27	-55	-13.7	1089	574	18	498	-10	-1.2
3	0	24	45	15	-84	-21.1	0	-70	-28	-57	-14.2	1198	559	40	600	35	2.5
5	0	29	43	17	-90	-22.4	0	-72	-29	-61	-15.2	1449	525	90	834	151	5.4
7	0	35	40	20	-96	-23.9	0	-75	-30	-66	-16.4	1754	486	151	1117	305	6.5
10	0	47	34	26	-107	-26.8	0	-81	-33	-75	-18.7	2334	414	267	1654	627	7.2

- - - - INFLATION OF SALE PRICE, INCOME, AND EXPENSE AT 15% ANNUALLY - - - - -

YR	GROSS INCOME	OPERATE EXPENSE	INTR	AMORT	CASH FLOW	% RE TURN	DEPREC IATION	TAXABLE INCOME	TAXES DUE	CASH FLOW	% RE TURN	SALE PRICE	DEBT REPAY	TAXES DUE	CASH FLOW	TOTAL PROFIT	% RE TURN
1	0	20	48	13	-80	-20.1	0	-68	-27	-53	-13.3	1035	587	7	441	-13	-3.1
2	0	23	46	14	-83	-20.8	0	-69	-28	-55	-13.9	1190	574	38	579	70	7.9
3	0	26	45	15	-87	-21.7	0	-72	-29	-58	-14.5	1369	559	74	736	170	11.2
5	0	35	43	17	-95	-23.8	0	-78	-31	-64	-16.0	1810	525	162	1123	432	13.3
7	0	46	40	20	-106	-26.6	0	-86	-34	-72	-18.0	2394	486	279	1629	798	13.8
10	0	70	34	26	-131	-32.6	0	-105	-42	-89	-22.2	3641	414	528	2699	1620	13.9

TABLE 17-2
Land Investment—No Depreciation (per $1,000)

LAND INVESTMENT -- NO DEPRECIATION (UNDEVELOPED) -- PER $1000

KEY FACTORS ARE ---

TOTAL INVESTED	---MORTGAGE TERMS---			---OPERATING & INFLATION ASSUMPTIONS---				----DEPRECIATION----			----TAX RATES----	
	AMOUNT	% INTR	LIFE	NET SALE PRICE	GROSS INCOME	OPERATING EXPENSE	% ANNUAL INFLATION	AMOUNT	LIFE	TYPE	INCOME	CAP GAIN
1000	600	10.00	20	900	0	20	10.0	0	0	0%	40%	20%

COMPUTED SUMMARY ---

EQUITY AMOUNT	---MORTGAGE TERMS---			% NET SALE TO TOTAL	% INCOME TO TOTAL	% EXPENSE TO INCOME	% INCOME TO TOTAL	% EXPENSE TO INCOME	% NET TO TOTAL	% DEPREC TO TOTAL
	% DEBT	MONTHLY	YEARLY							
400	60.0	5.79	69	90.0	0.0	0.0	0.0	0.0	-2.0	0.0

COMPUTED RESULTS ---

----HOLDING RESULTS BEFORE INCOME TAXES----

YR	GROSS INCOME	OPERATE EXPENSE	--MORTGAGE-- INTR	AMORT	CASH FLOW	% RETURN
1	0	20	60	10	-89	-22.4
2	0	22	59	11	-91	-22.9
3	0	24	57	12	-94	-23.4
5	0	29	55	15	-99	-24.7
7	0	35	51	18	-105	-26.2
10	0	47	45	24	-117	-29.2

----HOLDING RESULTS AFTER TAXES----

YR	DEPRECIATION	TAXABLE INCOME	TAXES DUE	CASH FLOW	% RETURN
1	0	-80	-32	-58	-14.4
2	0	-81	-32	-59	-14.8
3	0	-82	-33	-61	-15.3
5	0	-84	-34	-65	-16.3
7	0	-87	-35	-70	-17.5
10	0	-92	-37	-80	-19.9

----OVERALL RESULTS WITH SALE AT YEAR END----

YR	SALE PRICE	DEBT REPAY	TAXES DUE	CASH FLOW	TOTAL PROFIT	% RETURN
1	990	590	-2	402	-56	-13.9
2	1089	579	18	492	-25	-2.9
3	1198	567	40	591	13	1.0
5	1449	539	90	821	115	4.1
7	1754	504	151	1099	255	5.4
10	2334	438	267	1629	556	6.4

- - - - INFLATION OF SALE PRICE, INCOME, AND EXPENSE AT 15% ANNUALLY - - - -

----HOLDING RESULTS BEFORE INCOME TAXES----

YR	GROSS INCOME	OPERATE EXPENSE	--MORTGAGE-- INTR	AMORT	CASH FLOW	% RETURN
1	0	20	60	10	-89	-22.4
2	0	23	59	11	-92	-23.1
3	0	26	57	12	-96	-24.0
5	0	35	55	15	-104	-26.1
7	0	46	51	18	-116	-28.9
10	0	70	45	24	-140	-35.0

----HOLDING RESULTS AFTER TAXES----

YR	DEPRECIATION	TAXABLE INCOME	TAXES DUE	CASH FLOW	% RETURN
1	0	-80	-32	-58	-14.4
2	0	-82	-33	-60	-15.0
3	0	-84	-34	-62	-15.6
5	0	-90	-36	-69	-17.1
7	0	-98	-39	-77	-19.2
10	0	-116	-46	-94	-23.4

----OVERALL RESULTS WITH SALE AT YEAR END----

YR	SALE PRICE	DEBT REPAY	TAXES DUE	CASH FLOW	TOTAL PROFIT	% RETURN
1	1035	590	7	438	-20	-4.9
2	1190	579	38	573	56	6.3
3	1369	567	74	728	148	9.9
5	1810	539	162	1109	396	12.2
7	2394	504	279	1611	748	13.0
10	3641	438	528	2675	1549	13.3

TABLE 17-3
Land Investment—No Depreciation (per $1,000)

KEY FACTORS ARE ----

TOTAL INVESTED	---- MORTGAGE TERMS ----			---- OPERATING & INFLATION ASSUMPTIONS ----				---- DEPRECIATION ----			---- TAX RATES ----	
	AMOUNT	% INTR	LIFE	NET SALE PRICE	GROSS INCOME	OPERATING EXPENSE	% ANNUAL INFLATION	AMOUNT	LIFE	TYPE	INCOME	CAP GAIN
1000	750	8.00	20	900	0	20	10.0	0	0	0%	40%	20%

COMPUTED SUMMARY ----

EQUITY AMOUNT	---- MORTGAGE TERMS ----			% NET SALE TO TOTAL	% INCOME TO TOTAL	% EXPENSE TO INCOME	% NET TO TOTAL	% DEPREC TO TOTAL
	% DEBT	MONTHLY	YEARLY					
250	75.0	6.27	75	90.0	0.0	0.0	-2.0	0.0

COMPUTED RESULTS ----

YR	---- HOLDING RESULTS BEFORE INCOME TAXES ----						---- HOLDING RESULTS AFTER TAXES ----					---- OVERALL RESULTS WITH SALE AT YEAR END ----					
	GROSS INCOME	OPERATE EXPENSE	MORTGAGE INTR	MORTGAGE AMORT	CASH FLOW	% RETURN	DEPREC IATION	TAXABLE INCOME	TAXES DUE	CASH FLOW	% RETURN	SALE PRICE	DEBT REPAY	TAXES DUE	CASH FLOW	TOTAL PROFIT	% RETURN
1	0	20	59	16	-95	-38.1	0	-79	-32	-64	-25.4	990	734	-2	258	-56	-22.3
2	0	22	58	17	-97	-38.9	0	-80	-32	-65	-26.1	1089	717	18	354	-25	-4.4
3	0	24	57	19	-99	-39.8	0	-81	-32	-67	-26.8	1198	698	40	460	14	1.5
5	0	29	53	22	-105	-41.8	0	-83	-33	-71	-28.6	1449	656	90	703	117	5.6
7	0	35	50	26	-111	-44.3	0	-85	-34	-77	-30.7	1754	607	151	996	259	6.9
10	0	47	43	32	-122	-49.0	0	-90	-36	-86	-34.6	2334	517	267	1550	564	7.7

- - - - INFLATION OF SALE PRICE, INCOME, AND EXPENSE AT 15% ANNUALLY - - - - -

YR	GROSS INCOME	OPERATE EXPENSE	MORTGAGE INTR	MORTGAGE AMORT	CASH FLOW	% RETURN	DEPREC IATION	TAXABLE INCOME	TAXES DUE	CASH FLOW	% RETURN	SALE PRICE	DEBT REPAY	TAXES DUE	CASH FLOW	TOTAL PROFIT	% RETURN
1	0	20	59	16	-95	-38.1	0	-79	-32	-64	-25.4	1035	734	7	294	-20	-7.9
2	0	23	58	17	-98	-39.3	0	-81	-32	-66	-26.3	1190	717	38	435	56	9.5
3	0	26	57	19	-102	-40.7	0	-83	-33	-68	-27.4	1369	698	74	597	149	14.0
5	0	35	53	22	-110	-44.1	0	-88	-35	-75	-30.0	1810	656	162	992	398	16.0
7	0	46	50	26	-122	-48.6	0	-96	-38	-83	-33.3	2394	607	279	1508	752	16.0
10	0	70	43	32	-146	-58.3	0	-113	-45	-100	-40.1	3641	517	528	2596	1557	15.5

TABLE 17-4
Land Investment—No Depreciation (per $1,000)

KEY FACTORS ARE ---

TOTAL INVESTED	MORTGAGE TERMS			OPERATING & INFLATION ASSUMPTIONS				DEPRECIATION			TAX RATES	
	AMOUNT	% INTR	LIFE	NET SALE PRICE	GROSS INCOME	OPERATING EXPENSE	% ANNUAL INFLATION	AMOUNT	LIFE	TYPE	INCOME	CAP GAIN
1000	750	10.00	20	900	0	20	10.0	0	0	0%	40%	20%

COMPUTED SUMMARY ---

EQUITY AMOUNT	MORTGAGE TERMS			NET SALE PRICE		% INCOME TO TOTAL	% EXPENSE TO INCOME	% NET TO TOTAL	% DEPREC TO TOTAL
	% DEBT	MONTHLY	YEARLY	% NET SALE TO TOTAL					
250	75.0	7.24	87	90.0		0.0	0.0	-2.0	0.0

COMPUTED RESULTS ---

---- INFLATION AT 10% ----

YR	HOLDING RESULTS BEFORE INCOME TAXES						HOLDING RESULTS AFTER TAXES					OVERALL RESULTS WITH SALE AT YEAR END					
	GROSS INCOME	OPERATE EXPENSE	MORTGAGE INTR	AMORT	CASH FLOW	% RE TURN	DEPREC IATION	TAXABLE INCOME	TAXES DUE	CASH FLOW	% RE TURN	SALE PRICE	DEBT REPAY	TAXES DUE	CASH FLOW	TOTAL PROFIT	% RE TURN
1	0	20	74	12	-107	-42.7	0	-94	-38	-69	-27.6	990	738	-2	254	-65	-25.9
2	0	22	73	14	-109	-43.5	0	-95	-38	-71	-28.3	1089	724	18	347	-43	-7.7
3	0	24	72	15	-111	-44.4	0	-96	-38	-73	-29.1	1198	709	40	450	-13	-1.4
5	0	29	68	18	-116	-46.5	0	-98	-39	-77	-30.8	1449	674	90	686	72	3.5
7	0	35	64	23	-122	-48.9	0	-100	-40	-82	-33.0	1754	631	151	973	196	5.3
10	0	47	56	30	-134	-53.6	0	-104	-41	-93	-37.0	2334	548	267	1520	477	6.5

---- INFLATION OF SALE PRICE, INCOME, AND EXPENSE AT 15% ANNUALLY ----

YR	HOLDING RESULTS BEFORE INCOME TAXES						HOLDING RESULTS AFTER TAXES					OVERALL RESULTS WITH SALE AT YEAR END					
	GROSS INCOME	OPERATE EXPENSE	MORTGAGE INTR	AMORT	CASH FLOW	% RE TURN	DEPREC IATION	TAXABLE INCOME	TAXES DUE	CASH FLOW	% RE TURN	SALE PRICE	DEBT REPAY	TAXES DUE	CASH FLOW	TOTAL PROFIT	% RE TURN
1	0	20	74	12	-107	-42.7	0	-94	-38	-69	-27.6	1035	738	7	290	-29	-11.5
2	0	23	73	14	-110	-43.9	0	-96	-38	-71	-28.6	1190	724	38	428	38	6.5
3	0	26	72	15	-113	-45.3	0	-98	-39	-74	-29.6	1369	709	74	586	122	11.5
5	0	35	68	18	-122	-48.7	0	-103	-41	-80	-32.2	1810	674	162	975	353	14.2
7	0	46	64	23	-133	-53.2	0	-111	-44	-89	-35.6	2394	631	279	1485	689	14.6
10	0	70	56	30	-157	-62.9	0	-127	-51	-106	-42.6	3641	548	528	2565	1469	14.5

18

Home or Condominium Property

This chapter presents eight reference tables detailing the *implied* profitability of home or condominium ownership. No depreciation is allowed, but capital gains tax exclusions are available. Below is an index to this chapter's specific tables, showing their key factor values and summarized results.

Percent Mortgaged	Percent Mortgage Interest Rate	Percent Net Income to Total Invested	Percent Year 5 Rates of Return		Page Number of Table
			0% Inflation	5% Inflation	
60	8	6	7.2	17.9	222
60	8	8	13.2	23.4	223
75	8	6	8.6	23.8	224
75	8	8	18.2	32.1	225
75	10	8	14.8	29.6	226
75	10	10	24.6	38.0	227
90	10	8	28.3	53.1	228
90	10	10	52.7	72.3	229

TABLE 18-1
Home or Condominium Ownership—No Depreciation (per $1,000)

KEY FACTORS ARE ----

TOTAL INVESTED	----MORTGAGE TERMS----			----OPERATING & INFLATION ASSUMPTIONS----				----DEPRECIATION----			----TAX RATES----	
	AMOUNT	% INTR	LIFE	NET SALE PRICE	IMPLIED PROP. TAX GROSS INCOME	OPERATING EXPENSE	% ANNUAL INFLATION	AMOUNT	LIFE	TYPE	INCOME	CAP GAIN
1000	600	8.00	25	940	80	20	0.0	0	0	0%	40%	0%

COMPUTED SUMMARY ----

EQUITY AMOUNT	----MORTGAGE TERMS----		% NET SALE TO TOTAL	% INCOME TO TOTAL	% EXPENSE TO INCOME	% NET TO TOTAL	% DEPREC TO TOTAL
	DEBT MONTHLY	YEARLY					
400	4.63	56	94.0	8.0	25.0	6.0	0.0

COMPUTED RESULTS ----

YR	----HOLDING RESULTS BEFORE INCOME TAXES----						----HOLDING RESULTS AFTER TAXES----					----OVERALL RESULTS WITH SALE AT YEAR END----					
	GROSS INCOME	OPERATE EXPENSE	MORTGAGE INTR	MORTGAGE AMORT	CASH FLOW	% RETURN	DEPREC IATION	TAXABLE INCOME	TAXES DUE	CASH FLOW	% RETURN	SALE PRICE	DEBT REPAY	TAXES DUE	CASH FLOW	TOTAL PROFIT	% RETURN
1	80	20	48	8	4	1.1	0	-68	-27	32	7.9	940	592	0	348	-21	-5.2
2	80	20	47	9	4	1.1	0	-67	-27	31	7.8	940	584	0	356	19	2.5
3	80	20	46	9	4	1.1	0	-66	-27	31	7.7	940	574	0	366	59	5.1
5	80	20	45	11	4	1.1	0	-65	-26	30	7.6	940	554	0	386	141	7.2
7	80	20	43	13	4	1.1	0	-63	-25	30	7.4	940	529	0	411	225	8.0
10	80	20	39	16	4	1.1	0	-59	-24	28	7.1	940	485	0	455	356	8.5
	- - - - I N F L A T I O N O F S A L E P R I C E , I N C O M E , A N D E X P E N S E A T 5 % A N N U A L L Y - - - -																
1	80	20	48	8	4	1.1	0	-68	-27	32	7.9	987	592	0	395	26	6.6
2	84	21	47	9	7	1.9	0	-68	-27	35	8.7	1036	584	0	453	119	14.4
3	88	22	46	9	11	2.6	0	-68	-27	38	9.5	1088	574	0	514	218	16.6
5	97	24	45	11	17	4.3	0	-69	-28	45	11.2	1200	554	0	646	437	17.9
7	107	27	43	13	25	6.2	0	-70	-28	53	13.2	1323	529	0	793	685	18.0
10	124	31	39	16	38	9.4	0	-70	-28	66	16.4	1531	485	0	1047	1122	17.7

TABLE 18-2
Home or Condominium Ownership—No Depreciation (per $1,000)

KEY FACTORS ARE ---

TOTAL INVESTED	MORTGAGE TERMS			OPERATING & INFLATION ASSUMPTIONS				DEPRECIATION			TAX RATES	
	AMOUNT	% INTR	LIFE	NET SALE PRICE	IMPLIED PROP. TAX GROSS INCOME	OPERATING EXPENSE	% ANNUAL INFLATION	AMOUNT	LIFE	TYPE	INCOME	CAP GAIN
1000	600	8.00	25	940	110	30	0.0	0	0	0%	40%	0%

COMPUTED SUMMARY ---

EQUITY AMOUNT	MORTGAGE TERMS			% NET SALE TO TOTAL	% INCOME TO TOTAL	% EXPENSE TO INCOME	% NET TO TOTAL	% DEPREC TO TOTAL
	% DEBT	MONTHLY	YEARLY					
400	60.0	4.63	56	94.0	11.0	27.3	9.0	0.0

COMPUTED RESULTS ---

HOLDING RESULTS BEFORE INCOME TAXES

YR	GROSS INCOME	OPERATE EXPENSE	MORTGAGE INTR	MORTGAGE AMORT	CASH FLOW	% RE TURN
1	110	30	48	8	24	6.1
2	110	30	47	9	24	6.1
3	110	30	46	9	24	6.1
5	110	30	45	11	24	6.1
7	110	30	43	13	24	6.1
10	110	30	39	16	24	6.1

--- INFLATION OF SALE PRICE, INCOME, AND EXPENSE AT 5% ANNUALLY ---

YR	GROSS INCOME	OPERATE EXPENSE	MORTGAGE INTR	MORTGAGE AMORT	CASH FLOW	% RE TURN
1	110	30	48	8	24	6.1
2	115	31	47	9	28	7.1
3	121	33	46	9	33	8.2
5	134	36	45	11	42	10.4
7	147	40	43	13	52	12.9
10	171	47	39	16	69	17.1

HOLDING RESULTS AFTER TAXES

YR	DEPRECIATION	TAXABLE INCOME	TAXES DUE	CASH FLOW	% RE TURN
1	0	-78	-31	56	13.9
2	0	-77	-31	55	13.8
3	0	-76	-31	55	13.7
5	0	-75	-30	54	13.6
7	0	-73	-29	54	13.4
10	0	-69	-28	52	13.1

(AT 5%)

YR	DEPRECIATION	TAXABLE INCOME	TAXES DUE	CASH FLOW	% RE TURN
1	0	-78	-31	56	13.9
2	0	-79	-31	60	15.0
3	0	-79	-32	64	16.1
5	0	-81	-32	74	18.5
7	0	-83	-33	85	21.2
10	0	-86	-34	103	25.7

OVERALL RESULTS WITH SALE AT YEAR END

YR	SALE PRICE	DEBT REPAY	TAXES DUE	CASH FLOW	TOTAL PROFIT	% RE TURN
1	940	592	0	348	3	0.8
2	940	584	0	356	67	8.6
3	940	574	0	366	131	11.2
5	940	554	0	386	261	13.2
7	940	529	0	411	393	13.9
10	940	485	0	455	596	14.3

--- ANNUALLY ---

YR	SALE PRICE	DEBT REPAY	TAXES DUE	CASH FLOW	TOTAL PROFIT	% RE TURN
1	987	592	0	395	50	12.6
2	1036	584	0	453	168	20.3
3	1088	574	0	514	294	22.5
5	1200	554	0	646	569	23.4
7	1323	529	0	793	881	23.3
10	1531	485	0	1047	1424	22.8

TABLE 18-3
Home or Condominium Ownership—No Depreciation (per $1,000)

KEY FACTORS ARE ----

TOTAL INVESTED	MORTGAGE TERMS			OPERATING & INFLATION ASSUMPTIONS				DEPRECIATION			TAX RATES	
	AMOUNT	% INTR	LIFE	NET SALE PRICE	IMPLIED PROP. TAX GROSS INCOME	OPERATING EXPENSE	% ANNUAL INFLATION	AMOUNT	LIFE	TYPE	INCOME	CAP GAIN
1000	750	8.00	25	940	80	20	0.0	0	0	0%	40%	0%

COMPUTED SUMMARY ----

EQUITY AMOUNT	MORTGAGE TERMS			% NET SALE TO TOTAL	% INCOME TO TOTAL	% EXPENSE TO INCOME	% NET TO TOTAL	% DEPREC TO TOTAL
	% DEBT	MONTHLY	YEARLY					
250	75.0	5.79	69	94.0	8.0	25.0	6.0	0.0

COMPUTED RESULTS ----

- - - - - INFLATION OF 0 - - - - -

YR	HOLDING RESULTS BEFORE INCOME TAXES						HOLDING RESULTS AFTER TAXES					OVERALL RESULTS WITH SALE AT YEAR END					
	GROSS INCOME	OPERATE EXPENSE	MORTGAGE INTR	AMORT	CASH FLOW	% RETURN	DEPRECIATION	TAXABLE INCOME	TAXES DUE	CASH FLOW	% RETURN	SALE PRICE	DEBT REPAY	TAXES DUE	CASH FLOW	TOTAL PROFIT	% RETURN
1	80	20	60	10	-9	-3.8	0	-80	-32	22	9.0	940	740	0	200	-28	-11.1
2	80	20	59	11	-9	-3.8	0	-79	-32	22	8.8	940	730	0	210	5	1.0
3	80	20	58	12	-9	-3.8	0	-78	-31	22	8.7	940	718	0	222	38	5.3
5	80	20	56	14	-9	-3.8	0	-76	-30	21	8.4	940	692	0	248	106	8.6
7	80	20	54	16	-9	-3.8	0	-74	-29	20	8.0	940	662	0	278	177	9.8
10	80	20	49	20	-9	-3.8	0	-69	-28	18	7.3	940	606	0	334	290	10.4

- - - - INFLATION OF SALE PRICE, INCOME, AND EXPENSE AT 5% ANNUALLY - - - - -

YR	HOLDING RESULTS BEFORE INCOME TAXES						HOLDING RESULTS AFTER TAXES					OVERALL RESULTS WITH SALE AT YEAR END					
	GROSS INCOME	OPERATE EXPENSE	MORTGAGE INTR	AMORT	CASH FLOW	% RETURN	DEPRECIATION	TAXABLE INCOME	TAXES DUE	CASH FLOW	% RETURN	SALE PRICE	DEBT REPAY	TAXES DUE	CASH FLOW	TOTAL PROFIT	% RETURN
1	80	20	60	10	-9	-3.8	0	-80	-32	22	9.0	987	740	0	247	19	7.7
2	84	21	59	11	-6	-2.6	0	-80	-32	25	10.2	1036	730	0	307	105	19.8
3	88	22	58	12	-3	-1.3	0	-80	-32	29	11.5	1088	718	0	370	197	22.9
5	97	24	56	14	3	1.4	0	-80	-32	36	14.2	1200	692	0	508	402	23.8
7	107	27	54	16	11	4.4	0	-80	-32	43	17.2	1323	662	0	661	638	23.3
10	124	31	49	20	24	9.4	0	-80	-32	56	22.3	1531	606	0	925	1056	22.3

TABLE 18-4
Home or Condominium Ownership—No Depreciation (per $1,000)

KEY FACTCRS ARE ----

TOTAL INVESTEC	----MORTGAGE TERMS---- AMOUNT	% INTR	LIFE	----CPERATING & INFLATION ASSUMPTIONS---- NET SALE PRICE	IMPLIED GROSS INCCME	PROP. TAX OPERATING EXPENSE	% ANNUAL INFLATICN	----DEPRECIATION---- AMOUNT	LIFE	TYPE	----TAX RATES---- INCOME	CAP GAIN
1000	750	8.00	25	940	110	30	0.0	0	0	0%	40%	0%

COMPUTED SUMMARY ----

EQUITY AMCUNT	----MORTGAGE TERMS---- % DEBT	MCNTHLY	YFARLY	% NET SALE TO TCTAL	% NET SALE PRICE	% INCOME TO TCTAL	% EXPENSE TO INCCME	% NET TO TOTAL	% DEPREC TO TOTAL
250	75.0	5.79	69	94.0	11.0	27.3	8.0	0.0

COMPUTED RESULTS ----

----HCLDING RESULTS BEFORE INCCME TAXES----

YR	GRCSS INCCME	OPERATE EXPENSE	----MORTGAGE---- INTR	AMCRT	CASH FLCW	% RE TURN
1	110	30	60	10	11	4.2
2	110	30	59	11	11	4.2
3	110	30	58	12	11	4.2
5	110	30	56	14	11	4.2
7	110	30	54	16	11	4.2
10	110	30	49	20	11	4.2
---- INFLATICN OF 5% ----						
1	110	30	60	10	11	4.2
2	115	31	59	11	15	5.8
3	121	33	58	12	19	7.5
5	134	36	56	14	28	11.1
7	147	40	54	16	38	15.1
10	171	47	49	20	55	21.9

----HOLDING RESULTS AFTER TAXES----

YR	DEPREC IATION	TAXABLE INCOME	TAXES DUE	CASH FLCW	% RE TURN
1	0	-90	-36	46	18.6
2	0	-89	-36	46	18.4
3	0	-88	-35	46	18.3
5	0	-86	-34	45	18.0
7	0	-84	-33	44	17.6
10	0	-79	-32	42	16.5
INCOME, AND EXPENSE AT 5%					
1	0	-90	-36	46	18.6
2	0	-90	-36	51	20.3
3	0	-91	-36	55	22.1
5	0	-92	-37	65	25.9
7	0	-94	-38	75	30.1
10	0	-96	-38	93	37.2

----OVERALL RESULTS WITH SALE AT YEAR END----

YR	SALE PRICE	DEBT REPAY	TAXES DUE	TOTAL CASH FLOW	TOTAL PROFIT	% RE TURN
1	940	740	0	200	-4	-1.5
2	940	730	0	210	53	11.0
3	940	718	0	222	110	15.2
5	940	692	0	248	226	18.2
7	940	662	0	278	345	19.1
10	940	606	0	334	530	19.4
ANNUALLY ----						
1	987	740	0	247	43	17.3
2	1036	730	0	307	154	29.2
3	1088	718	0	370	272	31.8
5	1200	692	0	508	534	32.1
7	1323	662	0	661	833	31.2
10	1531	606	0	925	1358	29.8

TABLE 18-5
Home or Condominium Ownership—No Depreciation (per $1,000)

KEY FACTORS ARE ----

TOTAL INVESTED	MORTGAGE TERMS AMOUNT	% INTR	LIFE		OPERATING & INFLATION ASSUMPTIONS NET SALE PRICE	IMPLIED PROP. TAX GROSS INCOME	OPERATING EXPENSE	% ANNUAL INFLATION		DEPRECIATION AMOUNT	LIFE	TYPE		TAX RATES INCOME	CAP GAIN
1000	750	10.00	25		940	110	30	0.0		0	0	0%		40%	0%

COMPUTED SUMMARY ----

EQUITY AMOUNT	MORTGAGE TERMS % DEBT	MONTHLY	YEARLY	% NET SALE TO TOTAL	% INCOME TO TOTAL	% EXPENSE TO INCOME	% NET TO TOTAL	% DEPREC TO TOTAL
250	75.0	6.82	82	94.0	11.0	27.3	8.0	0.0

COMPUTED RESULTS ----

YR	HOLDING RESULTS BEFORE INCOME TAXES GROSS INCOME	OPERATE EXPENSE	MORTGAGE INTR	MORTGAGE AMORT	CASH FLOW	% RETURN	HOLDING RESULTS AFTER TAXES DEPRECIATION	TAXABLE INCOME	TAXES DUE	CASH FLOW	% RETURN	OVERALL RESULTS WITH SALE AT YEAR END SALE PRICE	DEBT REPAY	TAXES DUE	CASH FLOW	TOTAL PROFIT	% RETURN
1	110	30	75	7	-2	-0.7	0	-105	-42	40	16.0	940	743	0	197	-13	-5.1
2	110	30	74	8	-2	-0.7	0	-104	-42	40	15.9	940	735	0	205	35	7.3
3	110	30	73	9	-2	-0.7	0	-103	-41	39	15.8	940	726	0	214	83	11.6
5	110	30	71	11	-2	-0.7	0	-101	-40	39	15.5	940	706	0	234	181	14.8
7	110	30	69	13	-2	-0.7	0	-99	-40	38	15.1	940	682	0	258	282	16.0
10	110	30	64	17	-2	-0.7	0	-94	-38	36	14.4	940	634	0	306	439	16.6

- - - - INFLATION OF SALE PRICE, INCOME, AND EXPENSE AT 5% ANNUALLY - - - -

YR	GROSS INCOME	OPERATE EXPENSE	MORTGAGE INTR	MORTGAGE AMORT	CASH FLOW	% RETURN	DEPRECIATION	TAXABLE INCOME	TAXES DUE	CASH FLOW	% RETURN	SALE PRICE	DEBT REPAY	TAXES DUE	CASH FLOW	TOTAL PROFIT	% RETURN
1	110	30	75	7	-2	-0.7	0	-105	-42	40	16.0	987	743	0	244	34	13.7
2	115	31	74	8	2	0.9	0	-105	-42	44	17.8	1036	735	0	301	136	25.9
3	121	33	73	9	6	2.6	0	-106	-42	49	19.6	1088	726	0	362	245	28.8
5	134	36	71	11	15	6.2	0	-108	-43	59	23.4	1200	706	0	493	489	29.6
7	147	40	69	13	25	10.2	0	-109	-44	69	27.6	1323	682	0	641	769	29.0
10	171	47	64	17	42	16.5	0	-111	-44	87	34.7	1531	634	0	897	1267	27.8

TABLE 18-6
Home or Condominium Ownership—No Depreciation (per $1,000)

KEY FACTORS ARE ---

---OPERATING & INFLATION ASSUMPTIONS---

TOTAL INVESTED	---MORTGAGE TERMS---			NET SALE PRICE	IMPLIED PROP. TAX GROSS INCOME	OPERATING EXPENSE	% ANNUAL INFLATION	---DEPRECIATION---			---TAX RATES---	
	AMOUNT	% INTR	LIFE					AMOUNT	LIFE	TYPE	INCOME	CAP GAIN
1000	750	10.00	25	940	140	40	0.0	0	0	0%	40%	0%

COMPUTED SUMMARY ---

EQUITY AMOUNT	---MORTGAGE TERMS---			NET SALE PRICE	% NET SALE TO TOTAL	% INCOME TO TOTAL	% EXPENSE TO INCOME	% NET TO TOTAL	% DEPREC TO TOTAL
	% DEBT	MONTHLY	YEARLY						
250	75.0	6.82	82	940	94.0	14.0	28.6	10.0	0.0

COMPUTED RESULTS ---

YR	---HOLDING RESULTS BEFORE INCOME TAXES---						---HOLDING RESULTS AFTER TAXES---					---OVERALL RESULTS WITH SALE AT YEAR END---					
	GROSS INCOME	OPERATE EXPENSE	MORTGAGE— INTR	AMORT	CASH FLOW	% RE TURN	DEPREC IATION	TAXABLE INCOME	TAXES DUE	CASH FLOW	% RE TURN	SALE PRICE	DEBT REPAY	TAXES DUE	CASH FLOW	TOTAL PROFIT	% RE TURN
1	140	40	75	7	18	7.3	0	-115	-46	64	25.6	940	743	0	197	11	4.5
2	140	40	74	8	18	7.3	0	-114	-46	64	25.5	940	735	0	205	83	17.3
3	140	40	73	9	18	7.3	0	-113	-45	63	25.4	940	726	0	214	155	21.6
5	140	40	71	11	18	7.3	0	-111	-44	63	25.1	940	706	0	234	301	24.6
7	140	40	69	13	18	7.3	0	-109	-44	62	24.7	940	682	0	258	450	25.6
10	140	40	64	17	18	7.3	0	-104	-42	60	24.0	940	634	0	306	679	25.9

- - - - I N F L A T I O N   O F   SALE PRICE, INCOME, AND EXPENSE   A T   5%   A N N U A L L Y - - - -

YR	GROSS INCOME	OPERATE EXPENSE	INTR	AMORT	CASH FLOW	% RE TURN	DEPREC IATION	TAXABLE INCOME	TAXES DUE	CASH FLOW	% RE TURN	SALE PRICE	DEBT REPAY	TAXES DUE	CASH FLOW	TOTAL PROFIT	% RE TURN
1	140	40	75	7	18	7.3	0	-115	-46	64	25.6	987	743	0	244	58	23.3
2	147	42	74	8	23	9.3	0	-116	-46	70	27.8	1036	735	0	301	185	35.3
3	154	44	73	9	28	11.4	0	-117	-47	75	30.1	1088	726	0	362	321	37.8
5	170	49	71	11	40	15.9	0	-120	-48	88	35.1	1200	706	0	493	622	38.0
7	188	54	69	13	52	20.9	0	-122	-49	101	40.5	1323	682	0	641	965	37.1
10	217	62	64	17	73	29.3	0	-126	-51	124	49.6	1531	634	0	897	1569	35.7

TABLE 18-7
Home or Condominium Ownership—No Depreciation (per $1,000)

HOME OR CONDOMINIUM OWNERSHIP -- NO DEPRECIATION -- PER $1000

KEY FACTORS ARE ---

OPERATING & INFLATION ASSUMPTIONS-----

TOTAL INVESTED	MORTGAGE TERMS AMOUNT	% INTR	LIFE	NET SALE PRICE	IMPLIED PROP. TAX GROSS INCOME	OPERATING EXPENSE	% ANNUAL INFLATION	DEPRECIATION AMOUNT	LIFE	TYPE	TAX RATES INCOME	CAP GAIN
1000	900	10.00	25	940	110	30	0.0	0	0	0%	40%	0%

COMPUTED SUMMARY ---

EQUITY AMOUNT	MORTGAGE TERMS % DEBT MONTHLY	YEARLY	NET SALE PRICE	% NET SALE TO TOTAL	% INCOME TO TOTAL	% EXPENSE TO INCOME	% NET TO INCOME	% DEPREC TO TOTAL
100	90.0	8.18	98	940	94.0	11.0	27.3	8.0	0.0

COMPUTED RESULTS ---

---HOLDING RESULTS BEFORE INCOME TAXES--- | ---HOLDING RESULTS AFTER TAXES--- | ---OVERALL RESULTS WITH SALE AT YEAR END---

YR	GROSS INCOME	OPERATE EXPENSE	MORTGAGE INTR	AMCRT	CASH FLOW	% RETURN	DEPREC IATION	TAXABLE INCOME	TAXES DUE	CASH FLOW	% RETURN	SALE PRICE	DEBT REPAY	TAXES DUE	CASH FLOW	TOTAL PROFIT	% RETURN
1	110	30	90	5	-18	-18.1	0	-120	-48	30	29.7	940	891	0	49	-22	-21.8
2	110	30	89	9	-18	-18.1	0	-119	-47	29	29.4	940	882	0	58	17	9.5
3	110	30	88	10	-18	-18.1	0	-118	-47	29	29.0	940	872	0	68	56	20.7
5	110	30	85	13	-18	-18.1	0	-115	-46	28	28.0	940	847	0	93	137	28.3
7	110	30	83	15	-18	-18.1	0	-113	-45	27	26.9	940	818	0	122	221	30.1
10	110	30	77	21	-18	-18.1	0	-107	-43	25	24.8	940	761	0	179	355	30.4

- - - INFLATION AT 5% OF SALE PRICE, INCOME, AND EXPENSE AT 5% ANNUALLY - - - - -

YR	GROSS INCOME	OPERATE EXPENSE	MORTGAGE INTR	AMCRT	CASH FLOW	% RETURN	DEPREC IATION	TAXABLE INCOME	TAXES DUE	CASH FLOW	% RETURN	SALE PRICE	DEBT REPAY	TAXES DUE	CASH FLOW	TOTAL PROFIT	% RETURN
1	110	30	90	5	-18	-18.1	0	-120	-48	30	29.7	987	891	0	96	25	25.2
2	115	31	89	9	-14	-14.1	0	-120	-48	34	34.0	1036	882	0	154	118	52.9
3	121	33	88	10	-10	-9.9	0	-121	-48	38	38.4	1088	872	0	217	219	56.1
5	134	36	85	13	-1	-0.9	0	-122	-49	48	47.9	1200	847	0	352	445	53.1
7	147	40	83	15	9	9.1	0	-123	-49	58	58.2	1323	818	0	505	709	49.5
10	171	47	77	21	26	26.0	0	-124	-50	75	75.5	1531	761	0	770	1183	45.8

TABLE 18-8
Home or Condominium Ownership—No Depreciation (per $1,000)

KEY FACTORS ARE ---

TOTAL INVESTED	MORTGAGE TERMS			OPERATING & INFLATION ASSUMPTIONS				DEPRECIATION			TAX RATES	
	AMOUNT	% INTR	LIFE	NET SALE PRICE	IMPLIED PROP. TAX GROSS INCOME	OPERATING EXPENSE	% ANNUAL INFLATION	AMOUNT	LIFE	TYPE	INCOME	CAP GAIN
1000	900	10.00	25	940	140	40	0.0	0	0	0%	40%	0%

COMPUTED SUMMARY ---

EQUITY AMOUNT	MORTGAGE TERMS		% NET SALE TO TOTAL	% INCOME TO TOTAL	% EXPENSE TO INCOME	% NET TO TOTAL	DEPREC	% DEPREC TO TOTAL
	% DEBT	MONTHLY	YEARLY					
100	90.0	8.18	98	94.0	14.0	28.6	10.0	0.0

COMPUTED RESULTS ---

	HOLDING RESULTS BEFORE INCOME TAXES						HOLDING RESULTS AFTER TAXES					OVERALL RESULTS WITH SALE AT YEAR END					
YR	GROSS INCOME	OPERATE EXPENSE	MORTGAGE INTR	AMORT	CASH FLOW	%RE TURN	DEPREC IATION	TAXABLE INCOME	TAXES DUE	CASH FLOW	%RF TURN	SALE PRICE	DEBT REPAY	TAXES DUE	CASH FLOW	TOTAL PROFIT	%RE TURN
1	140	40	90	5	2	1.9	0	-130	-52	54	53.7	940	891	0	49	2	2.2
2	140	40	89	5	2	1.9	0	-129	-51	53	53.4	940	882	0	58	65	35.7
3	140	40	88	10	2	1.9	0	-128	-51	53	53.0	940	872	0	68	128	46.6
5	140	40	85	13	2	1.9	0	-125	-50	52	52.0	940	847	0	93	257	52.7
7	140	40	83	15	2	1.9	0	-123	-49	51	50.9	940	818	0	122	389	53.7
10	140	40	77	21	2	1.9	0	-117	-47	49	48.8	940	761	0	179	595	53.6

- - - INFLATION OF 5% ANNUALLY - - - - INFLATION OF SALE PRICE, INCOME, AND EXPENSE AT 5% ANNUALLY - - - - -

YR	GROSS INCOME	OPERATE EXPENSE	MORTGAGE INTR	AMORT	CASH FLOW	%RE TURN	DEPREC IATION	TAXABLE INCOME	TAXES DUE	CASH FLOW	%RF TURN	SALE PRICE	DEBT REPAY	TAXES DUE	CASH FLOW	TOTAL PROFIT	%RE TURN
1	140	40	90	5	2	2	0	-130	-52	54	53.7	987	891	0	96	49	49.2
2	147	42	89	5	7	6.9	0	-131	-52	59	59.2	1036	882	0	154	167	75.4
3	154	44	88	10	12	12.1	0	-132	-53	65	64.8	1088	872	0	217	294	77.0
5	170	49	85	13	23	23.4	0	-134	-54	77	77.0	1200	847	0	352	578	72.3
7	188	54	83	15	36	35.9	0	-136	-55	90	90.4	1323	818	0	505	904	68.4
10	217	62	77	21	57	57.0	0	-139	-56	113	112.7	1531	761	0	770	1485	65.1

Index

Index